Arthur
RACKHAM

Arthur
RACKHAM

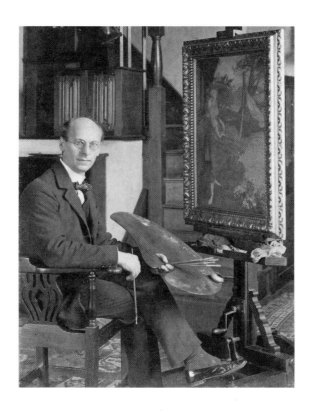

A Biography by
James Hamilton

Arcade Publishing · New York

Little, Brown and Company

For
KATE

**The author and publishers of this book would like to thank
The Paul Mellon Centre for Studies in British Art for their
generous financial support.**

FIRST U.S. EDITION

Library of Congress Cataloging-in-Publication Data
Hamilton, James.
Arthur Rackham / by James Hamilton. — 1st U.S. ed.
p.   cm.
ISBN 1–55970–096–3
1. Rackham, Arthur, 1867–1939.   2. Illustrators — England —
Biography.   I. Title.
NC978.5.R32H36   1990
741.6′092 — dc20
[B]   90–31806   CIP

Published in the United States by Arcade Publishing, Inc., New
York, a Little, Brown company

10   9   8   7   6   5   4   3   2   1

Designed by David Fordham
PRINTED IN ITALY

**Frontispiece: So valiantly did they grapple with him
that they bore him to the ground and slew him**
Pen and ink and watercolour, 1916
248 × 188 mm
Private Collection

Illustration to 'Cesarino and the Dragon: An Italian Tale', in
The Allies' Fairy Book. *Here, Rackham combines his feeling
for heraldry and the fantastic with his love of early Italian
painting appropriate to the nationality of the story. The head of
Cesarino is adapted from the head of the young horseman in
Uccello's* Battle of San Romano, *a painting which Rackham
recorded as being among his favourites at the National Gallery
in London.*

Title page illustration: Arthur Rackham photographed
in his studio at 16 Chalcot Gardens, c1915. His large oil
painting *Undine* is on the easel. (See pages 99, 151
and 193)
Private Collection

CONTENTS

ACKNOWLEDGEMENTS

ARTHUR RACKHAM HAD MANY FRIENDS IN HIS lifetime, but even he would have been surprised at the large number of new friends he has now, fifty years after his death.

In writing this life with illustration I have tried, with the indispensable help of many of Rackham's friends, to convey an idea of his personality and rescue him from the received view that categorizes him simply as a painter of fairyland. His talents were much more extensive, and if he must be categorized he deserves at the very least a bigger pigeon-hole.

From many of Rackham's friends I have received help, encouragement and a sense of purpose and direction. There are so many whom I want to thank, and in naming the following I am aware that there will be others whom I am omitting, and whose passing word, spoken or written, has added a trace more colour to mine.

W. Elisabeth Adams (neice), Pamela Adams, Gretel Akoglu, Dr John Andrewes, Dr Michael Andrewes, Janet Backhouse, Julian and Isabel Bannerman, Adrian and Mary Baulf, Tessa Beaver, Chris Beetles, Virginia Bennet-Clark, Victoria Blake-Tyler, Edgar and Charlotte de Bresson, Joanna Brown, Jane Byrne, Joann Chalat, Tessa Chester, Mary Coleman, Professor Philip Collins, Gwendolen Colthorpe, Bernard Crystal, H. M. Fletcher, Rodney Engen, Cara Denison, Charles and Rachel Eustace, Rowland and Barbara Eustace, Joan Jefferson Farjeon, Elizabeth FitzGerald, Dr Terry Friedman, Christa Gardner von Teuffel, Jonathan Gray, Kathleen Gee, Gregory Gillert, Nan Green, Francis Greenacre, John and Hilaire Gomer, Anne Goodchild, William Hallett, Patrick Hamilton, Georgina Hamilton-Fletcher, Rebecca Hamilton-Fletcher, Derek Hawley, Cathy Henderson, Michael Heseltine, George Hernandez, DL Hill, Sarah Hodson, Karen Hunt, Nesta Jenkins, Ann Jones, Professor Michael Kauffmann, Frances Kelly, Lionel Lambourne, the late P. R. Lazarus, Jeremy Maas, Rupert Maas, Sarah MacDonald, Catherine Martineau, Robert and Frances Maxwell, Stewart Meese, John Merton, Jean Miller, Anne Mitchell, Babs Nicholson, Rosemary Nicholson, Margaret Phaff, Fiona Price, Jane Roberts, Jasper Rose, Anthony Rota, David Rudkin, Richard Ryder, Ellen Scaruffi, Paula Sigman, Peyton Skipwith, Bob Smith, Delinda Stephens Buie, Jean Stralem, Nicholas Sursock, Heather Tanner, the late Courtney Theobald, Wynne and Diana Thomas, Ritchie Thomas, Stephanie Wiles, Lady Willink, Ruth Wilson, Graham Wontner-Smith, Carolynne Wright and Jeffery Young.

A handful of people, deserve a special mention and particular thanks and, had there been space, a citation. Ian and Betty Ballantine, Maggie Funderberg, Dorothy and George Gibbs, Dale Harris, Marie Korey, Kenneth Lohf, George T. McWhorter, Joseph Sedacca, Flo Smart, Roberta Waddell and Dr Mary Lou White, all of whom made me welcome in the United States of America; Professor Michael Kitson and the committee of the Paul Mellon Centre, London, who sent me there; Derek Hudson, Rackham's previous biographer, who was a consistent support; Anne Hobbs, Mary Hobbs, Harold Rackham and Professor Richard Verdi who read through my typescript and made valuable comments; Colin White who whispered my name to Russell Ash; Russell Ash, Steve Dobell, David Fordham and Joanne Rippin of Pavilion who converted the typescript into a book; my children Thomas and Elinor Hamilton who kept me going; and my wife Kate who, in marrying me, did not expect to be co-habiting with Arthur Rackham into the bargain. Finally, research would have been impossible without the constant encouragement, hospitality and friendship of Dr John Edwards and Arthur Rackham's daughter Mrs Barbara Edwards.

Much of this book was written in an upper room in Warwick, looking out westerly on to one of the great views of Europe. At sunset, Warwick Castle on the left and St Mary's Church tower on the right, joined by a fringed horizon of roofs, chimneys, trees and three or four street lights, formed a long, gilded silhouette that might have inspired Rackham. Instead, it inspired me.

JAMES HAMILTON, Warwick, 1989

The author and publishers would like to thank most warmly Mrs Barbara Edwards for her permission to quote from her father's writings and to reproduce his work in this book. They would like to thank the following libraries for permission to quote from papers in their possession. Art Workers' Guild, London; Arthur Rackham Collection, Rare Book and Manuscript Library, Columbia University; The Rare Book Department, Free Library of Philadelphia; Harry Ransom Humanities Research Center, The University of Texas at Austin; Henry E. Huntingdon Library, San Marino, California; Royal Academy Library, London; The Royal Watercolour Society; The Spencer Collection, New York Public Library; Arthur Rackham Memorial Collection, University of Louisville.

GLOSSARY

The following technical printing terms are used in the book:

LITHOGRAPHY:
The image is drawn with a wax crayon onto a porous limestone surface. The stone is then wetted, the water naturally avoiding the greasy wax and soaking into the stone around it. When the stone is inked for printing with a greasy ink, this is repelled by the wet area, but taken up by the lines the artist has drawn. These are thereby reproduced exactly – in reverse – on the paper pressed against them.

COLLOTYPE:
A variation of the above, in which gelatine coated with a light-sensitive ammonium bichromate stands in for the stone surface. The image is transferred photographically to the gelatine, whose cells harden in proportion to the light action. This, in turn, is controlled by the densities of the negative. The closer the grain of the exposed gelatine, the greater the amount of ink deposited, and thus the darker the printed area.

THREE-COLOUR PROCESS:
The mechanical process in general use in Britain in 1904 and 1905, which revolutionized colour printing. The original drawing was photographed through blue, green and red filters to make negatives which were then used to produce three printing plates registering the colour balance of the original. These plates were printed in the colours complementary to the negatives, ie yellow, magenta and blue-green, one on top of the other, to create a mix that approximated to the full colour of the original. It followed that if the original was painted in soft tones – as Rackham's illustrations were – the new and unsophisticated three-colour process could reproduce it the more faithfully.

ELECTROS:
Rackham (see p. 126) is referring to the electrotype process in which pages of type are reproduced by means of a copper-plated wax impression. These were cheap to produce and easily transportable, but printed poor quality text.

A QUESTION OF NERVOUS OUTPUT

HIS FACE WAS WIZENED AND WRINKLED LIKE a ripe walnut, and as he peered short sightedly at me out of his goggle spectacles I thought he was one of the goblins out of Grimm's Fairy Tales.'[1] This is how Arthur Rackham, at the age of about thirty-five, is remembered by his nephew, Walter Starkie. Whether Rackham wanted to be remembered in this way, however, is another matter entirely.

For eighty years Rackham's book illustrations have both charmed and terrified generations of children and adults all around the world. Now, fifty years after his death, the particular *frisson* that accompanies his combination of 'grace and grotesque', as E. V. Lucas described it,[2] has shown no signs of losing its power. This is because in dealing with issues of good and evil, pleasure and pain, comfort and misery, the beautiful and the grotesque, Rackham expressed in graphic form, and at their most elemental, feelings and qualities that every human has experienced, and probably always will. While at the same time helping to tell good stories, Rackham found and struck a chord in the human psyche, and continued throughout his life to harmonize upon it.

The texts he illustrated in his mature years were, with very few exceptions, classics of English and European literature. He rose to them to the extent that the greater the text, the more memorable and resonant his images became. His interpretations of *A Midsummer Night's Dream* and *The Wind in the Willows*, for example, have become definitive, and continue to challenge later illustrators to find new approaches. His illustrations to such books as *Snickerty Nick* or *Poor Cecco*, on the other hand, have sunk with their texts. Rackham could not breathe life into indifferent

Left: Windfalls
Pen and ink and watercolour, 1904
230 × 220 mm
National Gallery of Victoria, Melbourne

writing, but neither could he resist the inspiration of the best.

Rackham was a gentle man, witty and good company. He was brave in the face of hardship, enjoyed his fame, but was susceptible to panic and on occasion to depression and to waves of overwhelming emotion. An earlier writer, however, straining to be complimentary, described Rackham and his life as 'uneventful .... without eccentricity .... having no amusing myths or romantic legends .... to excite the curious.'[3] These words hardly accord with the counter image of Rackham as the embodiment of one of his own goblins.

This biography looks at Rackham's life with illustrations both from his surviving letters and from his abundant imagery. A count of his book illustrations shows he published more than 3,300 individual images and decorations, a figure that would be greatly increased if his magazine and miscellaneous illustrative work were added to it. His work has never been entirely out of print, and in its different ways it has affected childhood vision and imagination for four generations.

Writers, artists, filmmakers and even advertisers have expressed this influence through their work, while countless others have kept it quietly to themselves. Kenneth Clark wrote[4] of not daring to open the stories of Grimm on account of Rackham's illustrations, and of having his imagination stamped with images of terror if he caught sight of them before he was on his guard. For the 15-year-old C. S. Lewis 'the sky turned round' when he first set eyes on *Siegfried and the Twilight of the Gods*. 'Pure "Northerness" engulfed me:' he wrote, 'a vision of huge, clear spaces hanging above the Atlantic in the endless twilight of a Northern summer, remoteness, severity ....'[5] Graham Sutherland, too, became 'mad' on these illustrations as a boy. 'I used to copy them, or try to.'[6]

Gerda and the Little Robber Girl in the Robbers' Castle
Pen and ink and watercolour, 1932
325 × 255 mm
Private Collection

Illustration to 'The Snow Queen' in Harrap's edition of Hans Andersen's Fairy Tales. *The bold S-shape composition enables Rackham to create two centres of action. The rugs on which Gerda and the robber girl sit were owned by Rackham, and lay on his studio floor.*

Even the advertising agents for the *Sunday Express* 'You' magazine in the 1980s did not entirely escape the influence of Rackham's *Sleeping Beauty* in their TV advert. Rackham discovered and distilled a particular kind of chill spookiness which overtakes the vulnerable human – male, female, any age, just vulnerable – when placed in a desperate situation.

Rackham's illustrations to Grimm, Hans Andersen

Winter Frolic
Pen and ink and watercolour, 1924
379 × 562 mm
Private Collection

A large 'set piece' illustration for the 1924 Christmas issue of Pear's Children's Magazine. *Rackham illustrations of this kind, many of which were not linked to text, helped to keep magazine circulation figures buoyant.*

or Poe show him at his most imaginative and observant of human nature, while his gnomes, fairies and gnarled anthropomorphic trees in *Peter Pan in Kensington Gardens* or *A Midsummer Night's Dream* represent his more fantastic side, his 'fancy', as contemporary commentators put it. His fairies and their brother creatures, curious personages who show astringent traces of malice, also display other all-too-human traits like jealousy, rage and sulkiness, and rarely allow mere prettiness and sentimentality to creep in.

Rackham's sense of design, his *mise en page*, is unerring, and given the figure of sprites snowballing each other, robbers cavorting in a castle or a group of three monstrous blind old hags, he finds attitudes, expressions and a sense of space and excitement that complement and illuminate his texts. He was – and remains – a soloist in front of an orchestra, a player

with the responsibility to interpret and add a personal lustre to great works with variations of infinite subtlety and grace. His performances were courageous and spirited, and, as he himself described them in one of his vivid letters, were entirely 'a question of nervous output'.[7]

The chapter titles used in this book are, with three exceptions, drawn from phrases used by Rackham in his letters. The exceptions are Chapter Four, whose title is a quote from *The Daily Telegraph*, Chapter Five, which is a phrase used by Edyth Rackham and Chapter Eight, which is a line from Shakespeare.

CHAPTER ONE

AN UNFORGETTABLE AND EPOCH MARKING EVENT IN MY LIFE

ALFRED RACKHAM, A GENTLE, CHIPPER AND luxurious family man, was Arthur Rackham's father, and perhaps the single most formative influence on his early life.

Alfred's own background, firmly rooted in the education of the young, had an entrepreneurial flavour that set an example of self-sufficiency for his own children, and had prompted at least three of his immediate forebears to found their own private schools. Alfred (1829–1912) was the only surviving child of Thomas Rackham (*c*.1800–1874) and his wife Jane, née Harris (1801–1873). His paternal grandfather, Joseph Rackham, probably came from Norfolk, according to Alfred's own records, and died 'quite young', leaving a widow, Sarah, née Capel (1770s–*c*.1853), and two young children, Thomas and Joseph. Thomas, born in the Minories, in the East End of London, was a schoolmaster whose teaching career had begun in the school of his maternal uncle William Capel, in Vauxhall Walk. Thomas Rackham subsequently opened his own school across South London in Baalzephon Street, Bermondsey, in 1823, six years before Alfred was born.

Thomas's wife, Jane – Alfred's mother – was the daughter of another schoolmaster, James Harris,

Arthur Rackham's Parents:
Left: Alfred Thomas Rackham 1829–1912
Photograph c1899

Right: Annie Rackham 1833–1920
Photograph, c1900
Private Collections

whose school, in Prospect Row[1] near Elephant and Castle, was only a few miles away from Thomas's Baalzephon Street School. James Harris was a member of the Philosophical Society of London, a teacher *inter alia* of land surveying and navigation, and the author of *The Algebraists Assistant* (1818), a tutor's book for teaching elementary algebra.

Alfred's upbringing acknowledged the importance of a sense of responsibility for children, their care and their future, and for keeping them busy and amused. Other qualities that inevitably developed from such a background were an acceptance of – perhaps a desire for – high social status and ceremony in a small community, and a recognition of the importance of clarity

Left: The Hawthorne Tree
Pen and ink and watercolour, 1922
390 × 300 mm
Private Collection

Frontispiece, with an appropriate and punning title, to Nathaniel Hawthorne's A Wonder Book. The drawing was published in black and white but was later coloured by Rackham for exhibition and sale. It is a typical example of a tree with human attributes, the motif for which Rackham is perhaps best known.

of thought and of record. This upbringing, and, dare one say, the knowledge that he was the only one of his parents' children to survive, provided the impetus for Alfred to write out in 1902 two copies of his *Personal Recollections*, intelligent and articulate records of his own and his children's lives, with wide-ranging information about his forebears. In his firm and easy-going copper-plate hand, Alfred Rackham begins his story:

I am now 73 years old, and many memories of my relatives & myself will die with me unless I make a note of them. If one of my ancestors had made any such notes they would have been interesting to me; these will probably be of interest to my children & possibly to a later generation.[2]

In his writing, Alfred recorded those memories which exercised his considerable powers of description and his enjoyment of anecdote. His anecdotes, however, always contained a characteristic lesson. Writing of his maternal grandfather, the schoolmaster James Harris, he remembers 'he was very genial with children ... he once took some of us into a dark room, when he rubbed some chemical on his face & gave us a sort of luminous paint exhibition which I thought very wonderful.'

Further on, Alfred describes his first encounter with a telescope which the Southwark Astronomical Society had set up in Nelson Street, Bermondsey, near the family's home at 59 Long Lane. The Rackham family's early involvement with local scientific and educational activities shows the practical lengths to which they would go to fire Alfred's young mind:

... the Southwark Astronomical Society possessed a large refracting telescope, 30 feet long, mounted on an imposing wooden structure in the open air, the platform of which was reached by a wooden staircase. The Society had also a large room for lectures on various scientific subjects and a reading room. I remember as a boy of 7 or 8 attending lectures there with my Mother which were given by Wallis the astronomer, Dr. Birkbeck[3] and others. After the lectures we used on fine nights to go on the platform outside & look through the telescope at the moon & planets.

Despite his father's profession, Alfred Rackham was not sent to school. His mother, Alfred tells us, preferred her only child to be taught privately, away from other boys, by 'a very able woman, Miss Mary Sutherland'. With Mary Sutherland's tuition, and regular attendance from an early age at lectures by Wallis, George Birkbeck and others, Alfred's education was, even if secluded, broader and more imaginative than was normal in his day.

In January 1844, aged just fourteen, Alfred was sent as a Junior Clerk to the office of Mr Ormes, a Proctor[4] at Doctors' Commons. Doctors' Commons is described ('with the usual Dickens exaggeration,' sniffs Alfred Rackham) by Steerforth in *David Copperfield*, as 'a lazy old nook near St. Paul's Cathedral ... a little out-of-the-way place where they administer what is called ecclesiastical law, and play all kinds of tricks with obsolete old monsters of Acts of Parliament.... On the whole, I would recommend you to take to Doctors' Commons kindly, David. They plume themselves on their gentility there, I can tell you....'[5]

As if following Steerforth's advice to Copperfield, young Alfred Rackham did take kindly to Doctors' Commons. Looking back on his early life as a Junior Clerk, Alfred draws an expansive and affectionate picture of the Ecclesiastical and Admiralty Courts in which he served:

The Courts were held in the large Court of the College of Advocates.... The Judge at the farther end was on a raised dais; on either side of the Hall sat the Advocates facing each other and nearly on a level with the Judge.... Under the Judge sat the Marshal, with his Silver Oar and cocked hat on the table before him. At the sitting of the Admiralty Court there was a procession across the quadrangle from the chambers of the Judge Dr. Lushington on one side to the Court on the other. The Usher of the Court walked first with a silver tipped ebony wand, and was followed by the Marshal carrying the Silver Oar, then the Registrar and after him the Judge. On the first day of each term the Court looked very gay.

The high detail and clear recall of this description suggest that it had been well polished in the telling, and that this written account is just one of many repetitions of the story. Yet if Alfred sniffed at Dickens's words, as well might a man whose way of life was the butt of the novelist's incisive satire, his own description inevitably fades beside Dickens's. Alfred

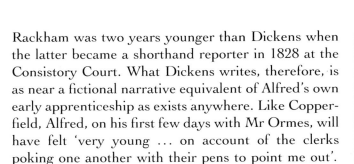

Left: Alfred Thomas Rackham, Admiralty Marshal, in procession with the silver oar at Doctor's Commons
Pen and ink, c1896–99
180 × 115 mm
Private Collection

Drawn by Arthur Rackham on a sheet of Law Courts note paper, presumably while watching his father in procession.

Rackham was two years younger than Dickens when the latter became a shorthand reporter in 1828 at the Consistory Court. What Dickens writes, therefore, is as near a fictional narrative equivalent of Alfred's own early apprenticeship as exists anywhere. Like Copperfield, Alfred, on his first few days with Mr Ormes, will have felt 'very young ... on account of the clerks poking one another with their pens to point me out'.

After two years with Mr Ormes, on a salary of £20 a year, Alfred was appointed to a full Clerkship at double the salary with Messrs Tebbs, also Proctors in Doctors' Commons. He was with Tebbs for eight years until 1854 when, with the Declaration of the Crimean War against Russia in March, he joined the Registry of the Admiralty Court, also in Doctors' Commons. This Court had responsibility for Naval Prizes taken in wartime, and the condemnation of ships and cargoes captured from the enemy, in addition, as Alfred records, 'to its usual jurisdiction in maritime causes generally'.

The Crimean War was the first Naval War since 1814, from which date the business and staff of the office had shrunk. The war, however, gave the office the opportunity to expand again, and 'mine was the first new appointment on the increased staff & owing to my knowledge of Admiralty business, acquired in Mr Tebbs' office, I commenced my Civil Service career at the age of 24 on the 2nd Class with a commencing salary of £200 a year – those coming after me being placed on the 3rd Class.'

Clearly, the first requirement of the commencement of a good war is the drawing up of a good-looking Declaration. This was Alfred's task, and, as Civil Servant 2nd Class, he took to the work with despatch, perseverance and without complaint:

At first we were extremely busy in preparing the Declaration of War & other papers required on the commencement of war with a civilized nation. On one occasion I remember hearing St. Paul's clock strike three in the morning while I was copying one of these documents for the Queen's Signature. It was on a large sheet of gilt-edged paper, and it had to be written out without any erasure or alteration. I was so dead tired from previous late hours and overwork that I essayed three times to copy it correctly but each time I made a fatal mistake and eventually felt compelled to give up the attempt. The next morning I went early to the office and satisfactorily accomplished the task....

This tenacity made him clearly suited to his work, and he was noticed. He continued at the Registry of the Admiralty Court in a secure job, with prospects and promotion. If not blessed with the meteoric rise experienced by Gilbert and Sullivan's lad, who served a term as office boy to an attorney's firm, and ended up as Ruler of the Queen's Navee, Alfred Rackham was at least soon in a sufficiently secure position to marry in 1861, aged 32, a girl whom he had met at the Great Exhibition ten years earlier. His bride was Annie Stevenson (1833–1920), the quiet and deeply religious second daughter of William Stevenson, a Nottingham draper, and his wife Elizabeth, née Roberts. His parents-in-law both came from extended Midlands trade and professional families whose interests combined the temporal security of lace manufacture and retail, with the spiritual certainty of the Baptist Church. Annie's maternal grandfather and three of her uncles were lace manufacturers, while her paternal grandfather, Thomas Stevenson, was a schoolmaster and General Baptist Minister at Baxtergate, Loughborough. Three other uncles on her father's side were Baptist ministers.

Alfred and Annie began their married life, after a month's honeymoon in Ventnor, Isle of Wight, and Paris, at what was then 210 South Lambeth Road, a house that was demolished after the Second World War to make way for flats. Alfred, however, tells us with precision that it was 'the next house to the corner on the South side of Mawbey Street'. By Alfred's own account, it was a happy place, in which strong family bonds were made:

'My mother and father lived with us until they died. My wife and I resided there until March 1882 – for over 20 years – and to us it was an eventful domicile. No similar memories can ever attach themselves to any other house. Here we began our married life, and here all our children were born. In it my Mother and Father died, and four of my children.'

The year after Alfred and Annie were married, their first child, Alfred William, was born, followed in 1864 by their second son, Percy. Before Percy had reached his first birthday, his elder brother had died of meningitis. Three other children, Margaret ('Meg', b. 1866), Arthur (b. 1867) and Harris (b. 1868), were born healthy and in quick succession.

Arthur Rackham grew up in a modest sized, respectable house, whose occupants ebbed and flowed in life and death restlessly around him. His elder brother, Percy, was an epileptic with a paralysed left arm. In 1873, by the time Arthur was six, Percy, now nine, was moved away from home to live with a clergyman, Dr Langdon Downs, by the River Thames at Hampton Wick. Alfred tells us that this was 'on account of his health', but whether it was less on account of Percy's health than on account of the peace of mind of his grandparents, parents and brothers and sisters, remains an open question.

By 1873, four adults and four children, as well as three servants and nursemaids, were living in the house,[6] two other children, Ethel and Leonard, having been born and died, aged two weeks and six months respectively, in 1871 and 1872. Arthur's grandmother died at home two weeks before Christmas 1873, and his grandfather six months later in June 1874. From the time Arthur was four in 1871 until his youngest brother Maurice was born in 1879, his mother had

The Old Man and his Grandson
Pen and ink and watercolour, 1900
In two parts, 140 × 50 and 178 × 126 mm
Private Collection

An adult rendering of a child's vision of the meeting of extreme youth and age. An illustration to Grimm's Fairy Tales, *drawn for the 1900 edition, but coloured and redated in 1904 for exhibition and sale in 1905.*

given birth to seven more children, and was always either pregnant, nursing an infant or both. Annie looked forward to her month in bed after giving birth, and always insisted on bathing the newest baby herself. In her copy of the poems of Elizabeth Barrett Browning she marked passages about the death of babies. Although she appeared to be placid and serene, Annie was ravaged by worries, which knitting socks, sewing exquisitely tucked shirts and attending religious meetings helped her to keep in check. Arthur, during his most impressionable years, until the age of twelve, was an enforced and perceptive witness to this intensive pattern of birth, sickness, life and death, at the most impressionable stage of his life.

their children, whom they happily expected both to see *and* hear, and their cultural interests and enthusiasm inevitably rubbed off. They took *Punch* and *Graphic* regularly, and these magazines gave Arthur his first grounding in the power and vitality of black and white art. As a child he was also given a copy of Arthur Boyd Houghton's *Arabian Nights*,[9] and some of Houghton's original drawings later became Arthur's most treasured possessions.[10] His first shilling paintbox was given to him before he could read,[11] and when he was nine he sent some sketches to his grandmother in Nottingham. She wrote to him: 'The sketches are from life, I suppose; the first one, Louisa & all you children having a nice romp in the nursery. Well, you have not made any of you very handsome,

Inevitably perhaps, amidst such a farrowing, Arthur was a mischievous and determined little boy. His younger sister, Winifred, remembered how he would smuggle pencil and paper into bed and draw until it became too dark to see. When this was discovered, and forbidden, he would still manage to secrete the pencil and draw on the pillows.[7] Winifred also recalls how he purloined successive nurses' thimbles, and stuffed them into a hole under the saddle of the family's rocking horse. All enjoyed the subsequent mysterious rattle as the children rode on it five at a time, two on top, one on each end of the rockers and one underneath.

Like most younger sisters, Winifred was the butt of her two big brothers' practical jokes. She later described how Arthur and Harris made her eat biscuits crushed up in water from a toy soup tureen. As an older man, in 1934, Arthur himself about his racketting childhood for a Junior Dictionary of Authors:

> .... my own boyhood was spent in a noisy, merry, busy little community of work and play almost large enough to be independent of outside engagements. I cannot remember the time when I hadn't a pencil in my hand and from the very first my bent was toward the fantastic and the imaginative.[8]

The Rackhams were an advanced and liberal family, Alfred and Annie lived in close contact with

Studies of mounted humming bird and dormouse
Watercolour, 1887 or 1888
Private Collection

Made by Arthur Rackham, aged 8 or 9 at the British Museum.

especially Louise [*sic*], what a nose she has....'[12] At this same period, Arthur was often taken to the British Museum, and from 1881 to the Natural History Museum in South Kensington, where he made 'endless' watercolour sketches.[13]

The Rackhams' house stood opposite Stamford House and Turret House, with their three-and-a-half acres of grounds. 'For nearly 17 years,' Alfred writes, 'we had the advantage of this open space in front of us, with all its fine old trees.' These, however, were no ordinary old trees, but a pedigree group which have their own place in garden history, descended from those planted by John Tradescant the Elder and Younger, gardeners to King Charles I.

Right: The Witches' Meeting
Pen and ink and watercolour, 1930s
380 × 267 mm
Rare Book Department, Free Library of Philadelphia

*A work which contains all the ingredients for the so called 'typical'
Rackham: the witches and their impedimenta, the gnarled trees and
a windswept landscape.*

Above: Three Grey Women
Pen and ink and watercolour, 1922
391 × 284 mm
Arthur Rackham Collection, Rare Book and Manuscript Library,
Columbia University

From A Wonder Book *by Nathanial Hawthorne, a collection of Greek
myths retold for children. In line with Hawthorne's atmospheric telling of
the stories, Rackham has used a bold spray technique, with scratching at
the top, to create the rays of light emerging from the single eye that the
women share.*

The Tradescants moved to Lambeth in 1626, and by the time of the Younger's death, their house had become famous as 'Tradescant's Ark'. It was visited by none other than King Charles I and Queen Henrietta Maria, and people of the eminence of the diarist John Evelyn. Tradescant's 'Closett of Rarities', the first catalogued public museum in Britain, later formed the nucleus of the Ashmolean Museum in Oxford. The garden to the house was planted with specimens collected by the Tradescants from expeditions they either supported or undertook themselves to Russia, North Africa, the Balearic Islands and Virginia.

The garden remained overgrown but extant until 1880, when it was sold for development for £16,150,[14] and Turret House was demolished. In the 1770s Dr William Watson described the gardens in a paper to the Royal Society: 'Mr. Tradescant's garden has now been many years totally neglected and the house belonging to it empty and ruined....'[15] According to John Loudon (1783–1843), the Scottish horticulturalist, among the trees and shrubs remaining in 1838 were lilacs, acacias and occidental planes.[16] A later rail traveller, however, noted in his Diary:[17]

Sat Nov 20th 1880: The railway traveller, hurrying from Clapham to Vauxhall Station, cannot fail to notice in South Lambeth a quaint, old fashioned house, with hammered iron gates standing apart from the noisy street as if conscious that it embodies in its bricks and mortar and narrow windows the well-to-do gentility which is vanishing from around it. Close by is a fine park with old yew trees and great shady elms, which seem strangely out of place in a neighbourhood where every rood of ground is worth a poor man's ransom. This was the house of the Tradescants....

By the time Arthur Rackham was old enough to take advantage of the garden, but young enough still to wonder at its mystery and silence, those old yew trees and great shady elms would also perhaps have been

19

The Trial of the Knave
of Hearts
Colour process plate,
1907

*Illustration to the
Heinemann edition of* Alice
in Wonderland *by Lewis
Carroll, and arguably a
visual parody of Alfred
Rackham's descriptions of
his work place, the
Ecclesiastical and Admiralty
Courts at Doctor's
Commons.*

overgrown, and even blighted and misshapen by the knots, gnarls and contorted root and branch structures that in later life Arthur was to make his own special preserve. How could any child, particularly one whose acknowledged bent was toward the fantastic and the imaginative, have resisted the magnetism of so strange a garden? So *was* this the place that launched a thousand drawings of possessed, demonic trees? And was this the place that launched Arthur on the career that, ultimately, was to affect the imaginative, literary and pictorial understanding of countless children and adults all around the world?

Rackham always considered himself to be a Cockney – a 'Transpontine Cockney' as he particularly described himself in the title of his 1934 *Self Portrait* – and it was from this breeding that he believed he derived his intense powers of observation, his obsession with the weird, and by extension perhaps his fascination with the historic trees he found himself to be born under: 'I could say something about my Cockney view,' he wrote in 1934,[18]

I'll only say I believe Cockneys are very observant of small, new, strange things: also I discover in myself that the *size* of the trees I almost always naturally draw, is a *middle* size – not a forest monster – & you know how fond I am of drawing bare winter trees & drawing them with black ink. Well it was almost a discovery for me when I found that tree-branches were *not* black in the country. This is a very youthful memory of course.

Arthur Rackham left no particular record of whether or not his father's work at Doctors' Commons also influenced his illustration, and so we can only guess. But for a son with such a vivid pictorial imagination to have a father with so picturesque and, to our eyes, exotic a profession, and still not be affected by it to a marked degree, would be stretching credibility rather too far. Arthur certainly watched the processions across the quadrangle as a young man, and made a quick pen and ink sketch on Law Court

20

paper of his father, as Admiralty Marshall, carrying the Silver Oar. Arthur's illustration of 'The Trial of the Knave of Hearts' from *Alice in Wonderland* (1907) is an image which evokes everything described by Alfred and satirized by Dickens: the King and Queen of Hearts sitting as Judges on a raised dais with a Gothic canopy; the White Rabbit with the scroll and accusation; and, nearly on a level with the Judges, the jury box crammed with the twelve jurors, while the Officers of the Court occupy the well below. The Officers may be playing cards, the jurors may be animals, and Exhibit A a plate of tarts, but nonetheless Arthur's visual parody of the scene parallels in telling detail his father's verbal recollection of Doctor's Commons.

Other images that recur in Rackham's work, and which are undoubtedly remnants of childhood memory, include those of someone hanging by his or her hair in brambles or branches, and of ominous shadows cast on an adjacent wall, preceding or dominating a figure. These both convey anguish and pain or the threat of it, and represent a darker side to Rackham's imagination which was perhaps rooted in his childhood. The pain of hair being pulled may, indeed, reflect Rackham's fascination during family Bible readings with the story of Absalom, who was caught by the hair in 'the thick boughs of a great oak'.[19] Every child knows the fear that shadows can hold, particularly a child who habitually drew on his pillows upstairs by the flickering light of a candle.

After the infant Mabel had been carried off by whooping-cough before she was 1 year old in 1876, and the mysterious and unfortunate Percy had died at his Thames-side lodgings in 1878, the shadow of death moved away from the Rackham household. In March 1882 they left number 210, and moved a few hundred yards across South Lambeth Road to a larger house, 27 Albert Square. Three years later they moved again, to 3 St Ann's Park Villas,[20] Wandsworth, within walking distance of Wimbledon Common.

For the first nine years of their married life, the Rackhams attended the Congregational Chapel in Claylands Road, Kennington, five minutes' walk from 210 South Lambeth Road. The chapel was run by James Baldwin Brown (1820–1884), the controversial and argumentative dissenting minister, pamphleteer and one of the leading opponents of the Doctrine of Annihilation. In 1870, Baldwin Brown led the majority of his congregation, including the Rackhams, to the new and more spacious Brixton Independent Church in Brixton Road. This had been built between 1869 and 1870 with money raised by the Claylands

The quicker he played the higher she had to jump
Colour process plate, 1900
Illustration to 'Sweetheart Roland' from *Grimm's Fairy Tales*

Rackham brought a terrifying and cruel reality to his drawings of figures caught by their hair, a memory, perhaps, of the story of Absalom heard during regular family Bible readings.

21

Left: Jack Sprat and his Wife
Pen and ink and watercolour, 1912
210 × 160 mm
Musée Nationale d'Art Moderne, Paris

Illustration to Mother Goose. *It was purchased from
Rackham by the collector Edmund Davis in 1913 for
presentation to the Luxembourg Gallery, Paris, with his
collection of 36 other works by contemporary British artists.*

Chapel congregation to celebrate Baldwin Brown's twenty-three year ministry.[21] The Rackhams were regular and keen attenders both at Claylands and Brixton Road, and advocates of Unitarianism, a branch of the Christian church which holds that 'each individual must be free to seek truth for himself, unaffected by official creeds'.[22]

Their most powerful influence at this time, however, was Frederick Denison Maurice (1805–1872), the great Victorian theologian and academic who, in 1846, became Chaplain of Lincoln's Inn. At his daily services and weekly Bible classes Maurice met many rising young men at all levels of the legal profession. One of his biographers, Olive J. Brose, has written of him: 'Maurice's magnetism was not that of a brilliant don or preacher like Newman.... It was more personal, limited to intense individual contacts, and hence was perhaps more profound.'[23]

Maurice, the son of a Unitarian minister, had studied for the Bar at Cambridge, but turned away from practising law before he became ordained into the Church of England in 1834. His career was one of the stormiest and most active of his day, and he played a leading role, with the Rev. Charles Kingsley, in the Christian Socialist movement which had such a damaging effect on the orthodoxies of the Established Church. He was also a founder of the Working Men's College movement, and in his own thought was rooted in the philosophical writings of Samuel Taylor Coleridge. Maurice was forced to resign his Professorship at King's College, London, on his refusal to withdraw his definition of Eternity which he had published in 1853, to which the Established Church deeply objected. Eternity, he maintained, had nothing to do with time or indefinite duration; 'not time extended', as L. E. Elliott-Binns pointed out, 'but time abolished'.[24]

Alfred Rackham, one of the thousands who heard Maurice preach, was drawn by his 'intense individual contacts', and in 1853 had left the Church of England as a protest against the Church's treatment of Maurice and Kingsley. As an official of Doctors' Commons, Alfred had further, professional, contacts with Maurice, when the latter took issue with Judge Dr Stephen Lushington's decision in 1861 on a case of false doctrine in the Ecclesiastical Courts.

The freedom of thought preached and practised by Maurice, and espoused by Alfred Rackham and many others like him, seems to be at odds with the Establishment formality required in Alfred's work as a civil servant. That Alfred maintained so rigorous a balance in his private and professional lives between a progressive social responsibility and a loyalty to an established system, speaks volumes for his energy, pragmatism, intelligence and tact. These qualities, which come over so strongly both in and between the lines of his *Personal Recollections*, were also those with which he imbued his children, and of which he built their foundations for life. In 1879, seven years after Denison Maurice's death, the Rackhams commemorated him in a most personal way by naming after him their youngest son, Maurice (1879–1927).

Perhaps the most tangible thread that links Denison Maurice, through Alfred, to Arthur Rackham, however, is their joint affinity with, and espousal of the writings of Samuel Taylor Coleridge. In his 42nd year in 1910, Arthur, addressing the Authors' Club as their Guest of Honour at a dinner,[25] acknowledged Coleridge as 'the most inspired critic and writer on art that I have come across'.

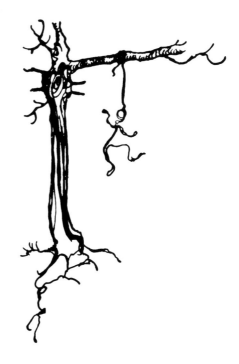

Alfred was meanwhile rising steadily in the hierarchy of the Admiralty Registry. He became Chief Clerk in 1875 ('salary £600, rising to £700'), and moved with his Department to Somerset House to temporary accommodation while the new Law Courts were being built in The Strand. In 1883 the Law Courts were completed, and the Registry moved the five hundred yards into the new building. Five years later, Alfred became Assistant to the Admiralty Registrar, and finally, in 1896, when his surviving children had all grown up, he was appointed to the rank of Admiralty Marshal and Serjeant at Mace of the High Court of Justice ('salary £800'), on the long-awaited retirement, aged 84, of the previous Admiralty Marshal.

Although the title of the post stresses its ceremonial aspect, the Marshal was in fact the Executive Officer of the Court, whose duties were to attend sittings and to arrest and keep in safe custody ships and cargoes proceeded against in the Admiralty Division. In wartime he had also the custody and sale of prizes taken from the enemy, and until the early years of the nineteenth century, the Marshal was responsible for the hanging of pirates and those condemned for murder on the high seas. Alfred writes: 'These criminals were hanged at Execution Dock down the River Thames, the gallows being erected on the shore between the flux and reflux of the tide. My father remembered having in his young days seen the bodies hanging in chains on the river's edge.' He adds: 'I am very glad that in my time this no longer formed part of the Marshal's duties.'

On Alfred Rackham's retirement in May 1899, six weeks before his seventieth birthday, and after a long, secure legal career in which he had reached the top of his profession, his eldest surviving son, Arthur, had still not yet had success of his own. Worse, he was the only one of the sons who had not found the academic or formal success, and the security that followed, of the kind approved of and striven after by their father.

In the year their father retired, Arthur's nearest brother, Harris (1868–1944), then aged 31, was a Senior Fellow at Christ's College, Cambridge, where he had graduated with 1st Class Honours in Pure Classics and Philosophy in 1891. The next brother, Bernard (1876–1964), nine years Arthur's junior, had the previous year been appointed Junior Assistant Keeper at the South Kensington Museum, straight from having taken a First in the Classical Tripos at Pembroke College, Cambridge.[26]

Stanley (1877–1937) had completed his agricultural studies at Aspatria Agricultural College, Cumberland, in 1898, coming first in the Annual Examination, and being made a Scholar of the College. Having won the Silver Medal and Free Life Membership of the Royal Agricultural Society of England in May 1898, and received a Diploma in Agriculture at Cambridge in July that year, Stanley went to Canada for a year in March 1899 for farming experience. The youngest brother of all, Maurice, left the City of London School in 1898 holding the school records for the mile, half mile and hurdles, and entered his brother Harris's College, Christ's, that autumn on a Classical Exhibition.

Here were the four brilliant younger sons of Alfred and Annie Rackham, bedecked with academic, athletic and agricultural honours. Every detail of their successes is recorded proudly by Alfred in his *Personal Recollections*. Arthur, however, now well into his thirties, who had witnessed their gestation and infancy, been about at their births and at the deaths of their infant brothers and sisters and of their grandparents, Arthur who had known and played with the absent and epileptic Percy, Arthur the mischievous and playful elder brother who would entertain them with caricatures, and so often sit just quietly looking about him, drawing and drawing, Arthur, the big brother, was apparently not doing quite so well.

Instead, he was earning a precarious living as a caricaturist, pictorial journalist, landscape and portrait painter and, to a limited extent, book illustrator. To all appearances, he was still a hack – indeed in later life, in a letter to W. E. Dawe in 1903, he describes 'not being able to embark on a professional career till I was nearly 25, & then for many years getting the barest living from my profession & having to do much distasteful hack work.'[27]

Throughout Alfred's *Personal Recollections* runs an acknowledgement of the importance of rank, status and success, for the sake of social and financial security and the future. At every promotion, Alfred

provincial draper's daughter, a senior official in an ancient profession, Alfred Rackham remained, however, a Company Man.

He was also tremendous fun. He had a wide general knowledge, which, peppered with jokes and anecdotes, he passed on to his children. The stories he tells in his notebook, surely the same as he told to his children at his knee, are full of visual imagery, and are the kind of stories that any wide-eyed and receptive child would love: the luminous paint exhibition given by his grandfather; looking through the telescope on fine nights in Southwark at the moon and planets; his struggling conscientiously at 3 a.m., as the White Rabbit might, with quill pen and parchment to finish the Declaration of War for the Queen to sign; the black- and red-gowned procession across Doctors' Commons, with the silver-tipped ebony wand and Silver Oar leading the way. Particularly potent and ghoulish is Alfred's story of bodies of pirates hanging in chains at Execution Dock,[28] 'on the shore between the flux and reflux of the tide', an image which so directly parallels Arthur's macabre drawing of 'The Dead Drummer' in *Ingoldsby Legends* (1898).

His father's rollicking presence kept slipping back into Arthur's memory, in both soft and hard focus, after Alfred's death in 1912. In his Foreword to *Mother Goose* (1913) Arthur reminds his readers that 'nursery rhymes have until recently been handed on only by oral tradition with its inevitable variations,' and adds, 'I have chosen those I knew and liked best in my own

Below: The Dead Drummer
Pen and ink, 1898
148 × 269 mm
Arthur Rackham Collection, Rare Book and Manuscript Library,
Columbia University

Silhouette tailpiece from The Ingoldsby Legends.

records his new salary, and the figure to which it would rise. He is proud to be a Civil Servant 2nd Class at 24, above those coming after him who were appointed on the 3rd Class grade. All his children's academic achievements are noted, complete with degree grades, scholarships and diplomas. He was nevertheless a most unusual Victorian paterfamilias, loving and beloved of his large family, genial and merry, precise and clear in his work, thought and opinions, and proud to the point of unreason of his children's achievements. He was God-fearing, with a commitment to religious radicalism and social responsibility, a free-thinking autodidact who read Ruskin, Morris and volumes of sermons. The son and grandson of schoolmasters, husband of a successful

nursery days, and I have kept to the version I was familiar with.... At home we had no complete book of them: most we knew came direct from our elders.'

Perhaps the clearest and fondest recollection of all, and a most touching memory that a son could have of his father, comes in a letter Arthur wrote to an unidentified recipient who had asked him in 1922 for his experiences of *Alice in Wonderland*: 'My experiences of the book are absolutely delightful ... it was read aloud to us (3 about the same age, 11, 10, 9 say) by my father & at once became a household word.... It is possible that my father's appreciation of it helped us children too. It was read to us with full dramatic effect, the songs sung and so forth. Altogether an unforgettable and epoch marking event in my life.'[29]

CHAPTER TWO

THE NECESSITY THAT SENT ME FIRST TO BUSINESS 1879–1898

Left: Portrait of Winifred, Aged 17
Watercolour, 1890
285 × 222 mm
Private Collection

Winifred, Rackham's younger sister, sat for him extensively in the 1890s and was his model for The Dolly Dialogues *cover and for* New Fiction *and Other Papers.*

I N SEPTEMBER 1879 ARTHUR, TOGETHER with his younger brother Harris, entered the City of London School,[1] then in Cheapside, across St Paul's Churchyard from the by now demolished Doctors' Commons. It was a day public school, and in sending all his sons there, Alfred, being 'not quite at one with my Mother's ideas on this point', gave them 'the advantage of association with others without being deprived of home influence as in a boarding school'. At school, Arthur was popular and happy, though he did not show signs of being particularly academic.

His ability as a caricaturist, and his friendly and agreeable character, made him many friends at school. The author of his Obituary in the school magazine tells how '… while still a boy [he] delighted his contemporaries with his drawings. One of his best remembered sketches showed the Fourth Form as a menagerie, with W. G. Rushbrooke, their master, as keeper….'[2] His caricatures of masters became famous in the school in other ways too – Rushbrooke caught him drawing some of these, and hauled him to the front of the class as a punishment to repeat them, for everybody's benefit, on the blackboard, to the accompaniment of gales of Fourth Form laughter.[3] Arthur seems to have been the class 'character', one of those boys who sat eternally at the back of the class, as he admitted to a school fellow, Howard Angus Kennedy: 'I settled down under Rushy, whose backbenches I occupied for a long time – never flying higher….'[4]

Arthur's precocity was, however, also given serious training by the schools' new and enthusiastic young drawing master Herbert Dicksee (1862–1942), and led him to win the school prize for Memory Drawing

Sun and Shade: Olives at Assisi
Watercolour, 1928
242 × 171 mm
Private Collection

This watercolour, exhibited at the RWS Summer Exhibition in 1929, demonstrates how Rackham continued throughout his life to seek out naturally contorted trees as subject matter.

in the Summer Term of 1883.[5] Dicksee, who had himself been a pupil at the school before leaving to study at the Slade, drew a portrait of Arthur as the School Prize for Drawing, which, in his last term, Christmas 1883, Arthur also won.

This high-spirited and intelligent boy did, however, win some other, more academic form prizes, two at least of which he kept until the end of his life, both being of significance for his later development. One, the Fourth Form Prize for Proficiency in Algebra and Trigonometry, Midsummer 1883, was a copy of *The Universe: or The Infinitely Great and the Infinitely Little*, a new book by F. A. Pouchet,[6] full of facts and information, illustrated with wood-engraved wonders of the natural world, the bizarre and the fantastic, and presented in a manner to capture any boy's imagination. The other prize was a copy of Paul Lacroix's *Manners, Customs and Dress during the Middle Ages and during the Renaissance Period*,[7] illustrated with chromolithographs and wood-engravings.

Despite his good humour and alertness, Arthur was not in good health. Because of this, his parents took medical advice from one of the leading physicians of the day, Dr (later Sir) Samuel Wilks (1824–1911), the Physician to Guy's Hospital. Wilks, as Alfred Rackham's *Personal Recollections* tell, recommended a sea voyage as the cure. Even though this entailed Arthur's leaving school at sixteen, Alfred and Annie took Dr Wilks's advice. The recent memory of the deaths of five of their children, one after the other, from a variety of sicknesses, made any other decision impossible.

Two friends of the family, Miss Liggens and Mrs Merrifield, were about to emigrate to Australia, and Arthur was booked on their ship, the SS *Chimborazo* of the Orient Line, to accompany them from London to Sydney and return on his own a few months later. Arthur's annotated passenger list of the outward trip survives.[8] They left Gravesend on 23 January 1884, forty travelling First Class (including Mrs Merrifield) and about eighty Second Class (including Arthur – there is no mention of Miss Liggens on the passenger list). Arthur's cheerful good humour evidently enabled him to mix well with his fellow passengers in the Second Saloon, though there is more than a trace of boyish prejudice in the words he used, in a tiny hand, to annotate their names on the passenger list.

Among the passengers were seven nuns, as well as Mr H. C. Champney ('Jumbo'); Mr J. A. Cohen ('jew'); Mr C. G. Cornwall ('fool – gin & bitters'); Mr R. Douglas ('Scotty'); Miss Edwards ('Chimpanzee'); Mr J. R. Forrester ('spitter'); Mr W. F. Jacob ('Revolver Jack … Tasmanian Devil'); Mr C. E. Livesey ('C. E. L. Esq'); Mr R. Lochhead ('Gold digger'); Mr A. K. Woolmington ('Wooly') and Mr & Mrs A. B. Booth and Family (6), whom he has annotated with the words 'Irish Farmers. Boycotted'. Arthur described himself, perhaps at sixteen the youngest travelling alone, as 'Me. The bantam'. Two passengers appeared, like Arthur, to be travelling for their health, and one, Mr C. Hunt, also travelling to Sydney, Arthur listed as an artist.

At the end of every day, Arthur recorded the distance run, and the latitude and longitude reached, to an accuracy of two decimal points. He noted the times of passing key landmarks – Cape Finisterre, Gibraltar, Sardinia, Straits of Messina, Suez, Aden – their crossing of the Equator on 21 February, and their arrivals at Adelaide (9 March), Melbourne (12 March) and disembarkation at Sydney (15 March). At the end of the voyage, he used his prizewinning mathematical skills to calculate the average speed over the 48-day voyage (1884 was a leap year) to be $260\frac{1}{3}$ miles per day, that is $10\frac{5}{6}$ miles per hour.

Arthur stayed in Sydney for two-and-a-half months, and according to the evidence of surviving watercolours worked tirelessly painting the sights: Sydney Harbour, Sugarloaf Bay, Balmoral Bay, Mossman's Bay Falls and Willoughby Falls. His Australian watercolours, made when he at last had the opportunity to give long stretches of time to painting, away from pressures of school work and the noise and chatter of his younger brothers and sisters, constitute the first focused body of work in which we can see an interesting – though no more than this yet – artist in embryo.

In later life, Arthur was asked to write 'In Praise of Water Colour', and tells with a light, engaging touch, of his paintbox, and what it had meant to him from childhood:

From the first day when I was given, as all little boys are, a shilling paint box with the legend printed along the space for the brush – 'Waste not, want not' (so I was informed, for I couldn't read then) – from that day, when I first put my water-colour brush in my mouth, and was told I mustn't, this craft we are celebrating has been my constant companion. On high-days (illuminating texts of a Sunday), off-hours and above all holidays. In the nursery, at school, and then during the long years when an office stool was my lot, my paint box was as impatient as I for the freedom of the holidays. Looking back I have one long memory of holidays and never one without my faithful friend. Such a modest silent convenient companion too. So light in weight and taking such little space. In he goes, brushes, water-bottle, and if the block is too big for my poacher's pocket, it takes no room to speak of in the rucksack.[9]

North Shore, Sydney
Watercolour, 1884
175 × 125 mm
Private Collection

Painted on his visit to Australia, and showing Rackham's growing fascination for bizarre and wonderful elements in nature.

Although there are earlier watercolours by Rackham surviving – one of the earliest is *Castle Rising, Norfolk*, August 1881, painted when Arthur was thirteen – the Australian group, though still juvenile, shows him beginning to achieve a mastery over his 'modest silent convenient companion'. Every one of the 24 views is inscribed, with infinite pains, with its title, date, and

when completed – for example *Middle Harbour, Sydney, from Folly Point April 1884 / Twemlow's Reef / Finished on homeward voyage*.

Another, *North Shore, Sydney*, shows trees, shrubs and a rocky outcrop whose textures, colouring and shadow are carefully and sensitively interpreted. The *genus* of the shrubs might not be discernible from Rackham's handling of the watercolour, but their differences certainly are, and the subject shows Arthur's growing fascination for the bizarre and wonderful in nature, the same fascination, no doubt, that ensured his enjoyment (and even his choice?) of *The Universe* as his Class Prize less than a year earlier. Arthur's interest in 'incident' also has an early showing here – his watercolour of *Sugarloaf Bay – Middle Harbour, Sydney, April 1884*, includes a dog looking quizzically at a crab, which waves its claws angrily in return.

His most ambitious painting in Australia, however, is the five-sheet panorama inscribed on the mount *PANORAMIC VIEW OF SYDNEY FROM NATURE, MAY 1884*. The view takes us across Sydney Harbour from Kirribilli Point, North Shore to Goat Island, MacMahon's Point and Lavender Bay. If pedestrian and laboured, unlike some of Arthur's single sketches around Sydney, it does prove his complete dedication as a painter, his application and perseverance to finish

a job – and further demonstrates that the paragraphs 'In Praise of Water Colour' were not merely an old man's rosy reminiscences of youth from fifty years on.

Three slight sketches survive from Arthur's voyage out to Australia, while from the way back there are 26, in addition to those Sydney views 'finished on the homeward voyage'. The boy worked very hard at his art, it is quite clear. No passenger list of the homeward voyage annotated by him survives, but from the record of the watercolours he left Sydney on Orient Line's SS *Iberia* at the end of May. The ship was near Adelaide on 2 June, off Cape Guardafui, Somalia, on 22 June, in the Red Sea on 25 June, and going through the Suez Canal on 28, 29 and 30 June. The passengers went on an excursion from the ship to see the Khedive's Palace, Lake Timsah at Ismailia on 29 June, and had reached the Bay of Naples on 6 July. To celebrate crossing the Equator on 17 June there was a Ship's Concert – and Arthur, ever the great joiner-in, designed the programme with its

Below and Right: Near Adelaide
Watercolour, 1884
175 × 125 mm
Private Collection

Both these watercolours were painted on board ship on Rackham's voyage home from Australia.

decoration of rope cartouches, flags, anchors, Britannia and the ship herself.

The most interesting and accomplished watercolours Arthur made since leaving England are those showing atmospheric sea and sky effects on the voyage home. *Near Adelaide / June 2nd 1884* is a Palmeresque vision of the moon and stars on a quiet, cloudless night. It is painted in a blue and white monochrome, with the moon on her back surrounded by a wide dark ring, and reflecting into a motionless sea. Six evenings later, the sea had become choppier, and Arthur painted the moon coming through a breaking cloud in the same blue and white. This little watercolour shows his growing understanding of the importance, indeed the power, of composition, and an attraction to the dramatic. If Arthur had left England

as a schoolboy, he was returning as an interesting and dedicated young artist.

Presumably the purpose of Arthur's trip to Australia, to improve his health, was accomplished, because nothing more is heard on the subject for nearly twenty years. The Australian trip also strengthened his resolve to become an artist, and gave him ample opportunity to develop a strategy to achieve this aim. In the summer following his return from Australia, Arthur visited Sussex with his family, making sketches of *Lancing* and of *Worthing Pier from Lancing*. He went on long walks with his father, and together they sat on cliffs drawing boats and the sea. Arthur had drawn in Lancing the two years previously, when his father had rented a pair of lodging houses to accommodate the family and its entourage on holiday, beginning an early affection for the county that throughout his life was to provide Arthur with inspiration, subject-matter and, in the 1920s, a home.

At sixteen, however, there was no question of his studying art full-time, or returning to any kind of formal education. His father in 1884 may have been approaching the top of his Chief Clerk's salary scale of £700 a year, but he was also keeping a family house in Albert Square, Lambeth, with staff, and had a wife and six other children to support.[10] Arthur inherited his father's belief in the importance of financial security and self-sufficiency, despite the fact that in the future he was to endure agonies in pursuit of it. Whether willingly or reluctantly, therefore, he accepted the compromise of attending evening classes at Lambeth School of Art in Kennington Park Road[11] the following autumn while at the same time looking for a job to help pay for his tuition and for his keep in his parents' house.

At Lambeth, Arthur studied under William Llewellyn (1858–1941), the landscape painter, who had himself studied under Poynter and in Paris in the studio of Ferdinand Cormon.[12] 'With me or in most cases just before me at the school but surviving in influence,' Rackham wrote years later to Ethel Chadwick, 'there was a rather remarkable run of students,'[13] and he goes on to list Charles Shannon, Charles Ricketts, Leonard Raven Hill, Reginald Savage, F. H. Townsend, Thomas Sturge Moore and Oliver Hall. That many of these artists made their names and their livings by selling their work for reproduction by printers reflects the success of the School's training of artists for the ceramic, metal, stone or printing industries.

Arthur remained loyal to the friendship and example of his student colleagues throughout his life, but from the distance of age remembered some of them more clearly than others. Shannon, for example, he discussed in a letter to Kerrison Preston: 'I do not know Charles Shannon personally but he was a senior

student at Lambeth, & a little god, when I was a junior there.'[14] He wrote about Ricketts to Mrs Edward Parsons, a New York collector:

Charles Ricketts was, indeed, an inspiring influence & a class-mate, a senior when I was a junior & very properly approached with the deference that 2 or 3 years seniority demanded.... But I had other student companions who have won fame & though I was very restless under the necessity that sent me first to business, I have since appreciated the good fortune that took me to evening classes where I got such training as I ever had.[15]

One of these student companions who won fame was Thomas Sturge Moore (1870–1944), the poet and wood-engraver, who remained a close friend until Arthur died in September 1939. They were in correspondence in June of that year, reminiscing, in an inconsequential way, about the rosy past. Sturge Moore wrote to Arthur during the legendary hot summer before war was declared: 'This weather reminds me of the summers we had and which seemed so normal in our youth, though they seem so rare now.' Discussing A. J. Finberg's *Life of J.M.W. Turner*, then just published, Sturge Moore goes on to say: 'Poor

Landscape with Barn
Oil on panel, c1890s
117 × 197 mm
Private Collection

One of the many small oil and watercolour landscapes, reflecting a knowledge of Impressionism, that Rackham painted in London and the South of England during his years as an art student and a young insurance clerk (1885–92), and subsequently as an illustrative journalist.

Wimbledon Common
Watercolour, 1890's
222 × 185 mm
Private Collection

Finberg died about 3 months ago.... Did you know him at Lambeth? Off and on I knew him quite a lot....'[16]

Throughout his life Arthur remained convinced from his own experience of the importance of formal study for young artists, and the provision of good teaching for them. He was fortunate in his own youth in being taught by Dicksee and Llewellyn, two artists who were themselves at the beginnings of distinguished careers[17] and both fresh with the latest ideas from France. Years later, writing to a Mr Wilson, an art teacher whose students had presented him with a pipe, Rackham said: 'But of one thing I am *quite* sure & that is that you, all of you, get real joy of the highest kind in your studies.'[18] Again to Wilson, he adds: '... I cannot conceive how anyone can be doing more valuable work than you are to pave the way for a finer awakening – a new renaissance....'[19]

To earn his keep, Arthur applied for a job at the Westminster Fire Office, and in November 1884 was possibly one of fourteen candidates to pass the arithmetic examination for the two vacant probationary posts of Junior Clerk (4th Class).[20] He was supported by a pair of glowing references from his school teachers, his former Headmaster, Edwin Abbott, pointing out that 'as regards ability, knowledge, character and gentlemanly bearing, Mr. Arthur Rackham would be well suited to the clerkship he is now seeking in the Westminster Fire Office.'[21]

Arthur was not, however, successful in the subsequent ballot to choose the lucky two appointees, and does not appear as a fully fledged Junior Clerk (4th Class) until he is recorded as having completed his probationary period, usually six months, on 20 May 1886.[22] Therefore it is unlikely that he joined the Fire Office much before Christmas 1885. On a starting salary of £40 a year, with an annual £10 increment, Arthur was one of twenty-three 3rd and 4th Class and Junior Clerks[23] employed at the Covent Garden office of the Company.[24] They were 'plain copying clerks, and juniors learning the business', and were paid at a rate much lower than that paid by comparable insurance offices at that time.[25]

Although Arthur was the kind of young man who gave life the benefit of the doubt, and superficially at least was characteristically disposed to be cheerful, he was nevertheless bored and frequently dispirited by his job at the Fire Office. In his article 'In Praise of Water Colour'[26] he writes of 'the long years when the office stool was my lot', but nevertheless he was realist enough to know that his office stool was merely a means to an end. The advice he gave to the aspiring artist W. E. Dawe, written when he was at the height of his success, looks at the issue from a parental point of view, and may not necessarily be the kind of advice he himself would have welcomed as he sat on his office stool. It may well, however, echo the advice that Alfred Rackham, who knew what it was like to be a Junior Clerk, actually gave to *his* son:

As a profession, [art] is one to which no parent would be justified in putting a son without being able to give him a permanent income as well. Then, of course, if he fail, he will have something to live upon: I know several such, &, believe me, their bitter disappointment at their professional failure is only just prevented from being misery by the possession of an independent income.[27]

During the 1880's when Arthur was undergoing the change from schoolboy to student and junior clerk, he

made friends for life, travelled in Britain developing his technique as an artist, gave his time to charitable causes, and fell in love.

During the summers of the late 1880s, and at weekends throughout the year, Arthur and his friends went on sketching trips near at home on Wimbledon Common, and further afield. The Rackhams – with Arthur – had by now moved to Wandsworth, an easy walk away from the Common where such a wide variety of subjects were to be found. Two of Arthur's early oil paintings of the Common survive, one dated 1888, and one watercolour dated January 1885, as well as a number of other landscape subjects. These include the churches at *Winchelsea* and *Rye* (pencil, both May 1885), *Leith Hill, Surrey* (1887), a pen and ink view of *Cadgwith, Cornwall* (1889) and an undated and highly accomplished oil on canvas of a *Snowy Landscape*, painted with enthusiastic knowledge of French Impressionism.

Already in the late 1880s, Arthur was beginning to make his own important formal achievements as an artist. In 1888 his watercolour *Winchelsea from the Marsh* was accepted for the Royal Academy Summer Exhibition (no. 1446), and the following year another watercolour, *Cottages at Pett, Sussex*, was selected (no. 1297).[28] Both were submitted from his parents' address, 3 St Ann's Park Villas, Wandsworth, and both were sold, albeit to people whom Arthur knew, and who knew him, and who were supporting him for friendship's sake, too. Mr Hunter, 'late of Admiralty Registry',[29] a colleague of Alfred Rackham, bought *Winchelsea* for 2 guineas, and F. G. Ryves, a colleague at Westminster Fire Office, paid 3 guineas for *Cottages at Pett*. He was also showing landscape paintings at the Royal Society of British Artists, two oils and a watercolour of Southern English scenes in 1889, an oil

of *Chiddingstone, Kent* in 1890, and an oil of *Shoreham, Sussex* in 1890/91.[30]

During this still shadowy period of his life, Rackham was beginning to submit drawings to some of the illustrated magazines of the day. It was a buoyant market for artists still, despite the looming threat of new techniques that would soon transform the magazine industry with photographic illustrations. Decorative head and tailpieces, however, became a new and fertile area, and one in which Rackham and many others excelled. The magazines that accepted Rackham's illustrations in the 1880s were *Scraps* and *Illustrated Bits*.[31] Perhaps in an attempt to head off assiduous researchers into his early work (which he often quite understandably wished would disappear), he wrote to the keen Frederick Mason, a Londoner trying to build up a Rackham collection: 'You'll *never* find "Scraps". I think it was a $\frac{1}{2}$d weekly. A sort of illustrated forerunner of Tit Bits. And the paper it was printed on has decayed to dust. Years ago when I had

Arthur Rackham, seated, centre
with his brothers, sisters and friend.
Photograph, 1890
Private Collection

a print it broke actually like rotten egg shell in my hands.'[32]

Arthur's first recorded love affair, an ultimately Platonic interlude, came to nothing. He had set his cap at Amy Tompkins, who came up to London every other day from her home at Lee in Kent,[33] between 1885 and 1887. She was driven to London by her father in his Phaeton, with her white Pomeranian, Puff, to ride in Hyde Park while her father went to his club to gamble. As Amy rode up and down Rotten Row, Arthur looked after Puff, as his series of small pen and ink sketches, one inscribed 'Love me, Love my Dog', suggests. During the courtship Arthur was invited by, or even followed, Amy to Yarmouth, where the Tompkins family spent their summer holidays. Five of the sketches are now at Columbia University, New York, but a sixth, recording the dénouement of the courtship, was not acquired. The lovelorn Arthur, like Freddie in *My Fair Lady*, having travelled to the street where she lived, is coolly described in a sale catalogue as: 'Silhouette of male figure, carrying top hat, being kicked out and down the front steps of a house.'[34] Exit little Cockney insurance clerk, who sketched.

Walter Freeman and Donkey Cart
Pen and ink and watercolour, 1889
Arthur Rackham Collection, Rare Book and Manuscript Library,
Columbia University

Drawn while on holiday with Freeman in Cornwall. Rackham shows himself closing the gate in the background.

One of his great friends and holiday companions of this period was Walter Freeman, a young journalist who later wrote for *The World*. Together they helped to run a Christian cadet corp, the Boy's Brigade, in Kingston, where Freeman lived with his parents,[35] and together they travelled on holiday to Cornwall in the latter years of the 1880s. After one of these trips, Freeman was instrumental in introducing Arthur to one of his most important early sources of employment. He showed Arthur's pen and ink drawing of *Cadgwith* (1889) to the then Editor of *Punch*, and this, Freeman's daughter claimed, 'got [Arthur] his start with that paper.'[36]

On the same holiday Arthur produced a laboured but clear pen, ink and watercolour drawing of Freeman driving a donkey cart and Arthur, in the background, closing a farm gate behind them. Though laboured – maybe because of it – this drawing does demonstrate Rackham's concern at this early stage in his career to get details right. The donkey cart and harness are shown with clarity, and we can see how both operate, though the donkey itself appears to be little more than a four-legged pudding with long ears.

Self Portrait, Aged 24
Oil on card, 1892
210 × 160 mm
Arthur Rackham Collection, Rare Book and Manuscript Library,
Columbia University

Despite Arthur's professed loathing of gadgetry, he was always at pains to make equipment look as if it would work when, for the purposes of an illustration, equipment had to be included. One particularly poignant case in point came right at the end of his life when, an old, sick and bedridden man, he fretted about having forgotten to put the oars in Mole and Ratty's boat in his illustration to *The Wind in the Willows*, and insisted on using some of his last few ounces of strength to put the error right. A less emotive case is the drawing *Common Objects at the Seaside by Our Goblinesque Artists. Studies for Goblin Tapestry*, made for the *Punch Almanack* of 1905. Here analysis goes far beyond humour, and we see Arthur observing *inter alia* the workings of an overloaded dinghy in full sail, a fishing rod under extreme tension, a lobster pot containing a doleful lobster, a collapsing artist's easel, and many other wacky objects and incidents.

Arthur had remained at Lambeth School of Art until at least 1890,[37] and at the Fire Office until February 1892, when he resigned.[38] He soon moved out of his parents' house to rooms of his own, first at 12 New Court, Carey Street, Lincoln's Inn, where he lived in 1893 and 1894,[39] and then to Buckingham Chambers, 11 Buckingham Street, The Strand, where he lived from 1895 until 1897.

New Court, a red-brick block of chambers designed by Alfred Waterhouse RA around a central courtyard and completed in 1884 (now demolished), was densely inhabited by a curious mix of barristers and artists, as well as architects, trade wood-engravers and legal shorthand writers.[40] Rackham's section, number 12, had nineteen residences alone, and he shared the busy staircase with an architect, Henry Leonard Hill, wood-engravers Iago and Crossfield, artists Kate Banning, Lindsay Butterfield and Reginald Dick, nine Barristers, a Queen's Counsel, and three firms of Solicitors. The Attorney-General, Sir Charles Russell QC, MP, kept rooms nearby at number 10. Rackham's second London residence, Buckingham Chambers, stands in a street which for two hundred years had been the home of eminent artists and literati, including Samuel Pepys, Robert Harley, William Etty and Clarkson Stanfield, all of whom had at different times lived at number 14. Henry Fielding, Samuel Taylor Coleridge and 'Strata' Smith, the father of modern geology, had also lived in the street, and Thomas Hume and J. J. Rousseau had been visitors.[41] Rackham shared number 11 with the offices of The Pure Literature Society, The Royal Canoe Club, Irish Church Missions to Roman Catholics, Missions to Seamen and others.[42]

All this serves to underline the fact that Rackham was extremely careful and particular about his choice of dwelling. As buildings, both New Court and Buckingham Chambers were good to look at and of high architectural quality, and as places with conducive historical connections and interesting neighbours they had a certain *cachet*, important to a working artist who needed contacts and connections to survive, and one who was naturally gregarious.

Rackham was determined upon a career as an artist, as his listings in the Trades section of successive *Kelly's Directories* for London demonstrates. He judged that he had now achieved the level of skill and had

Right: Common Objects at the Seaside
Pen and ink and watercolour, 1904
460 × 365 mm
Private Collection

A drawing commissioned originally by Punch *for their Almanack of 1905. The subtitle inscribed onto the margin of the drawing reads 'Studies for Goblin Tapestry by our Goblinesque Artists'. There appear to be at least four self portraits of Rackham among the figures.*

THE BRITISH HOUSEWIFE AS ANDROMEDA.

THE THAW.
PLUMBER PERSEUS TO THE RESCUE.

The Thaw
Illustration to *Pall Mall Budget*, Jan 1891

Rackham drew and painted many serpents, as the illustrations in this book show. This, however, is his only known drawing of a domestic serpent.

developed enough contacts to attain the success he had longed for and was brave enough to pursue. With characteristic prudence, however, he waited until he had had a full year's series of illustrations published by the *Pall Mall Budget* throughout 1891 before leaving the Fire Office to join the *Budget* staff, with a source of income assured.

The *Pall Mall Budget*, owned by William Waldorf Astor, was a general interest magazine for adults, with a regular children's section. It had a liberal outlook, reporting on politics with a critical and satirical eye, and knew how a varying mixture of crime, sensational trials, confessions, hangings, deaths, royalty and religion, combined with a sprinkling of art, theatre and fashion, would keep circulation figures buoyant.

Arthur's life now began to open out. He was despatched to cover light opera and comedy, the music hall, a Christmas party for '2,000 little waifs and strays of the Ragged School Union',[43] and the death and funeral of the Duke of Clarence, where his pen lingered over the bizarre shop window display of mourning merchandise, such as black Liquorice Imperials and dark brown Chocolate Bricks.[44] 'Our

artist', as he was from time to time anonymously described, was present at the announcement of the death of Pastor Charles H. Spurgeon (1834–1892), the fiery preacher at the Metropolitan Tabernacle,[45] and even at the digging of Spurgeon's grave in Norwood Cemetery.[46] He got up early to witness winter bathing on the Serpentine,[47] and joined a return day trip by coach from London to Dorking, with stops at inns and stables on the way.[48]

Arthur got everywhere. Perhaps the most exciting, certainly the liveliest assignment of this part of his journalistic career came when he was sent to St James's Hall to cover a Votes for Women meeting.[49] Bernard Shaw, speaking in support of the bill to extend women's franchise, made a 'precise taunt' which upset the opposition and caused a rush towards the platform during which the reporters' table collapsed. The *Budget* reported: '...for a few minutes there was a hand-to-hand fight. The massive brass railings in front of the platform ... were wrenched down; the din was fearful; shrieks and shouts rent the air, and for ten minutes or so one of the most remarkable disturbances ever chronicled in St James's Hall was in full swing....' Arthur's spirited sketches show the opposition (four men in hats) barracking the meeting from the Gallery, portraits of ten of the women speakers, the storming of the platform amid fisticuffs and the collapse of the reporters' table, and the lone figure of Bernard Shaw raising the storm in the Gallery with the words: 'I was not referring to you gentlemen when I mentioned persons possessing a grain of political intelligence.' Later in life, Arthur and Shaw became friends – though whether they first met in the *mêlée* at St James's Hall, or on some other occasion, is not clear.

When his time permitted, Arthur was also doing his own work, and in particular examining a subject that was closest to him, his own face. A *Self Portrait* (1892) shows a young man with pronounced features, a high forehead with fair brown hair and soft grey eyes.[50] He wears a formal black suit with a winged collar, and has an expression of quiet determination and confidence.

Arthur's attachment to the *Pall Mall Budget* ended when he moved across to the *Westminster Budget* at New Year 1893. The progressive Lewis Hind had

taken over as Art Editor of the *Pall Mall Budget*, and Rackham was succeeded there by Aubrey Beardsley, whose portrait of Sir Henry Irving in drawings of the cast of *Becket* soon made, in Beardsley's words, 'the old black-and-white duffers sit up'.[51] On the *Westminster Budget*, Rackham continued as a general reporter, though none of his assignments were quite so dangerous as the St James's Hall episode. He was also contributing to the *Westminster Gazette*, where he was given his first piece of fiction to illustrate for publication. This was *The Dolly Dialogues* by Anthony Hope (1894), in which he used his younger sister, Winifred, as the model. *The Dolly Dialogues* was followed by a cover design for a collection of reactionary literary and art criticism entitled *The New Fiction: A Protest Against Sex Mania* by The Philistine, published by the *Westminster Gazette* in 1895. Rackham's cover shows a young woman – a Beardsley parody also modelled by Winifred, his regular unpaid model in the 1890s – distraught at what she has been reading, dropping her books and pulling her hair. Perhaps through contacts made on the paper he drew twenty pen and ink illustrations (many captioned as from photographs) for *To the Other Side* (1893), a journalistic account of a trip from Britain to the USA and Canada by Thomas Rhodes, designed to sell tickets on transatlantic steamers and American and Canadian railways.[52]

Nearer home, he was sent by his employers to Chelsea to make some drawings of Carlyle's House for *The Homes and Haunts of Thomas Carlyle* (1895), a series of articles which were subsequently issued as a book, and to Hawarden Castle in Cheshire to draw *Gladstone in the Evening of his Days* (1896) for the same purpose.

In later life he expressed genuine surprise when, because of his fame, he saw his early books fetching comparatively high sums. Writing to N. Carroll in Malden, Massachusetts,[53] he discusses *The Dolly Dialogues*: 'It is *very* bad (*my* work, I mean). Quite, quite stupid & uncongenial. I have original *sketches* for much of this old work, though the actual drawings reproduced have mostly vanished (waste-paper basket in most cases I hope & believe). I have destroyed much.'

Arthur's drawings at this time were his employers' property and the papers were free to use them as and when they chose. For another collector,

M. D. McGoff of Liverpool,[54] he recalled that *Homes and Haunts of Thomas Carlyle* 'was a by-product of the paper's.... There were several. I don't think my work was used in many of them but I shouldn't know if it had been. I was at that time on the staff of the paper.... They used to publish an Academy Extra: Zoo Guides: Natl Gallery Guides: &c all of which grew out of the usual labours of their staff. Work of mine crops up in unexpected ways – adapted for unforseen and unintended purposes.'

The Zankiwank

Line block illustration from The Zankiwank and the Bletherwitch *by S. J. Adair-Fitzgerald, 1896.*

During his period on the *Westminster Budget* and *Gazette*, Arthur began to diversify. It was at this time that his first books appeared, and between investigating Carlyle and Gladstone for the *Gazette*, he produced four illustrations for Washington Irving's *The Sketch-Book of Geoffrey Crayon, Gent* (Holly Edition, 1894) and travelled around East Anglia making up to one hundred drawings for *Sun-Rise Land*, a guide to the region by Mrs Alfred Berlyn (1894).[55] In the same year he took part in his first joint exhibition, organized by the publishers J. M. Dent at the Institute of Water Colour Painters' rooms in Piccadilly. This was held in September and October to celebrate the completion of Dent's edition of *Morte Darthur*, with Aubrey Beardsley illustrations, and included the work of Beardsley, Rackham and other young artists who were at that time providing work for Dent's publications.[56]

In 1895 and 1896 he contributed, with others, illustrations to two more books by Washington Irving, *Tales of a Traveller* and *Bracebridge Hall*, beginning a relationship with an author's work which he was to bring to classic status in 1905 with his illustrations to *Rip Van Winkle*. Rackham's main achievement of 1896, however, was the production of 41 illustrations to S. J. Adair Fitzgerald's fantasy story for children *The Zankiwank and the Bletherwitch*, published by J. M. Dent. Here, in the imaginative silhouettes of the attenuated, weirdly double-jointed ostrich-like figure of the Zankiwank, Arthur is finding a commercial, even a career outlet, for the 'fantastic and the imaginative' which had preoccupied him from an early age. Forget Carlyle's house, forget Gladstone in his dotage – here at last is the real Rackham breaking out as, inevitably, he must. Even the title page lettering in its three neat blocks above the image, indebted as it may

Above: Mit Gedult Kommt Alles [All things come with patience.]
Pen and ink and watercolour, 1890s
Private Collection

A calligraphic panel by Rackham for Frederick Andrewes as a consolation when Frederick's first proposal of marriage was refused.

Below: Crack! Went the Rope . . . Cover illustration to *Chums*

be to Charles Rennie Mackintosh, shows a beginning towards the ragged serif face of his own invention that emerges on the cover or title pages of *The Ingoldsby Legends* (1898), *Gulliver's Travels* (1900), *Grimm's Fairy Tales* (1900) and books beyond.

At the same time, Arthur was continuing to make blood-and-thunder and romantic illustrations for books and magazines, many of which were owned by Cassell. He supplied cover illustrations to *Chums*, of the flavour of '"Crack!" went the rope ...',[57] and, regularly from 1896 to 1905, pictures for a variety of stories in *Little Folks*,[58] edited by his friend Sam Hamer.[59] With his full-page popular novel illustrations in the Hugh Thomson manner of girls sighing in gardens and of young officers slapping each other on the back, Rackham had by now developed a well-deserved reputation as an illustrator who could turn his hand to the widest variety of subjects, and produce good and popular work on time. Even crime paid: for Cassell he contributed a number of pen and ink drawings for their three-volume *Mysteries of Police and Crime* (1898), including a macabre drawing of a floating young female corpse captioned: 'Her body ... was found in the water.'

It was not long before publishers and editors – many of whom were or became his friends – began to realize that the balance was shifting, and people were beginning to buy books *because* they were illustrated by Arthur Rackham. The title page of *The Zankiwank* announces that the book has '41 pictures by Arthur Rackham', while Charles Lever's popular novel

Charles O'Malley the Irish Dragoon (1897) carries the title page note 'With Sixteen Illustrations by Arthur Rackham'.

The 1890s was the period in which Rackham travelled in England, Europe and Scandinavia whenever opportunities allowed. His circle of friends had widened by this time to include Frank Keen, Sam Hamer and the two Andrewes brothers, Herbert and Percy.[60] Together they took part in amateur dramatics for which Arthur designed and painted sets, in particular mounting productions of Gilbert and Sullivan. They performed *Box and Cox* in 1891, and also during this period *Ruddigore* (1897) and *Pirates of Penzance*, at St Christopher's Hall, Wigmore Street, London under the direction of their friend Octavia Hill (1838–1912), the housing reformer and founder of the National Trust.

The five formed themselves into a kind of jolly walking club, which they called the *Fünfverein* (Five Club). Their English holidays took them to Dartmoor from a base at Kelly College, Tavistock, and European holidays to France, Austria, Switzerland and Germany. Rackham's dated watercolours, such as *Oberammergau* (1896), *Olden* (1898) and *Rothenburg* (1899), give a hint of the trail they followed. In a letter of condolence written to Rackham by Percy Andrewes on the news of the death of Maurice Rackham, Percy recalls:

I shall never forget the trip I had with you and your brother – in 1901 if I recollect rightly – when we went to Eisenach, Munich & Seefeld, where we joined Sam Hamer & Frank Keen.... My old programmes tell me we saw Meistersinger & Tristan there.[61]

Above: Study for Bookplate
for Herbert Andrewes
Charcoal, 1890's
254 × 165
Private Collection

Herbert Andrewes became a distinguished authority on black beetles. His bookplate reflects the early stages of this interest.

Left: Gulliver's Combat with the Wasps
Colour process plate, 1909

Illustration drawn for Rackham's second edition of Gulliver's Travels, *an image inspired by Alfred Rackham's account of his own battle with a swarm of flies during a walk in the Alps.*

Memories of their holidays remained strong with Frank Keen, too. A decade later, he wrote a congratulatory letter to Rackham on the birth of his daughter Barbara, adding: 'Can you assure us that both hands & both feet are duly adorned with the emblems of the fumpfverein [*sic*] & that nature has not added "noch ein" anywhere?'[62]

It is possible that the *Fünfverein* extended their 1898 German tour with a sailing holiday in Norway. Rackham himself certainly went on to Norway, for during the holiday he met an elderly book collector, Dr Hans Reusch of Christiania, who signed his name in Rackham's sketchbook of the trip.[63] Later, a correspondence developed between the two men. Reusch wrote to Rackham:

It was very pleasant to meet you in the splendid "ocean racer" which took us from Nordfjord. – I hope that you think with pleasure on your stay in Norway and that I may have the fortune to meet you again soon. I beg you to pay my compliments to the amiable young gentlemen who accompanied you.[64]

Germany was Rackham's favourite holiday destination, and the country which, apart from England,

had the single most important influence on his art. His visits to Germany were not, however, without their disappointments. He went to Bayreuth to see *The Ring* in 1897, and 'returned deceived' because in his view the pedantic and over-detailed setting destroyed the atmosphere.[65] This was the period of Cosima Wagner's direction of the Bayreuth Opera House, and Rackham saw *The Ring* performed among sets designed the previous year by Max Brückner. He was not alone in his dislike, as Stewart Houston Chamberlain (1855–1927), Cosima's English-born son-in-law, wrote of Brückner and his sets: '…familiar stuff, without a trace of invention or imagination…. Frau Wagner and her son can do a lot, but they cannot inject talent into that man.'[66]

Arthur Rackham returned to Bayreuth in August 1899, when *Parsifal*, *The Ring* and *Die Meistersinger* were in repertoire,[67] having spent a week in Switzerland joining his parents and sisters Meg and Winifred on their summer holiday. It was on this trip that Arthur's father once more provided him with a graphic account of an event that was later to emerge as an illustration. In his diary of the holiday, Alfred Rackham writes:

Tuesday 11th [July]: My birthday.... Walked up the ravine towards the top of the Mountain but after an hour's saunter were fairly driven back by the flies great beasts & little beasts all sorts & sizes the most terrifying being the shape of a blue bottle but over an inch long with rather a pointed abdomen (going off to a point almost like a tail). This brute thought my frieze coat was an animal's hairy skin & did its hardest to sting me through it but it was too thick for it to get thro'. Mother [*Annie Rackham*] said there were sometimes 20 or 30 of them on my back at the same time....[68]

Rothenburg
Watercolour, 1899
250 × 177 mm
Private Collection

Painted on one of Rackham's European walking tours

In the 1909 edition of *Gulliver's Travels* this image surfaces once again in the illustration of a hard-pressed Gulliver engaged in mortal combat with six enormous wasps. More particularly, on the flyleaf of the copy of *Gulliver* that Rackham inscribed and gave to his parents,[69] he has drawn a large hand picking up a Liliputian waspman by the scruff of its neck, a private reference that firmly connects the incident of the flies on the mountainside to the wasp illustration in *Gulliver*.

In 1897, Rackham was thirty years old. His achievements, however, had come nowhere near the proportions of those of Aubrey Beardsley, three years his junior, and also for a while a clerk in a London fire

43

insurance office, the Guardian Life. Beardsley had been able to leave his fire office early in 1893, the year after Rackham had made his own escape, to take up a contract with J. M. Dent to supply 350 designs for *Morte Darthur*. Three years after putting Beardsley under contract, Dent commissioned the *Zankiwank*

illustrations from Rackham, when Beardsley's own genius and fame were at their height, with his *Rape of the Lock* illustrations (1896), and his contributions to *The Savoy*.

Although Rackham often mentioned his colleagues and rivals in friendly terms in letters, writings and

A Bend in the Semois
Watercolour, 1891
259 × 183 mm
Rare Book Department, Free
Library of Philadelphia

*Rackham here conscientiously
attempts to master the tradition of
English landscape watercolourists,
aiming particularly at a kind of
Pre-Raphaelite intensity. This
watercolour, possibly done on the
spot, was the basis for a drawing in*
Pall Mall Budget *(16.7.91)
illustrating an article on French
rivers.*

reminiscences, there seem only to be two references to Beardsley, of whose work and fame Rackham was of course well aware[70] – indeed Rackham owned a set of the two-volume Dent edition of *Morte Darthur* illustrated by Beardsley.[71] It is clear that Rackham regarded Beardsley very highly as an artist, and included his name in a list of the '33 Greatest Painters of the XIX Century' written out in his own hand among his papers.[72] Eleven of the artists on his list he describes as 'exclusively (virtually) black and white illustrators', and these are, in roughly chronological order, Thomas Bewick, Thomas Rowlandson, William Blake, Samuel Palmer, Arthur Boyd Houghton, Frederick Sandys, Charles Keene, Randolph Caldecott, Phil May and E. J. Sullivan, as well as Beardsley. Nevertheless, Rackham made a lampoon on Beardsley's work, much more caustic than his later *New Fiction* cover, for the *Westminster Budget* at the height of the controversy over Beardsley's illustrations in *The Yellow Book*. The drawing is captioned *Nightmare: Horrible Result of Contemplating an Aubrey Beardsley After Supper.*[73]

Beardsley's exotic nature and talent, which has defined the *fin de siècle* mood of the period, had the effect of disturbing the creative and commercial outlet of Rackham's own expression. Rackham, though still a young man, was probably included in Beardsley's swipe at 'old black-and-white duffers'. When Beardsley died of consumption in 1898, the gap left in the publishing market enabled Rackham's own career to begin to take off with *The Ingoldsby Legends* followed by *Grimm's Fairy Tales*, and he never looked back.

CHAPTER THREE

IT IS NO GOOD SITTING LAZILY 1898–1906

B Y 1898, RACKHAM HAD BECOME THE MASTER of a repertoire of three areas of style. The first, and perhaps the style which had brought him the greater part of his income to date, was the blood-and-thunder boy's adventure story manner of such magazines as *Chums*, and of books such as *The Money-Spinner* (1896) and *Charles O'Malley* (1897). Its serious side derives from magazine tradition and from the work of Academicians of the latter part of the nineteenth century, such as Sir Ernest Crofts (1847–1911), Sir John Pettie (1839–1893) and W. F. Yeames (1835–1918), whose historical costume pieces were so popular at Royal Academy Summer Exhibitions. Its more jovial aspect was practised by artists such as the illustrator Hugh Thomson (1860–1920), and Dendy Sadler (1854–1923), whose paintings of jollified monks, exhibited in the Royal Academy in the 1880s and widely reproduced, were an inevitable source for some of Rackham's illustrations to *The Ingoldsby Legends*.

Right: Headpiece for *Country Life*

Left: Sir Galahad draws the sword from the floating stone
Pen and ink and watercolour, 1902
244 × 176 mm
Private Collection/Sotheby's

Illustration to Stories of King Arthur *by A. L. Haydon*

The second area, more fluid in its use and application, is seen when Rackham exaggerates and

stylizes the human and animal form for either humorous or decorative effect, often in silhouette. Rackham used this manner for head and tailpieces and small text illustrations in magazines, whether for adults, as in the elegant headpieces of *Ladies' Field* and *Country Life*, or for children, as in *Cassell's Magazine* or *Little Folks*. The children's illustrations of this type frequently have a whimsicality that borders on the mawkish, but those which go out of their way to be funny have a waggish humour that reflects Rackham's own character and sometimes anticipates William Heath Robinson. Occasionally the humour backfires, as in '*A couple of dozen dynamite shells would wreck the Metropolis*' in Cassell's Magazine,[1] published long before London suffered any kind of aerial bombardment, and no longer quite so funny when the Zeppelin air raids began in the First World War.

The third area, which takes something from both of the two previous styles, is the 'fantastic and the imaginative', as Rackham himself described it. The illustrations to *The Zankiwank* introduced the manner, while its first mature phase is defined in *The Ingoldsby Legends* (1898). At this time, as J. M. Dent pointed out,[2] Rackham was not yet known as a colourist, but

only as a black and white artist as colour printing techniques were still in their infancy.

Despite the fact that Rackham is best known for his fantasy illustrations, which reached their finest expression in *Peter Pan* and the 1908 edition of *A Midsummer Night's Dream*, he kept the two other areas in his back pocket throughout his life for use when required. A sophisticated version of the blood-and-thunder manner reappears in 1935, for example, in *Poe's Tales*, while its more jovial, domestic aspect can be seen again in *The Vicar of Wakefield* (1929). Rackham's waggish manner reappears in *The Sleeping Beauty* (1920) and *Where the Blue Begins* (1925), as well as in other books such as *The Night Before Christmas* (1931) and *The King of the Golden River* (1932).

In 1898, which was to be a watershed year for Rackham, Dent invited him to produce one hundred black and white illustrations for R. H. Barham's quaintly medievalizing poems and stories *The Ingoldsby Legends of Mirth and Marvels*. The £150 fee for this important commission bought, in addition, ownership of the originals and copyright.[3] The stories had been originally published in *Bentley's Miscellany* and *The New Monthly Magazine* from 1837, and first collected in 1840. Their episodic nature and superficial, rollicking humour were well suited to Rackham's talents, presenting him with endless opportunities to exercise his talent for the macabre and the inventive, the fantastic and the knockabout comic. Despite his relatively advanced age – he was 32 – Rackham was still a new artist, and had not been fully stretched in an important book. At the same time he was hedging his bets, and investigating other avenues of journalistic employment, holding, for three months only, the Art Editorship of the new magazine *Ladies' Field*.

The *Ingoldsby Legends* commission was soon followed by another from Dent, for the eleven illustrations to

'At length for my seared and writhing body there was no longer an inch of foothold on the firm floor of the prison.'
Pen and ink and watercolour, 1935
274 × 190 mm
HRHR Art Collection, Harry Ransom Humanities Research Center, University of Texas at Austin

Illustration to 'The Pit and the Pendulum' from Poe's Tales of Mystery and Imagination.

'Who has been eating off my plate?'
Pen and ink and watercolour, 1900
240 × 195 mm
Rare Book Department, Free Library of Philadelphia

Illustration to 'The Seven Ravens' in Grimm's Fairy Tales.

Bundoran
Watercolour, 1899
172 × 248 mm
Private Collection

*Painted in County Donegal,
Ireland, on a fishing holiday
with Herbert Adams.*

Harriet Martineau's *Feats on the Fjord* (1899). To be quite sure of getting the detail in the Norwegian costume right, Rackham sought the advice of Dr Hans Reusch, the friend he had made in Norway the year before. Reusch told him:

What costumes the peasants had in the Solitelma region about 1750 I think nobody knows. Gentlemen and ladies had the common .... dress (never though the latest mode in far away Norway). For peasants' dress I send you some suggestions. A peasant in full state then had generally his ox with him....[4]

For the Haddon Hall Library, which J. M. Dent launched in 1899, Rackham contributed cover designs and head and tailpieces. The nine titles with Rackham's decorations included *Wild Life in the Hampshire Highlands* (1899), *Fly Fishing* (1899) and *Hunting* (1900). The country life subject-matter of this series,

covering outdoor recreations and delights, suited Rackham's personal tastes for energetic country walks and long days fishing.

Despite the pressure of deadlines, and his own conscientious attitude to his work, he allowed himself time away on walks and fishing expeditions, alone or with friends. He had at least two fishing holidays in Ireland with his future brother-in-law Herbert Adams, making a watercolour of *Bundoran* on the 1899 holiday. He enjoyed his own company, and in 1933 gave an idyllic, reflective picture of his holidays alone with his fishing rod and his 'modest silent convenient companion', as he described his paintbox:

I will choose .... a river .... below the Alps. We will wander not too far, and when we've found our resting place, we'll sling the rucksack off our shoulders, and take out the bottle of wine and sink it carefully in a cool little cranny under the river

Landscape
Etching, 1898
89 × 124 mm
Private Collection

*One of only two etchings Rackham is known to have made. There are two
known states of this etching, the second being signed and dated.*

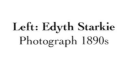

Left: Edyth Starkie
Photograph 1890s

bank.... We've got a fishing rod with us, and it will do your credit .... with the wilderness-singer no wrong if a couple of trout, broiled on the embers of a wood fire, add character to the simple menu – the sausage, the hard-boiled eggs with their little screw of salt, oranges, grapes, nuts, delicious bread.

But that won't be till one o'clock or so. Meantime not only will my silent companion have begun his modest part, but the sunny warmth of the gleaming water may well have tempted a secret nudist plunge.... Or the scene may have been high up among winter snows. Roasting on the sunny side of a hay-chalet with skis standing sentinel. No trout, no bathing, but the inevitable little paint box, and what an appetite! Or – but this is praise enough. Like the sundial, my paint box counts no hours but sunny ones.[5]

From 1897 to 1899 Rackham lived in Tufnell Park, at 2 Carleton Rd, and, from 1898, at 8 Brecknock Studios, 114A Brecknock Road,[6] a bicycle ride away from his friends in Highgate.[7] By 1901 he was using a Hampstead studio at this time, 6 Wychcombe Studios, England's Lane, where he made a new friend, Edyth Starkie.

In 1897 Edyth Starkie, and her mother Mrs Frances Starkie, had rented 3 Wychcombe Studios. Edyth was studying at the Slade School under Henry Tonks, and was soon to become noticed as a portrait painter. She exhibited at three Royal Academy Summer Exhibitions in the 1890s with *Miss M. D.* (1895), *Lilla* (1897) and of *St Cecilia* (1898).[8]

Edyth's and Arthur's backgrounds, though very different, did have certain areas in common. While Arthur was the son of a legal official, the kind of man whose role it was to uphold and maintain the Establishment, Edyth Starkie's father, William Robert Starkie JP, a member of an Irish landowning family, upheld the law in his way as an Irish Resident Magistrate. Edyth had been born in 1867 on the West Coast of Ireland at Westcliff, near Galway, the youngest of six children. For most of her youth, however, she lived at Cregane Manor, Roscarbery, near Cork.

Barbara Edwards, the daughter of Arthur and Edyth Rackham, later described Cregane Manor as

.... a curious mixture of a house with considerable Victorian additions, but Victoriana purified by the simplicity of material and stark position on a headland overlooking Roscarbery Bay. It had whitewashed walls, gothic doorways, castellations, and a jumble of soft blue-grey slate roofs, ringed round by a grove of windswept trees. Dotted about the grounds were the little whitewashed cottages of the tenants who ministered to the estate in various ways, digging the land, grooming the horses, plucking the geese, fishing in the bay, providing their children as boot-boys and their grandmothers to sit and poke the fire and tell apocryphal stories of Starkie ancestors for my mother to pass on to me.[9]

Barbara Edwards draws a picture of a mixture of poverty and lively Irish gaiety: butlers waiting at table still smelling of horses; furniture propped up with books; of girls sitting up in bed all night, sometimes two nights, before a ball, so as not to disturb their coiffure which had been dressed by a peripatetic hairdresser; of long carriage journeys to the balls and of pranks played on the guests – such as one by Lady Bandon who urged all the gentlemen to try out the new fire escape, which she had aimed to send them all flying, in full evening dress, into the lake.

These stories of her childhood, which Edyth told later to her husband and daughter, say as much about Edyth's own zest for life as they do of her particular experience of Ireland at the time, the Ireland of the mass emigrations to America and England, and the Ireland of Somerville and Ross. Edyth rode to hounds, sailed in the Bay, teased her brothers' tutors, and was terrified by nurses who told her that the pointed stones in the courtyard were the corners of coffins whose inmates would rise up and haunt her if she were naughty. One of her nurses made her wear a vest in the bath, lest, she was warned, the Virgin Mary should see her naked. There were Banshee stories too, and Edyth firmly believed she heard a Banshee wail when her father died.

Edyth's father, the Resident Magistrate, taught himself to play the violin, and as often as not performed his duties as Magistrate by reading the newspaper on the Bench until lunchtime and then saying, 'The Court is adjourned for today.' Edyth's mother, Frances Starkie, was much more active than her husband. When Edyth was sixteen, Frances shut up the house, put her husband into rooms in Cork, and set off with Edyth on a Grand Tour lasting two or three years. They had never been out of Ireland before, even Dublin was a rare adventure, so they found the capitals of Europe entrancing. Frances Starkie trusted and made friends with everybody.

Portrait of the Artist's Mother, Aged 66
Oil on canvas, 1899
700 × 570 mm
Private Collection

Rackham was 32 when he painted this mature, accomplished portrait. Its subdued colours and sombre atmosphere reflect an understanding of the portraits of Whistler and Sir Hubert Herkomer.

'Good morning, Mr. Maple'; 'Lovely weather Mr. Schoolbred', she would say to the commissionaires of the big London stores, imagining them, in their finery, to be the owners. The only warning she gave her daughter when going out alone was never to tread on gratings in the street as they were liable to be designed by white-slave traffickers to open and swallow up young girls.

In 1884 they were in Paris, where Edyth studied art

at the Académie Julien under Jules Lefebre and Tony-Robert Fleury, and then went on to Germany, where she continued her studies, and where one of her brothers, Rex, was an officer in the German army. In Cassel, Edyth became engaged to a Prussian officer,[10] causing a major scandal when she finally broke it off because she could not stand the stiff Prussian attitudes; her fiancé would insist on challenging to a duel any man whom Edyth so much as smiled at in the street. After a brief return to Ireland to bury William Starkie, mother and daughter settled in London, first at 118 Adelaide Road (1895) and, two years later, at 3 Wychcombe Studios.

Edyth and Arthur met over the garden wall, and quickly became friends. During the period of their subsequent courtship they were both making considerable progress as artists. It was the period in which Arthur, too, was painting portraits, notably the highly accomplished *Portrait of the Artist's Mother* which he completed in 1899, and in some respects the pair were at first friendly rivals.

In 1901 Rackham was just emerging from the twelve-year gap in which he exhibited rarely, and which amounted to a long, informal apprenticeship as a black and white artist. He showed nothing at the RA between these years, the 'very thin time', which he lucidly described with hindsight in 1925:

I think I may say that for a good many years at the beginning of my career I had far from an easy time. I was working mainly as a free-lance for various illustrated journals and magazines. Work was hard to get and not well paid, and such efforts as I made along the lines I have since followed received little encouragement. And then came the Boer War. That really was a very thin time for me, and may be considered the worst time I ever had. The kind of work that was in demand, to the exclusion almost of all else, was such as I had no liking for and very little aptitude. It was also clear that the camera was going to supplant the artist in illustrated journalism, and my prospects were not encouraging. But my work became less immature, and before long my special bent began to be recognized – by artists first. I was elected to membership of one or two exhibiting societies, my work was welcomed, dealers and publishers became interested, and the worst was passed.[11]

Life – Soul Stirring Drama by Gad!
Charcoal and wash, 1890s
268 × 358
Private Collection

A study for an untraced magazine illustration.

Arthur and Edyth became engaged in the summer of 1901, and noticed how the whole of London seemed to be celebrating and sharing in their happiness with bunting and ER and AR monograms in The Mall and other important positions in Central London.[12] Although these were actually proclaiming the Coronation of Edward VII and Queen Alexandra, Arthur and Edyth quite properly took it that London was celebrating for them.

This was a very happy and positive period for them both. In 1902 Arthur had been elected an Associate of the Royal Watercolour Society, an organization of which he was proud to be a member, even if he was at times impatient of it. Around the time of his own election as an ARWS he wrote about Edmund J. Sullivan (1869–1933) to W. T. Whitley:

It was at my urging that [Sullivan] put up at the RWS & I am really very proud of the Society for having elected so rare a man. It removes a good deal of the stigma of old-fashioned fogeyism with which some have been wont to label them for E.J.S. is about as unconventional as possible.[13]

This is continuing and loyal support of a man to whom Rackham had lent the considerable sum of £50 in July 1900,[14] only four guineas of which had been repaid eighteen months later.[15] Rackham put his benevolence into practice on an official level too. He organized a fund-raising drive on behalf of the Artists' General Benevolent Institution at Christmas 1902, eliciting donations from artists and others including Robert

Anning Bell, George Clausen, Thomas Cooper Gotch, HRH The Princess Louise, Briton Rivière, Henry S. Tuke and W. L. Wyllie. He had a relaxed style when asking for money – as relaxed as that which he adopted when he lent it – but was hardly surprised when he found that 'folk are very slow at answering though I get some pleasant letters when they do.'[16] (Illus. page 57.)

After his long period of absence as an exhibitor at the Royal Academy, Rackham returned there in 1901 with *Evening – Switzerland* (no. 1101),[17] and in 1902 with three subjects from Grimm. He was included in the 1901 Loan Exhibition of Modern Illustration at the Victoria and Albert Museum and the Museum of Science and Art in Edinburgh, and first showed at the Royal Watercolour Society in the Summer Exhibition of 1902 (*The Four Ravens*, *The Wizard* and *Alpine Dawn*). This was the year of his election to the RWS, and he contributed to group exhibitions there twice a year, summer and winter, virtually

'Appy 'Ampstead
Pencil and watercolour, 1903
253 × 353 mm
Leeds City Art Galleries

The Goose Girl
Pen and ink and watercolour, ?1900
270 × 365 mm
Private Collection

*Possibly intended as an illustration to 'The Goose Girl' in
Grimm's Fairy Tales, but not used.*

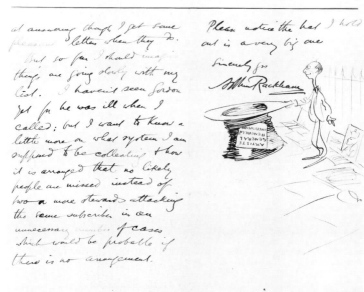

Illustrated Letter 1902
Rare Book Department,
Free Library of Philadelphia

Alpine Dawn
Body Colour, 1902
200 × 283
Private Collection

An allegorical mountainscape, inspired by Rackham's travels in the Alps, and particularly reminiscent of The Punishment of Luxury *(1891, Walker Art Gallery, Liverpool) by the Italian artist Giovanni Segantini.*

The Witch's Pool
Watercolour and bodycolour, 1904
275 × 152 mm
Private Collection

58

without a break until 1938, the year before he died. His exhibits at the RWS settle into a pattern of being part fantasy, part pastoral subjects, a balance with which he prudently kept his options open. Because of this he remained known both to collectors and to his artist peers as a painter who was not limited to the fantasy subjects for which his books were beginning to earn him a wider fame.

It was Edyth's influence, however, that persuaded Arthur to show fantasy subjects at the RWS at all. According to a family story, Arthur was afraid people might mock his fantasy pictures, and was reluctant to exhibit them in the company of the work of orthodox watercolourists. Edyth, however, rejected this diffidence and encouraged him to put *Grimm* and *Morte D'Arthur* illustrations into the RWS Winter Exhibition of 1902, alongside two pastoral watercolours of Arundel. All ten of these sold, for a total of £60.14.0, the first significantly high figure Rackham had

'Good dwarf, can you not tell me where my brothers are?'
Pen and ink and watercolour
210 × 152 mm
Private Collection/Chris Beetles Gallery

Illustration to 'The Water of Life', Grimm's Fairy Tales.

Following pages: Left: The Rescue of Guinevere Right: Beaumains Defeats the Green Knight
Pen and ink and watercolour 1902
244 × 176 mm
Private Collection

Two illustrations to Stories of King Arthur *by A. L. Hayden.*

made for any exhibited body of work. Gradually things were improving, and for the warm reception of his fantasy work he had only Edyth to thank. Later, he showed another fantasy painting, this time an enlarged version in oil of his *Rumplestiltskin* for Grimm at the 1903 Society of Oil Painters exhibition. The painting was welcomed by one critic, who wrote:

Perhaps one of the most interesting new-comers in oil painting is Mr. Arthur Rackham. He is a man with a special kink in his mind, a faculty for exaggerating certain odd developments of humanity to the pitch of monstrosity, yet with an affectionate liking for the monster. The Cockney Leno-like character that, trodden on, comes up smiling, he expresses in quintessential fancy. He shows as a flatterer, but a flatterer of wit, and even a little pathos.... Oil painting does not really suit him; it is, oddly enough, too easy a medium.... I should like to see him do wood carving.[18]

The following month his *Danae* from *Greek Stories* was welcomed at the RWS: 'Here the vision of the romantic poet is well combined with the true pictorial quality.'[19] Reviews like this encouraged Rackham,

Round the fire an indescribably ridiculous little man was leaping, hopping on one leg and singing.
Pen and ink and watercolour, 1900
215 × 164 mm
Private Collection

Illustration to 'Rumplestiltskin' in Grimm's Fairy Tales. *The drawing was coloured and redated for exhibition and sale in 1906. Rackham made an oil painting (Arthur Rackham Collection, Rare Book and Manuscript Library, Columbia University, New York) of the same composition for exhibition in 1903.*

and by 1902 he had been elected a member of the Langham Sketching Club, a society of professional artists in Central London. This was an off-shoot of 'The Artists' Society for the Study of Historical and Rustic Figures', founded in 1830, and among its past members were Edward Duncan, Charles Keene, John Tenniel, Hablot Brown ('Phiz') and George Vicat Cole.

By the time Rackham had become a member, the Langham met weekly on Friday evenings[20] and all sessions followed a prescribed pattern. A subject, usually with literary or narrative potential, such as *The Rendezvous*, *Spring Morning* or *The Magic Cup*,[21] would be announced, and the members would be given two hours to produce a sketch in whatever medium they liked, without the use of a model or other visual aid. At the end of the two hours all the sketches, whether finished or not, would be exhibited to the members present. A. L. Baldry analysed the routine:

The whole process is an exacting one because of the conditions under which the work is done and the high pressure in execution which is necessitated by the time limit; but it has at all events the effect of obliging each artist to be decisive in his statement of opinion, and to make up his mind with all possible promptness. He has no time for hesitating over alternatives, and must not delay in his selection of the directest method of giving form to his imaginings.

There is another technical difficulty he has to face, the accommodating of his colour interpretation to the artificial light in which he has to work. As the meetings of the Sketching Club are held in the evening, all the drawings and paintings have to be done by gas light, so that there is upon all the workers the obligation not only to keep intensely active their sense of pictorial expression, but as well to give constant attention to the agreement of colours which do not as they are put down produce the same effect that they will present when they are seen in daylight. This implies a particular kind of experience, and colour judgement of an unusually educated type.[22]

For Rackham this was the ideal kind of gymnasium for his manual and mental skills, an amusing but exacting limbering-up session in preparation for the meeting of publishers' deadlines. It had the added benefit of being a place where friends were made and kept, and contacts cultivated. Other members included William Cubitt Cooke[23] and George Haité. Meetings always ended with a supper presided over by the Chairman, an office which required affability and good humour, and one to which Rackham was elected for the two consecutive years 1905/06 and

Old Man Standing Under a Street Light
Watercolour, 1900
280 × 140 mm
Private Collection

Inscribed to Jack Sullivan, 19.4.1900.

1906/07. He remained a member of the Langham until 1920, after which he ceased to pay annual subscriptions, because on Friday evenings he was beginning his weekends at Houghton House, his Sussex home from 1920, and so could no longer attend.

Although models were not used in the Langham meetings, they were an integral part of Rackham's processes as an artist in his daily work. From before 1897 he kept a notebook[24] with names and addresses of his models, listing their physical qualities and, in detail at first, what costumes they had used out of his extensive studio stock. George Riches, of '32 Fifth Avenue, Queen's Park, W., for example, dressed up as a Parson, a Barrister, a Monk and other figures; Miss Florence Pinto, of 119 Hampstead Road, used the Spanish Dancing, Moorish, Empire and Mantilla costumes; and Mr Sargeant, of Coverdale Road, Shepherd's Bush, put on Rackham's Dervish costume, his toga and a grey beard. Others, such as Mr W. J. Lavington, of Cricklewood, is described as 'tall: bald: beard: middle aged: well dressed', and modelled for him in 1898. Twelve models are 'dated' 1898, three men, one 'little boy of 6' and eight women, showing that already Rackham had a busy and productive studio system, well organized and professional. Undoubtedly some, if not all, of these models will have been used for *The Ingoldsby Legends* illustrations, and so perhaps George Riches posed for the monk up to his knees in brown stout, or Miss L. Cooke, whom Rackham notes as having worn his 'Empire' costume, for the pretty young woman in the subtle pink floral

Study for 'Up to his Knees in Brown Stout'
Pencil, 1898
215 × 165 mm
Private Collection

Drawn direct from the model, for The Ingoldsby Legends.

Empire line dress in '*Making court to their Polls and their Sues*' from 'The Dead Drummer' in *The Ingoldsby Legends*.

By the early years of the century, Rackham was managing his models in an efficient and professional manner and indulging, through them, his love of painting richly patterned fabrics. His notebook clearly details those who would model nude for him (marked 'Figure' or 'F') and those who preferred not to ('Not Figure' or 'NF'). He kept up with them, and hired them again and again as he required them. Many of

the names record address changes, two or three in some cases, suggesting a continuing loyalty on the part of the model and need on Rackham's part.

Occasionally the integration of model with picture is less successful than it might be. For his illustration '*Half blinded, he staggered to the gangway...*' in *Brains and Bravery*, a collection of stories by G. A. Henty and others (1903), Rackham has drawn the two staggering figures from poses, and merely turned the sheet through nearly ninety degrees, adding the backdrop of the burning ship.[25] There is no sense of the figures falling or being in any way concerned about their dire plight, and a regard for the stiff upper lip has inadvertently been carried rather too far.

When, as it usually does, a posed composition succeeds, as in the '*Making court*' illustration, Rackham skilfully

Making their Court to their Polls and their Sues
Pen and ink and watercolour, 1898
149 × 98 mm
Spencer Collection, New York
Public Library, Astor, Lenox and
Tilden foundations

Illustration to The Ingoldsby Legends, *published as a black and white drawing in the 1898 edition, and reworked and coloured for the 1907 edition. Rackham's handling of decoration was, on rare occasions, too subtle for his printers to reproduce. The pink floral dress of the girl on the left is clear for the first time in this printing.*

integrates figures and furnishings to make a harmonious, rhythmic whole. The two groups of figures, though back to back and separating themselves from each other, are linked visually by the wooden framework of the balcony, whose rigid lines are counterpoised by the catenary curve of the rope. Rackham adds further interest and drama – he is after all helping to tell a good story – by leading the eye from the minute foreground detail of the wood grain and rope to the decorative and dramatic effect of the figures in the middle ground and the background view of the ships which will all too soon remove the sailors from their Polls and their Sues. Rackham's design has a cinematic quality, which is particularly potent in other *Ingoldsby* and *Grimm* illustrations, such as the dramatic and witty scale-shift in '*When Tom Thumb had said goodbye to his father…*', where the tiny Tom sits on the enormous brim of one of the two strangers' hats, waving to his distant and thus equally tiny father.

Books that Dent commissioned from Rackham of the quality of *The Ingoldsby Legends*, *Lamb's Tales* (1899) and *Gulliver's Travels* (1900) were not enough to keep him fully employed. While Dent paid £150 for the one hundred *Ingoldsby* illustrations, this fell to £24 for the production and copyright (though not the ownership) of twelve drawings for both *Lamb's Tales* and *Gulliver*. In 1900 he was still a regular illustrator for *Cassell's Magazine*, *The Ladies' Field* and *Little Folks*, and this provided the bulk of his income. His papers tell us that in 1901 he earned £430 gross, a figure which fell drastically to £271 for 1902 before climbing back in 1903 to £484 and in 1904 to over £700. These figures add flesh to Rackham's remark, published in 1925, that the years 1899 to 1902, the period of the Boer War, were a 'very thin time' for him.

Arthur and Edyth were married at St Saviour's Church, Hampstead, on 16 July 1903 at 'really very short notice',[26] the ceremony being delayed because Arthur had had to undergo unspecified, though essential, surgery.[27] Only days before the wedding, his younger brother Harris advised him to put it off if he was not 'feeling pretty well recovered'.[28] Neither Arthur nor Edyth were in particularly good health, and later on in their lives illness was to be a recurring preoccupation for them both.

Edyth's family was not at first enthusiastic about the match, dismissing Arthur as a 'tuppenny-ha'penny Cockney artist',[29] and even on the wedding day their fears resurfaced. As Edyth was arriving at the church with her brother Robert, who gave her away, Arthur was seen dashing off in the opposite direction in a Hansom Cab. 'There you are, Edyth,' Robert said. 'He's left you already.' Arthur had in fact just forgotten the ring and was hurrying home to find it. Friends of the couple, however, were a great support to them. Writing to Arthur just before the wedding a close

Gulliver is struck with fear at the first sight of the Brobdignagian reapers
Pen and ink and watercolour, 1900
224 × 128 mm
Spencer Collection, New York Public Library, Astor, Lenox and Tilden Foundations

friend of Edyth's family, Mina Welland, expresses her joy at the match, adding:

[Edyth] is one of the most beautiful, graceful women I have ever known & loved…. She was always very sensitive, perhaps too much so, but out of that sensibility has developed a keen sympathy, I suppose the best gift of an artist. I don't think she can ever stand too much fatigue or excitement, or much worry; though she is so well & strong now she was for years very delicate, & even now her nerves are not strong & she puts her best strength into her work, & it suffers if she is not up to the mark. Nobody would suspect this if they had only known her in health, but I know.[30]

Barbara Edwards wrote later of her mother that 'everybody liked her and many people loved her. I don't think she was conventionally beautiful, but people instantly thought that she was. She had a smooth pink and white complexion, wide open blue eyes and, from an early age, snow white hair. She made people laugh without ever really saying anything particularly witty, and could give great comfort without much useful advice.'

The couple spent their honeymoon in North Wales, near Cader Idris and Lake Talyllyn. Arthur described the holiday in a letter to his brother Stanley after their return:[31]

Edyth & I had a very good time in every way. Even weather which has been shocking in most parts was quite fairly fine. We found some excellent places in Wales. The fishing was far from good – trout fishing is never really good in midsummer but it was enough to keep us pleasantly pottering & boating.

Though I was a fortnight just beneath Cader Idris I never went up it though I went nearly to the top to a tarn to fish twice. Weird fishing it was too – a lonely forbidding place like a volcanic crater with a very deep pool about 300 yards across – and raging wind that tore the water into smoke every now & then, & sometimes great clouds of rain that hid the cliffs down to a few feet from the water.

Although he does not discuss it in correspondence, Arthur characteristically took to his paintbrush during the honeymoon. One work, the mature and impressionistic *Lake-Side, Talyllyn, Evening*, with its glimmering lights and reflections in a New English Art Club

manner, sums up the idyllic, atmospheric and relaxed nature of their holiday.

After the honeymoon, the Rackhams returned to live at Edyth's Wychcombe Studio, while Arthur also worked at 54A Parkhill Road. In September they

The Dance in Cupid's Alley
Pen and ink and watercolour, 1904
325 × 595 mm
The Tate Gallery, London

An absorbing allegory, illustrating Austin Dobson's lines 'O Love's but a dance, where Time plays the fiddle!' Father Time provides the music in the background, while ships ready to depart await some of the foreground dancers.

moved together to 3 Primrose Hill Studios, one of a quiet group of artists' studios down a long passageway off Fitzroy Road. There was room for them both to work, and just enough living accommodation. Arthur described to Stanley the alterations he was going to make, adding a small sketch:

We want the addition of a bedroom & dressing room & I think it can be arranged by a balcony in the bigger studio & part of the underneath shut in. It will give us a queer compact little place with no room to spare but I really think we could manage even if there was a family for a few years; as another tiny room could be cut off the studio under the balcony.[32]

Despite this cheerful optimism, Arthur also describes some of the realities of his work as an artist to Stanley, who was himself facing the realities of life as a pioneer farmer in the North West Territories of Canada:

I do not think I am by any means devoted to the dress-clothed & cultured life: and short of a berth such as father's & Maurice's there is just as much anxiety & doubt for the future. And in a profession like mine income stops, of course, the instant I stop work. I think we in London are often really spoilt. We grow up thinking that one's livelihood will be made pretty easily by just doing some pretty easy work, pretty well, pretty punctually between 10 & 4 – certain for life & a pension to follow.

Father for instance has never experienced what I have to experience frequently. That is, having done all the work one has had ordered & having not a stroke more in hand to do &, temporarily, being quite unable to get any more. Sometimes for a week or two I have been unable to keep from getting very

blue. It has seemed as if the work had all fallen away from me. Of course it is no good sitting lazily – there are things one can & must do to remedy it – assiduously look up one's old connection, try to see new people, or do drawings 'on spec'. All the same, one has often very disheartening times.

One has to cultivate a happy go lucky disposition to some extent & be content that one has, after all, got something to eat & to wear for the time being & try not to look forward where one can see nothing, but just lay one's plans as wisely as one can & trust to them turning up trumps.

The continuance of good notices and the regular exposure of Rackham's work in books and magazines made a breakthrough inevitable. He was invited in September 1903 to contribute five drawings to the 1904 St Louis Exhibition,[33] and in April 1904 his mastery was acknowledged with the words: 'beyond dispute a master of his craft, and he occupies a position no-one can be said to share with him.'[34] Around

the middle of 1904, certainly by July,[35] Ernest Brown
and Phillips commissioned 50 colour illustrations to
Rip Van Winkle, and purchased the originals and all
rights for 300 guineas. The publishing rights were
then resold in a complicated deal to Heinemann,
before the illustrations were exhibited at Brown and
Phillips's Leicester Galleries in March 1905, with 39
other works by Rackham. Most of the *Rip* drawings
were sold at the exhibition, and by October they had
all found purchasers.[36]

Brown and Phillips's investment, made secure by
the keenness of Rackham's purchasers, was not let
down by the reviews his work received:

'[Rackham] reminds me of Cruikshank, but he is a far more
accomplished draughtsman, owing much, no doubt, to the
study of Dürer's etchings, and the engravings of the little
masters of the German Renaissance....' *Birmingham Post*[37]

'His work has much of the quality of a good etching.... His
line is full of meaning and suggestion ... comparable among
living artists only to that of Sattler....' *Daily Chronicle*[38]

The comparison with the German artist Joseph Sattler (1867–1931), whose work had been featured
twice by 1905 in *The Studio*,[39] is significant because not
only do he and Rackham share Dürer as an influence,
but both dwell on the grotesque and the morbid in
their subject-matter. When, in September 1905, *Rip
Van Winkle* was published, comparisons between
Rackham and German artists continued to be voiced,
The Times remarking on 'the marvel of his Düreresque
detail'.[40]

The illustrations, all gathered together at the back
of the book, are 'tipped in', that is, printed on coated
paper and stuck on to thicker card because it was then
technically impossible to print in colour on text pages.
The 51 illustrations, for a story of not more than five
thousand words, enables the story to be told twice,
once through Irving's words, and once again, image
by image, through Rackham's pictures with their text

Above: These Fairy Mountains
Pen and ink and watercolour, 1904
253 × 215 mm
Rare Book Department, Free Library of Philadelphia

Illustration to Rip Van Winkle

extracts printed as titles on India paper flyleaves. In
his illustrations, Rackham pays homage not only to
Dürer, Cruikshank and Dutch seventeenth-century
painting, but to contemporary artists too, such as
Clausen, Stott, La Thangue, Stanhope-Forbes and
other artists associated with the New English Art
Club, as well as – arguably – Sattler.

Interspersed with the genre scenes of village life are the imaginative subjects such as little mountain men, ghosts, and the squaw spirit 'who hung up the new moons in the skies and cut up the old ones into stars.' It was subjects such as these which were to run away with Rackham's reputation, and influence our perception of his genius for lively human characterization.

One critic compared Rackham's Rip to the definitive theatrical portrayal by the American actor Joseph Jefferson (1829–1905). Jefferson had brought Washington Irving's story, reworked as a play by Dion Boucicault, to London in 1865, where it was an immediate success in the autumn season at the Adelphi Theatre. Memories of the performance clearly lingered, as *The Atheneum* reminded its readers: '… Mr. Rackham's conception of Rip Van Winkle will somewhat disappoint those who know him as presented by Jefferson. Mr. Rackham's Rip is a silly, even weak-minded person, whereas the true Jeffersonian Rip was conspicuous for his shrewdness.'[41]

Rackham himself greatly regretted that he had never seen Jefferson in performance as Rip,[42] but avoided making a clear statement on whether or not Jefferson was a source for his Rip. He told Eleanor Farjeon, a friend and neighbour in Hampstead, and also Jefferson's granddaughter:

One feels that it was [Jefferson] who made the character for all time the great and living entity that it is,' adding that he doubted whether the story would have become so immovably established 'if Jefferson hadn't given Rip the living personality we now recognise him by.[43]

In giving Eleanor Farjeon material for a magazine article she was preparing about him, Rackham said of Jefferson's performance:

The Kaatskill mountains had always been haunted
Pen and ink and watercolour, 1904
390 × 300 mm
Private Collection

Illustration to Rip Van Winkle

I think [his] Rip is one of the most remarkable of created characters. Created as the sherest [*sic*] piece of pleasant moralising, acknowledging even that it was cribbed from old-world sources – here is Rip firmly fixed in the hearts of all good Americans, as any genuine myth. I can think of no other such instance.[44]

Although he is no longer in the grip of public imagination, Joseph Jefferson was one of the great actors of his day, and his characterization of Rip was also known to Americans through widely distributed engravings, photographs and statuettes.

Rackham was always less concerned with what the critics might say than he was about the opinion of his artist and writer colleagues. E. V. Lucas, on seeing the *Rip Van Winkle* exhibition, wrote to him:

Hitherto one has had to go to the Continent for so much mingled grace & grotesque as you have given us. The drawings seem to me to be extraordinarily successful & charming. The only thing I quarrel with is the prevalence of 'Sold' tickets....[45]

When the book appeared, Clayton Calthrop, the *Punch* illustrator, described *Rip* as 'one of the most beautiful illustrated books I have ever seen and one of the most perfect in conception.... One can never in the future think of "Rip" without the perfect commentary of your drawings.'[46]

The *Rip* exhibition ended at the Leicester Galleries in April 1905, and the pictures were barely off the walls before Brown and Phillips had written to Rackham engaging him on another contract.[47] They told him that they had just concluded arrangements with Hodder and Stoughton[48] for the publication of J. M. Barrie's *Little White Bird* 'or whatever title may be decided for it', and accepted the terms Rackham himself had stated to them the previous month. These were that Brown and Phillips should pay 5 guineas apiece for the copyright of fifty drawings illustrating Barrie's work, 'the drawings to be commenced at once and the whole to be delivered to us by the 1st of September 1906, the cover and title page to be included.' The letter from Brown and Phillips added that an exhibition, with 'at least 20 drawings beyond those illustrating the book', would be held at the Leicester Galleries in November 1906.

Rackham's success with *Rip* had now enabled him to name his own terms. For *Rip*, Rackham had accepted 300 guineas for fifty drawings, i.e. 6 gns each, passing the originals and copyright over to Brown and Phillips, who sold them in their turn. For *Peter Pan in Kensington Gardens* (the title later decided on for this edition of Barrie's book), however, Rackham sold the copyright of the drawings for 5 guineas

They crowded round him, eyeing him from head to feet with great curiosity
Pen and ink and watercolour, 1904
330 × 270 mm
By courtesy of W. R. Fletcher

Rip Van Winkle returns to the village after a twenty-year sleep, to find his wife dead, his house in ruins and the world changed.

each, but retained ownership of the originals. This was a prudent move, as sales at the exhibition totalled £1851.3.0.[49] Five guineas a drawing and retention of ownership seems now to have been Rackham's current price, as these were the same terms he had given to Routledge in reply to their invitation to him to illustrate Trollope.[50]

Rackham now had before him a clear run at a book. With nearly eighteen months to go before the delivery

The Widow Whitgift and her Sons
Pen and ink and watercolour,
1906
308 × 245 mm
Courtesy of the Board of
Trustees of the V&A/
Bridgeman Art Library

Rackham is here parodying the Newlyn School paintings of fishermen and their lives by Stanhope Forbes and others. An illustration to 'The Dymchurch Flit' in Puck of Pook's Hill *by Rudyard Kipling in an edition published only in America.*

date, at least twice the length of time he had been given to complete *Rip*, he was well on with the work by October 1905.[51] Arthur and Edyth were still living and working in their tiny Primrose Hill studio, and it was here that the *Rip* and *Peter Pan in Kensington Gardens* illustrations were made. It was here also that they prepared for their first child. Edyth became pregnant soon after the couple were married, but the baby, a girl, was stillborn prematurely in March 1904.[52]

The young Walter Starkie (1894–1976), Edyth's nephew, stayed with the couple while Arthur was at work on the *Peter Pan* illustrations. He wrote later that

… my new uncle took me on many exciting journeys through London, but the most enjoyable days were those when [he] allowed me to accompany him on a painting expedition. We would sally forth early on a sunny morning and my uncle, loaded with all his paraphernalia of paints, paint-brushes and easel, reminded me of one of the kobolds I had read about in Andrew Lang's *Blue Fairy Book*; but when we were in Kensington Gardens and the painter had armed himself with his palette and paint-brush, he became in my eyes a wizard who with one touch of his magic wand would people my imagination with elves, gnomes and leprechauns. He would make me gaze fixedly at one of the majestic trees with massive trunk and tell me about Grimm's fairy tales, which he had illustrated, and about the little men who blew their horns in elfland. He would say that under the roots of that tree the little men had their dinner and churned the butter they extracted from the sap of the tree. He would also make me see queer animals and birds in the branches of the tree and a little magic door below the trunk, which was the entrance to Fairyland. He used also to tell me

stories of the primitive religion of man which, in his opinion, was the cult of the tree; but he made my blood run cold when he told me of the punishment meted out to those who injured trees. This consisted of impaling the culprit by the navel to the trunk and winding his guts round and round. And he told me to warn any little boy I noticed cutting the bark of a tree of the punishment that would be inflicted upon him for his barbarism.[53]

It is in Walter Starkie's later writings that we see the most imaginative contemporary portrait of Rackham. Starkie also tells us more about Rackham's working processes and his own literary approach to his subjects. The account of the punishment for injuring trees, for example, comes straight out of J. G. Frazer's *The Golden Bough*,[54] a book that was published serially in twelve volumes between 1890 and 1915, and which clearly Rackham was reading.

J. M. Barrie, the creator of Peter Pan, was a great admirer of Rackham's drawings for *Peter Pan in Kensington Gardens*. His reactions, however, were less elemental than Starkie's, and have a feyness that reflects only a partial understanding of Rackham's art. '[The exhibition] entranced me,' he wrote to Rackham after visiting the Leicester Galleries. 'I think I like best of all the Serpentine with the fairies, & the Peter in his night gown sitting in the tree. Next I would [*sic*] the flying Peters, the fairies going to the ball (as in the "tiff" & the fairy on cobweb) – the fairies sewing the

Below: An afternoon when the gardens were white with snow
Pen and ink and watercolour, 1906
263 × 352 mm
Rare Book Department, Free Library of Philadelphia

Illustration to Peter Pan in Kensington Gardens. *Kensington Palace
is visible in the background behind the naturalistic screen of trees. The
sometimes overcharged sentiment of Rackham's humanised trees is
avoided here.*

The fairies have their tiffs with the birds
Pen and ink and watercolour, 1906
253 × 278 mm
Private Collection

Illustration to Peter Pan in Kensington Gardens.

leaves with their sense of fun (the gayest thing this) and your treatment of snow. I am always your debtor....'[55]

Reacting to Barrie's missing of the point of his work, Rackham was himself critical of Barrie who had confusingly created two Peter Pans. Barrie had chosen to develop the Peter Pan of Never-Never Land, and in his view had thereby missed the opportunity of creating a new, popular and localized myth of Kensington Gardens. Rackham expressed these views to Eleanor Farjeon in their talks together for her 1914 article, though forbad her to report them:

Right: After this the birds said they would help him no more in his mad enterprise
Pen and ink and watercolour, 1906
320 × 215 mm
Private Collection

Illustration to Peter Pan in Kensington Gardens.

**The Serpentine is a lovely lake and there is a drowned forest
at the bottom of it**
Pen and ink and watercolour, 1906
525 × 355 mm
Private Collection

Illustration to Peter Pan in Kensington Gardens.

Peter Pan might have lived as the same local character [as Rip] if his author had not created two entirely different Peters, that result in the Kensington Peter being a palpable invention & the other Peter a typifying of everlasting boyhood. I always think this is rather a pity. The play, of course, has entirely eclipsed the book in its power of appeal, but I regret that the chance has been let slip of permanently peopling Kensington Gardens as the book might have done it. I think Never Never lands are poor prosy substitutes for Kaatskills & Kensingtons, with their stupendous powers of imagination. What power localising a myth has. The Rhine. The Atlas Mountains. Olympia. The Brocken. Dick Whittington. King Arthur. Even girt Jan Ridd [*a character in* Lorna Doone]. Even the musicians of Bremen. But what the dooce! This won't help you.[56]

Having welcomed Rackham warmly with *Rip*, the critics gave him a rougher time with *Peter Pan in Kensington Gardens* – as much a swipe at the publisher's decision to produce an expensive de luxe edition of this children's story, as at the illustrations. Although the *Liverpool Post*[57] predicted it would be the 'book of the year', the *Manchester Guardian*[58] was less happy:

… Has [Rackham] unloosed a new troop of strange figures to haunt us afterwards as we look at familiar places and things? I think he has quite failed to do that. His fairy dancing on a gossamer thread with a spider's web spread below her like an

acrobat's net, seems to show why he failed. It impressed one as very ingenious … rather than inventive.… [he] is undoubtedly a genuine artist with a future, but I do not think it will be along the avenue into which his admirers will be hurrying him.

The Times felt that:

… the appeal again seems to be addressed to the drawing room rather than the nursery. It is all very subtly contrived to catch the fancy of (self) indulgent elders at Christmas time.… It will remain, we may be sure, 'downstairs', where, in fact, illustrations and text will both be best appreciated.[59]

This was a view echoed by the *Daily Express*.[60]

Rackham's particular achievement with *Peter Pan in Kensington Gardens* was to work within the technical limits of the three-colour printing process available to him, and to make a virtue of the necessity of using the kind of spare outline and subdued colouring that could be reproduced faithfully. *The Star* commented:[61]

**The chrysanthemum heard her and said so pointedly, 'Hoity-
toity, what is this?'**
Pen and ink and watercolour, 1906
200 × 150 mm
Private Collection

Illustration to Peter Pan in Kensington Gardens.

As an illustrator Mr Rackham has been forced to consider the means by which [his illustrations] are reproduced.... The line process gives a hard and mechanical look to a drawing, and the half tone a smudgy and indistinct look. Rackham combines the advantages and minimises the disadvantages. Pen and ink foundations keep his forms secure, which the delicate washes ... weave ... into a kind of rhythm.... The device is quite simple and logical, and we may expect to see it taken up by artists who work for reproduction.

With *Rip Van Winkle* and *Peter Pan in Kensington Gardens*, Rackham had created two series of illustrations in which a sense of place was firmly established and conveyed. Although his settings for *Rip* came from his imagination, and echo his memories of European mountains, German or Norwegian forests and English village life, *Peter Pan* is an imaginative distillation of a place that Rackham – and countless others – knew intimately. The Broad Walk, St Govor's Well, the Round Pond and the Serpentine were all parts of the Gardens against which a localized myth of the kind that Barrie invented could be played out. It was also the ideal background to set Rackham's own imagination alight. Such is the importance of reality to him as a spur for his imagination, that Rackham's gnomes and fairies, almost outnumbered by boys, girls and grown-ups, live among real railings, dance on newly spun cobwebs, and flit about the Serpentine at dusk as the gas lights come on in the background.

CHAPTER FOUR

A TENDER, FLICKERING LIGHT OF IMAGINATION 1906 – 1914

R ACKHAM'S SUCCESS WITH *RIP*, and the coming of the new *Peter Pan* illustrations, encouraged him and Edyth to take the major step of buying the lease[1] on a house of their own and, at their joint age of 39, at last starting life in the style of successful married professionals. The years of hack work were over. Arthur was a respected artist on the verge of becoming a 'personality', now able to plan his work over the extended period of eighteen months, hitherto an unheard-of luxury for him.

He had the added, if questionable, luxury of being able to turn down commissions and invitations to exhibit, on the grounds of having a full order book. While in the midst of producing his *Rip* illustrations, he was invited by George Routledge & Sons to illustrate Trollope, but turned the offer down because he had 'so much in hand that at present I could hardly undertake anything further. I have work that will virtually take me all my time until the end of the year.'[2] He 'declined regretfully'[3] an invitation from the Société Internationale d'Aquarellistes in Paris to exhibit at their November 1905 inaugural exhibition, presumably on the same grounds that had led him in October 1905 to turn down Robert Bateman's invitation to exhibit at the Whitworth Institute in Manchester:

Left: Jewels from the Deep
Pen and ink and watercolour,
1909
356 × 253 mm
Harris Museum and Art
Gallery, Preston

A watery subject which is perhaps connected with Undine, *the book which Rackham was illustrating in 1909.*

At the present moment I have literally nothing I could submit to you – all the drawings for Rip Van Winkle found purchasers & I have since been almost entirely occupied with commissions which will take most of my time for a whole year. Among other things I have another book to do of a similar nature to Rip … this will I believe contain some of my best work.[4]

The house they chose was 16 Chalcot Gardens, an elegant detached building at the end of a short road set back from the traffic, running parallel to England's Lane, Hampstead. It had been designed by Charles Voysey in 1881, and altered by him in 1898[5] for the artist Adolphus Whalley. Before moving in, Rackham commissioned Maxwell Ayrton to adapt the house once again, to provide studios both for himself and for Edyth.[6] This was a period of intense activity for them both. As builders were moving in and out of Chalcot Gardens, removing and then replacing the studio roof, raising its walls and making an upper and a lower studio, Rackham was at work in Primrose Hill Studios finishing off the *Peter Pan* illustrations, while Edyth had resumed her portrait painting, exhibiting *The Grebe Hat* at the RA in 1907 after an eight-year break.

At Chalcot Gardens, Rackham's studio was on the new first floor, with an external staircase down to the garden. It was described in 1907 in

16 Chalcot Gardens, Hampstead
Photograph, c1908
Rackham is standing on his first floor studio balcony

Walter Freeman's newspaper *The World* as 'fine and beautifully lighted ... volumes of fairy lore, ancient and modern, are well represented among the contents of the well-lined bookshelves.'[7] Another journalist, writing in 1908, reported it to be 'a most delightful place, cool, airy and quiet, with its polished floor and wide spaces, the walls bare but for a stray watercolour sketch or two, for there is little furniture besides a big drawing easel and a few deep, low and most comfortable chairs. A few books lie scattered about, but otherwise an air of order ... prevails; ... lovely outlook over a leafy garden, with its rolling green lawns and fine old trees.'[8]

Yet another report, this time for an American magazine, described the studio in 1914:

It was of ordinary size, with both side and top windows. Its walls were stained a light brown and it contained a few good rugs and pieces of furniture, among them a bookcase filled mostly with illustrations, of which he has an interesting collection, all so exquisitely fresh and in good order. A bar ran across the room from which hung a trapeze.... There were fine drawings on the walls, one or two of his wife's pictures, but no special studio furniture.... The centre of interest in this room is the work table ... adjustable in height and angle, unusually small for a work table. Over it hung, on a level with the eye, an electric light.[9]

These observations, written over a seven-year period, agree on the fundamental points that Rackham's studio was light, airy, and not over-furnished, that he was surrounded by his collection of books, and that he did not allow clutter. Everything, it seemed, had its

Rackham in his studio at
16 Chalcot Gardens
Photograph, c1908

80

place, and everything, when not in use, was put away. The fact that there appears to be hardly any change in the studio in the years between the 1908 and 1914 articles, indicates a tranquillity and a desire on Rackham's part for continuity, harmony and domestic peace.

The studio was the hub of Rackham's life, and he welcomed family and visitors into it. 'I always like being disturbed at my work (I believe in their hearts most artists do),' he wrote to Alfred Mart, an architect friend from the Tufnell Park days, now living in Sussex.[10] He had the enviable facility of being able to carry on a conversation and draw at the same time, sometimes unconsciously making weird grimaces as he did so, to try out the new expression that he required for a character.[11] He was never disturbed by the people and conversation around him, and when he wanted to break off from work he would run a comb through the hair of his cat, Jimmie, named after Sir James Barrie, or take a turn on the trapeze which he hung for amusement, exercise, and for his models to pose upon, from the studio roof. Nor was he ever upset by the fearsome characters he invented. 'Oh yes,' he said to Gladys Beattie Crozier, 'I can always call up any number of entirely freshly created and horrible beasts and hobgoblins at a moment's notice before my mind's eye when they are wanted as

Arthur Rackham c1909

models for my work, and banish them as easily directly I have done with them.'[12]

Talking to Clara Mac Chesney, he revealed that he did not work with laboured preliminary studies. 'I dash off an idea which comes to me and often very vaguely. I build as I go on, and the idea develops as I work. I always, however, plan beforehand and I always use models.'[13] Another critic, A. L. Baldry, gives his own valuable account of Rackham's method, telling how 'with a general idea of his composition in mind, he begins by setting down the surroundings of the figures before he draws in the figures themselves – he builds up, as it were, the scene before he brings on his characters to play their parts on the stage.'[14] This is akin to the method of a storyteller who will describe the background and setting of his story before moving on to more detailed characterization. A rare survival of an unfinished drawing of 1907 from a cancelled edition of *Sleeping Beauty*,[15] shows just how Rackham

Soldiers Caught in Brambles
Pencil, pen and ink, 1907
376 × 271 mm
Courtesy of the Board of Trustees of
the V&A

*Unfinished illustration to the cancelled
1907 Heinemann edition of* Sleeping
Beauty.

builds up his picture from the outside in, and from the back to the front, even completing the signature flourish and date while the main 'character' of the illustration is still an uncertain swirl of pencil lines.

At 39, Rackham was approaching middle age, and settling comfortably into a pattern of success, and delighting in his celebrity. Photographs show him as neat and alert, wearing a high collar and tie or spotted bow-tie, and a tweed or blue serge jacket 'heaven knows how old, ragged & worn till it is so threadbare & shining that it could claim respectability as an alpaca.'[16] His tailor made him a new suit every so often of exactly the same cut and colour as the last, which was then relegated to end its days as his studio suit. His hair had begun to recede by the time he was forty and, always, he wore a pair of steel or gold-rimmed spectacles. Were it not for the multitude of pens and pencils visible behind his tilted drawing-board in a photograph published in 1909,[17] Rackham would pass for a thoroughly professional and organized, characteristically punctual, senior clerk, architect or accountant.

His tastes, however, remained simple, and because of his Spartan early years he found it hard to spend money on pleasure or to waste it on unnecessary expense. He would recycle his old newspapers, then still a rare kind of thrift among the wealthy. Old newspaper had a multitude of uses for him: as blotting paper, as wrapping, for keeping warm in bed, for filing, for drying out damp shoes, as a table-cloth and for eating sardines off.

If the studio was the hub of Arthur's life, downstairs Edyth took charge of all the decorating, entertaining and running the house. 'Servants and tradesmen adored her,' wrote Barbara, 'and she only had to paint a room a certain colour for all her friends to want to copy it. She loved experimenting in interior decoration, and often became very daring, covering chairs with bits of old petticoat and other fancies, and arranging flowers in saucepans.'

The Rackhams shared their house freely with their friends, organizing regular parties and musical evenings. George Bernard Shaw was on their guest list, and wrote to chide Rackham before one musical evening took place: 'I am greatly hurt at your calling me a slight acquaintance. I regard you as quite an old pal.'[18] Charles Holroyd, Director of the National Gallery, enjoyed the same evening with the Rackhams so much that he wrote afterwards requesting the address of the entertainer.[19] Other regular guests included artists such as Edmund Sullivan and his wife, Walter and Gilbert Bayes, Briton Rivière, his son and grandchildren, and the *Punch* illustrator Lewis Baumer. Neighbours, too, became friends, and regular visitors: the Farjeons, the Underhills and the Raes among them. Calvert Spensley lived next door, and took Barbara to London Zoo, of which he was a Fellow, allowing her to have monkeys and boa constrictors out of their cages. Friendships were sealed when neighbours became patrons, and of Rackham's neighbours who bought his original work from exhibitions were the Raes, the Underhills and the Spensleys.

Barbara remembers her father's regularity of habit and appearance:

He seemed to me always to look much the same, small and thin, with a deeply grooved but clear-cut face, and smooth pepper-and-salt hair at the sides of his bald head. If he grew slightly balder, more wrinkled and silvery during the years, it hardly altered his general appearance. He was active and precise in all he did, whether working or playing, in which there was really little difference since he enjoyed his work and took his play seriously.

Perhaps without realizing it, Rackham was at this period beginning to establish the image which was to

82

Arthur Rackham at his drawing board
Photograph, 1909

precede him for the rest of his life and for subsequent years. This neat, precise man, who had already often introduced his own self-portrait into his work, because his was the most convenient and ever ready face to draw, had presented his image as a hostage to fortune for subsequent writers and journalists to do with what they would.

His own personal idiosyncrasies reinforced the point, and created irresistible copy for writers. Walter Starkie confessed to thinking Rackham *was* a goblin when he saw his uncle 'in his shabby blue suit and carpet slippers, hopping about the studio with a palette on one arm, waving a paint brush in his hand.'[20] Rackham professed to loathe modern inventions, despite the fact that he and his younger brother Harris had happily carried out chemistry and physics experiments at home as children, and together had constructed an electric battery.[21] Eleanor Farjeon recorded his declaration that cars and motorcycles, telephones and typewriters were at the root of most modern evils. 'I would rather,' he told her, 'have a page of handwriting I couldn't read than a typewritten manuscript.'[22] Nor would he wear a wrist-watch ('new fangled' – he had a gold Hunter instead) or have horn-rimmed spectacles (also 'new fangled', fancy and impractical). It was a favourite assertion of his, too, that the fall of man began with the invention of the wheel, though this remark smacks of being more of a tease than a sincerely held conviction.

Despite these assertions, and his reluctance to travel by car, he enjoyed and was indebted to his bicycle, and rented an automatic player-piano from a pianola-roll supplier because, as Eleanor Farjeon added, 'he must have music at any price, [and being]

incapable of playing common time with one hand and triple time with the other ... has had to fall victim to a machine.' His wilful conservatism extended to his abhorrence of modern changes in pronunciation, and Barbara tells how he would harry bus conductors by insisting on tickets to 'Tibbalds Road', 'Simmery Axe' or 'Marrerbun' [Theobald's Road, St Mary Axe and Marylebone]. He even subdivided his London loyalty by saying, 'Of course I was born South of the Thames. I'm a Surrey man', though we may take it that talking in Cockney slang to bus conductors was probably just another way he had of amusing his daughter.

Rackham's anachronistic, self-generated image inevitably affected the way others saw him. There is only a short step between a young reader such as Walter Starkie seeing the artist's self-portrait as a gnome in one of his drawings and imagining he is one. Even writers of the intelligence of Eleanor Farjeon exploited this, giving her article the title 'The Wizard at Home':

Landscape with Stream and Cows
Watercolour, 1909
175 × 254 mm
Arthur Rackham Memorial Collection, University of Louisville

The watercolour is inscribed to Dr George Savage, a friend and frequent companion of Rackham's on fishing trips.

[My family and I] knew Arthur Rackham's *Rip* before we knew Arthur Rackham. I always had the impression that [he] ... was a kind of wizard; that he only pretended to call himself Arthur Rackham, and hobgoblins really hailed him by some more mystic name on stormy nights on Hampstead Heath.... Acquaintance has not entirely allayed my suspicion.... He watches you from behind the Spectacles of Cunning, and there's a whimsical line on his face that can translate itself into the kindliest of smiles. He is light and spare and alert....'[23]

Farjeon's article, written for the American magazine *St Nicholas*, probably did more than any other to reinforce the received image of Rackham as some kind of busy little gnome, acquainted with the fairies. On the principle of the wish becoming father to the thought, it had the subsequent effect of encouraging other writers to think along the same lines. At the same time, Farjeon reinforced the allied image of the scatty, forgetful artist. Describing how he searched for a letter in her presence, Farjeon recalls Rackham's words:

You see ... but I must read you that letter ... where *is* that letter? Did I leave it in Barbara's room? ... No I can't find it.... You really should hear the letter, but it isn't here or here – let me look once more.... Of course, this is where it ought to be.... Ah! *now* you see the mistake of putting things in their proper places....

Rackham wrote at least three letters to Eleanor Farjeon commenting on her text, and suggesting amendments. He nervously persuaded her to tone down his views on James Barrie:

I *must* not criticise Barrie. I *think* it all as you've reported. But – I mustn't have it published.... Mention if you like as mine my preference for the imagination-stirring Kaatskills & Kensington to the imaginative Never-Never Land.... I can't bear to have my views (which I express far too freely & foolishly) put into cold print. I'm much too careless a talker to bear reporting....[24]

Other views, too, he wanted to keep to himself: 'Also, about [Walter] Pater. I mustn't give opinions in this way. Also I had rather not publish my views on

Cubism. And Edyth doesn't like the suggestion of aloofness & severity that is unavoidable with that reference.'

Although the views on Pater and Cubism that Rackham successfully suppressed have gone unrecorded, he did not complain of the 'wizard' analogy that Farjeon used in describing him, so one can only conclude that he approved of it and the slant that it gave to the portrait drawn by the article. The pigeonhole that Rackham thereby put himself into may have been good for business, but it had the additional effect of allowing the myth to develop which led ultimately to such appellations as 'The Goblin Master' and 'Court Painter to King Oberon and Queen Titania'.

Rackham attempted a justification of his retiring attitude in an article he wrote in 1926, in which he ignored the constructive effect that good criticism, as opposed to gossip, can have:

Contemporary criticism should rather be intended for the consideration of the public than for the author, and so long as it prepares the ground for the production of genuine art it justifies its existence. I do not think I have found the published criticism of my own work of any value to me as an artist and, after a very brief experience, years ago, of a press cuttings agency,[25] I do not now seek to read it.... There is no doubt that an author had better now read the contemporary reviews of his work. The writers cannot mean them for him or they would have written to him privately.... So, when we have put forth our effort, let us quietly retire to our workshops again and try to do better next time.[26]

In the meantime, after the success of *Peter Pan*, Rackham embarked on a new edition of *Alice in Wonderland* which, at Christmas 1907, was coming out of copyright. Tenniel's illustrations, first published in 1865, had established the story in the public mind, and *Alice* was the first important and popular work, with genuinely loved illustrations, to be submitted to a public process of re-illustration. Inevitably, even the thought of this was a source of controversy, and the drums started to beat in advance of the new edition's appearance:

The statement that Mr. Arthur Rackham is following up his *Rip Van Winkle* and *Peter Pan* books with an illustrated *Alice in Wonderland* is very interesting, but it does not give me, for one, unmixed delight.... Few people can less desire a new pictorial treatment of the Mad Hatter and the Duchess.... Sir John Tenniel fixed the type, and any alien treatment will ... simply be unwelcome. I waive the question of taste which each artist must decide for himself.[27]

Heinemann had anticipated just such an attack, and were ready with a blast of justification when their *Alice* appeared. This was not only conveyed by clever

Mad Hatter's Tea Party
Colour process plate, 1907
Bridgeman Art Library

Illustration to Alice in Wonderland. *In what is perhaps his most famous self-caricature, Rackham depicts himself as The Mad Hatter.*

advertising, but also by clever editorship. To precede the main text, Heinemann commissioned Austin Dobson to write a four-verse 'Proem', which has appeared in all reprints of the edition since. Describing Alice as 'enchanting', Dobson writes:

But still you are a Type, and based
In Truth, like LEAR and HAMLET;
And Types may be re-dressed to taste
In cloth-of-gold or camlet.

Here comes a fresh Costumier, then;
That Taste may gain a wrinkle
From him who drew with such deft pen
The rags of RIP VAN WINKLE!

Rackham's model for Alice – and later for Cinderella and the Sleeping Beauty – was Doris Jane Dommett, a girl who herself later became a miniature painter.

85

Right: They all crowded round it, panting, and asking 'but who has won?'
Pen and ink and watercolour, 1907
235 × 165 mm
Private Collection

Illustration to Alice in Wonderland.

Above: An unusually large saucepan flew close by it, and very nearly carried it off
Pencil, pen and ink and watercolour, 1907
387 × 259 mm
Private Collection

A preliminary study for the illustration in Alice in Wonderland, *set in Rackham's own kitchen at Chalcot Gardens. His cook at the time, a temperamental Irish woman called Mrs Fitzpatrick, is seen throwing the plates.*

She recalled the sittings soon after Rackham's death: 'He chose me from a number of little girls and I was so pleased he copied my print frock exactly, because it was one my mother had allowed me to design myself. The woollen stockings I wore were knitted by my old French nannie, Prudence. They were thick to keep out the cold, and how they tickled! Nannie went with me to Mr. Rackham's studio in Chalcot Gardens. She stood in some awe of him, and thought artists a little odd. But I loved to watch him when he was drawing the Mad Hatter, because his own face took on the expression he was trying to get. In the mad tea party picture, he set out Mrs. Rackham's best china on the long table, and I sat in his big wing-back chair – I've loved such chairs ever since. Nannie approved of this picture because I am so prim and proper in it.'[28] For

the kitchen scene Rackham's own kitchen, and his cook, were the models. 'Will she throw plates?' Jane asked Rackham. 'Oh no, they've been broken already,' the artist replied, as he had already thrown a few to make sure the detail was right.

When the book appeared, four other new *Alices* were published at the same time: those illustrated by Charles Robinson (Cassell), Millicent Sowerby (Chatto & Windus), W. H. Walker (John Lane) and T. Maybank (Routledge).[29] Of these, only Rackham's has survived despite, or perhaps because of, a flurry of hostile criticism. *Punch* published a cartoon[30] on the subject by E. T. Reed, with the remark:

If ... it was either desirable or necessary to re-draw Sir John Tenniel's unsurpassable and immortal illustrations to *Alice in Wonderland*, Mr. Rackham may be said to have performed the task as well probably as any draughtsman could for he is an artist with a rare sense of grotesque fancy and humour and an extraordinarily delicate and sensitive line. But it were better, we think, for him to employ his imagination upon his own rather than other men's business....[31]

The Times[32] was only slightly less harsh:

Tenniel was [Alice's] predestined illustrator.... Of the Rackham edition (for the other four are negligible) it may at least be said that the artist feels his privilege and his responsibilities.... His humour is forced and derivative, and his work shows but few signs of true imaginative instinct.... The best that can be hoped for is that neither Mr. Rackham nor any other too adventurous draughtsman may venture further to experiment on *Through the Looking Glass*.[33]

Arthur Rackham [signature]

Left: At this the whole pack rose up in the air, and came flying down upon her
Pen and ink and watercolour, 1907
Private Collection/Bridgeman Art Library

Illustration to Alice in Wonderland, *Rackham's Alice, modelled by Doris Dommett, was described by the* Daily Telegraph's *critic as 'older and more sophisticated [than Tenniel's Alice]; but at the same time has a tender, flickering light of imagination in her eyes.'*

Right: Advice from a Caterpillar
Pen and ink and watercolour, 1907
245 × 160 mm
Private Collection

Illustration to Alice in Wonderland.

Alice and the Caterpillar
by Sir John Tenniel, 1865

The Daily Telegraph, however, had a few days earlier published a review in favour of Rackham's treatment:

The Alice ... is not the heroine of Sir John Tenniel's imagination; she is older and more sophisticated; but at the same time she has a tender, flickering light of imagination in her eyes, which lifts her out of the domain of the merely pretty and childish.... Mr. Rackham's inexhaustible imagination, working over and embroidering the ground-work of Tenniel's types, has added a really wonderful wealth of uncanny, dreamlike mystery to the story ... [and] extraordinary feeling into the drawing of the hands.[34]

The controversy fuelled the sales of Rackham's book, 14,322 copies of the six shilling edition being sold in the first six months of publication,[35] nearly twice the number of copies that the *Peter Pan* trade edition had sold in its first nine months,[36] and a rate of sales that Rackham was not to reach again. As well as buying the book, the public, strangers and friends came to

Rackham's defence. The etcher H. R. Robertson of Haverstock Hill, Hampstead, claiming modestly to be a stranger to Rackham, wrote: 'I felt I *must* express my indignation at the injustice of the "Times" criticism. However, I am certain that Time is on your side, and that nothing but prejudice prevents your superiority being recognised now. Your delightful Alice is alive and makes by contrast Tenniel's Alice look a stiff wooden puppet.'[37]

Edyth, now like Arthur aged 41, was pregnant for the second time when Arthur was working on the *Alice* illustrations, and Barbara, their only surviving child, was born in January 1908, just over a month after the publication of *Alice*. Inevitably, in the mass of letters the couple received from friends, many congratulated them on the birth of their own 'Alice'. Claude Shepperson sent his congratulations on the birth, adding the pious hope that the 'new little "Alice's" adventures in this Wonderland ... will always be happy and bright ones.'[38] Brown and Phillips' mixed references

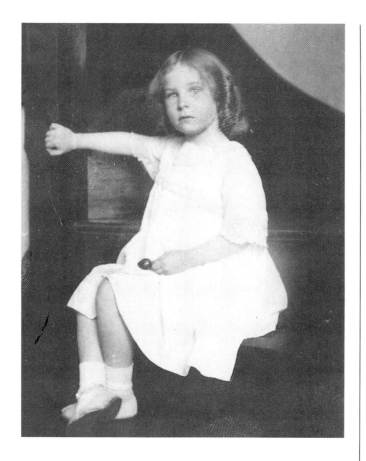

Above: Study of Barbara as a baby
Pencil, 1908
Private Collection

Left: Barbara Rackham
photographed by Eleanor Farjeon
1913

to three subjects illustrated by Rackham in their five-line letter, thus indicating how deeply entangled and identified Rackham had already become with his subjects: 'Let us congratulate you on the birth of little Alice. May all the good fairies attend her Christening. Perhaps little Peter will follow in due course.'[39]

Only Arthur and Edyth's close friend Hugh Rivière touched obliquely on the importance of Barbara's birth to the couple, being aware, as all their circle must have been, of the tragedy of Edyth's earlier still birth: 'It is only since we have had the joy of our little one that one has really understood what it means to be without them and our long waiting for ours was nothing to what you & your wife must have been through.'[40]

The birth of a child to the wife of Arthur Rackham was news.[41] By now he had become a celebrity, and it is significant that it is *his* Alice that is particularly lampooned in E. T. Reed's *Punch* cartoon, while Reed shows the other new Alices cowering anonymously in the corner. Rackham's face, and the fact that he had caricatured himself as the Mad Hatter, were already sufficiently well known to be parodied to effect by Reed, the other artists *being nowhere*. Parodies of Rackham's work even extended into children's magazines, such was his fame. *St. Nicholas* published a story whose headpiece by Reginald Birch depicted a gnome and a Rackham Alice look-alike standing below a Rackhamesque tree, in whose branches is the sign: 'NO TRESPASSING by Order of A. Rackham.'[42]

Another side-effect of his fame was that he was courted by the press for his views on issues only tangential to his work. At the time of the launch of *A Midsummer Night's Dream* the year after *Alice*, the *Daily Mirror* invited Rackham to give his views on dolls, and he took the opportunity to propound, rather too earnestly, his wider moral feelings:

There is one doll in particular to which I have a very strong aversion ... the repulsive red-nosed policeman. We have had more than enough of the "red-nose" cult on the music halls and elsewhere, and to introduce such hideousness into the nursery is to familiarise childhood with an ugly idea from which it should be kept free. Drunkenness under the most charitable interpretation is a form of disease....[43]

The *Daily Mirror* gave him no chance to amend his views before they appeared in cold print, and Rackham talked on:

Golliwogs and punches I look upon as grotesque ... but I should prefer to give my little girl a nice warm woolly bear as being a representation of a natural creature.... Little girls – and little boys as well – use their dolls to cultivate the dramatic instinct that all children possess ... and for many years of their after life they retain in their minds the picture of the hero or heroine of their early days. It is because of the lasting qualities

of childhood impressions that these should be made beautiful and not repulsive.... In a fairy story the good fairy always gets the better of the wicked fairy, as the child knows this there is no harm in showing it a picture or representation of a bad fairy, dark and ugly, but not deformed.

His views on the art of illustration, too, were sought, and he was invited in January 1910 to be Guest of Honour and speaker at a dinner given by the Author's Club,[44] where he gave a clear statement of his own purpose. He reminded his listeners of 'the essential differences of aim between a work of art that is enclosed between the covers of a book and one that is to be exposed upon a wall', and appealed for them to be judged from different standpoints. 'A picture both in subject and treatment must be considered as a work for constant contemplation – a permanent companion. An illustration, on the other hand, is only looked at for a fraction of time, now and then, the page being turned next, perhaps, to a totally different subject, treated, it may even be, in a totally different way. In this branch, bizarre and unusual effects of arrangement, violent actions, exaggerations and other matters of spasmodic interest may find a place almost forbidden on the walls of a room. In addition there are the different technical requirements of association with the printed page, even of scale, and of distance at which the work will be considered by the spectator.' Rackham went on to point out that 'in some ways we book illustrators are more in touch with artists of certain periods of the past than are those following many other branches of art. While the modern painter usually paints what he likes, the early painter almost invariably worked to order. And so, too, do most modern illustrators, almost invariably.'

Rackham's main points, however, were that the illustrator should be regarded as a partner of the author, not as his servant, nor as an aid 'like gold leaf on the cover' to selling more books. 'Any attempt to coerce [the illustrator] into a mere tool in the author's hands can only result in the most dismal failure. Illustration is as capable of varied appeal as is literature itself; and the only real essential is an association that shall not be at variance or unsympathetic.'

Rackham described three main roles of illustration: firstly to say what the author failed to say clearly; secondly to add some fresh aspect of interest to a

Father Christmas
Pen and ink and watercolour, 1907
368 × 286 mm
Private Collection/Chris Beetles Gallery

The Wolf and the Goat
Pen and ink and watercolour, 1912
210 × 140 mm
Private Collection

*'Pray take my advice and come down here
where you will find plenty of better food.'
Illustration, later coloured, to Aesop's
Fables.*

subject which the author has already treated interestingly from his point of view ('a partnership that has often been productive of good'); and thirdly and most fascinatingly of all, the expression by the artist of an individual sense of delight or emotion aroused by the accompanying passage of text.

Pointing out that authors do not always recognize the difference in technique and limitations between their work and that of illustrators, Rackham adds:

It is easy enough to refer in words for instance to the charm of a beautiful woman. No more than the mere mention is necessary to bring a picture to the mind of the reader which, if it were fully realised by a painter, would merit for his work a resting place in the National Gallery and for his body a resting place in St. Paul's.

Rackham also addressed the issue of illustrating the literature of writers of the past citing *Moll Flanders* and *Tom Jones* as cases in point:

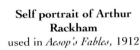

[The illustrator] can revive for the present generation a view of the past ... so as to bring to its readers a power of appreciating the times written of that they could not have without his help. What would we give now if only some of the great works of the past had been illustrated fully in their own day by even a reasonably able artist, and with real desire to show the environment of the stories?

Finally, Rackham takes another tilt at photography, the art that ultimately ousted him and other artists of his generation from illustrative journalism

Now your work, all your work, should be regarded as work of imagination, as art. You are not copying-clerks or phonographers or recording angels. Yet there is some tendency now to illustrate even poetic works and fiction by photographs. Surely to place before your readers ... the actuality you had before you when writing, is ruthlessly to rub off all the bloom of imagination, of temperament, of personal view, of atmosphere, which are your chief, your only, great claim to consideration.

In this brief address to his author colleagues – to him partners, not masters – Rackham underlines points that concerned him throughout his career, that illustration was literally as its name described, the adding of lustre, of light, to a text, a means of giving it a new dimension, a kind of road sign to help the reader around the 'environment of the stories'.

Another off-shoot of the lionization of Rackham was the award to him of prizes from foreign art institutes. This was the direct result of his beginning to exhibit in group exhibitions in Europe and of his publishers then bringing out foreign-language editions of his books. His first European foray was the inclusion of *The Young Count and the Frogs* (*Grimm*) in the Düsseldorf International Exhibition of 1904, the same year that he was invited to show in the St Louis International. Two years later, he exhibited *The Battle between the Air and the Earth*, also from *Grimm*, in the Milan International, where it was awarded the Gold Medal. Building on this success, his new publishers, Heinemann, brought out an Italian edition of *Alice*, selling two thousand trade copies and 150 de luxe to the Instituto Italiano in Bergamo in November 1907,[45] and leading Bernard Rackham to remark, in his letter congratulating the couple on Barbara's birth, 'I see you are advertised in the Italian papers as "Arturo Rackham".'[46]

Success in exhibitions abroad led to further success in publishing, and at Christmas 1908 Heinemann published French, Italian and German editions of *A Midsummer Night's Dream*, in addition to the English-language version for Britain, the United States and the Colonies. In 1909 the Italian edition of *Alice* was reprinted, and in March 1910 one thousand French trade copies were sold to Hachette in Paris. And so it went on: Rotterdam Arts and Crafts Society asked for 25 drawings from *Rip Van Winkle* and *Peter Pan* for their winter 1907 exhibition, *Illustrative Arts*,[47] but because of the new demand on his work for exhibition and sale, had to be content with six illustrations from *Ingoldsby Legends* and two other works. The Venice

Left: The Crooked Man
Pen and ink and watercolour, 1913
265 × 216 mm
Arthur Rackham Collection, Rare Book
and Manuscript Library, Columbia
University

Illustration to Mother Goose.

**The ducks which he had once saved
dived and brought up the key from the
depths**
Colour process plate, 1900

*Illustration to 'The Queen Bee' in the 1900
edition of* Grimm's Fairy Tales, *reworked for
the 1909 edition. Before reworking this
drawing, Rackham told its owner that 'the key
is rather a bald statement, & the ducks
themselves might have a little more "quality".'*

International exhibition included three Rackhams, in 1908 followed by two in 1910.

This flood of requests put great pressure on Rackham, who had to combine the satisfying of these demands with the need to allow adequate time to think about and work on his next book. 'But you do not work at night?' Clara Mac Chesney asked him. 'Not much,' he answered dubiously. 'Altogether too much,' Edyth quickly added.[48] He was also forced to review his committee work, resigning from the Picture Committee of the United Arts Club in 1909 because of continuing irregular attendance.[49] He found himself having to go back to the purchasers to borrow work not only for exhibitions[50] but to make reissues of earlier books too. Writing to Alfred Mart in 1909, he asks to borrow back two drawings from *Grimm* so that they can be rephotographed by Constable, 'who are bringing out the book again with better repros in colour', adding the sweetener: 'The publishers will be glad to send you an edition de luxe of the book when it comes out in the autumn.'[51]

The bandwagon rolled on. Dent had taken advantage of the launch of *Alice* to reissue *The Ingoldsby Legends*,[52] as had Cassell to reissue five of Rackham's illustrated stories to *Little Folks* in a collection entitled *The Land of Enchantment*. The new edition of *Ingoldsby Legends* had a new frontispiece and some new plates, with earlier plates reworked and many recoloured. The agreement with Dent gave Rackham the opportunity to win back some at least of the *Ingoldsby* drawings he had sold to Dent in 1898 as part of the original

agreement, by insisting on 'all drawings altered or coloured becoming mine'.[53] In November 1909, as Rackham's book for that year, *Undine*, was launched by Heinemann, Dent brought out *Gulliver* and *Lamb's Tales from Shakespeare* in a 7s 6d trade and a de luxe edition, paying Rackham £500 for 'Old drawings altered, cancelled and added to'.[54] Not to be outdone, Constable, who had bought the rights from its previous publisher, Freemantle & Co., reissued Rackham's *Grimm* with revised, redrawn and recoloured illustrations.

This amounted to a battle of the books, with Rackham as the weapon used by one publisher against another, while he himself quietly worked away reaping the rewards. Collectors were sometimes called on to give more than just their permission to lend. Again to Mart, he wrote: 'I wonder whether you will allow me to work on it a little. Not to any great extent ... the key is rather a bald statement, & the ducks themselves might have a little more "quality". But only if you don't mind.... In this new edition I am overhauling my old work where it seems to want it. A very little sometimes makes a great improvement.'[55]

Following on from the Gold Medal in Milan in 1906, Rackham won the First Class Medal at the Sixth International Exposition of Art at Barcelona in 1911. This was awarded for his seven exhibits in the Drawing section, which included illustrations from *A Midsummer Night's Dream*, *Undine* and *The Ring*, as well as *The Imp of the Smoke*, which Barcelona Museum subsequently bought. In 1912 he was elected an

Twilight Dreams
Pen and ink and watercolour, 1912
340 × 520 mm
University of Liverpool Art Gallery and Collections

Conceived as endpapers for the 1912 edition of Peter Pan in
Kensington Gardens, _the drawing was later coloured and
dated for exhibition and sale in 1913._

Associate of the Société Nationale des Beaux Arts,[56] after exhibiting 79 works in a room given over to him entirely at the Grand Palais in Paris. This was a great honour for any artist, and particularly for an Englishman, as _Le Gaulois_ reported: 'Arthur Rackham was received yesterday at 5 o'clock by the Committee of the S.N.B.A., who have awarded him the exceptional distinction of the medal of the Society, to commemorate his fine manifestation of art. As is known, the S.N. does not distribute any awards. It is then in this case a testimonial of the most flattering kind.'[57]

This sort of attention and lionization had its disadvantages. Hodder and Stoughton, who still had control over the _Peter Pan in Kensington Gardens_ illustrations, reissued the book in a smaller format version in 1910, much to Rackham's despair. Margaret Farjeon, Eleanor's mother asked him to sign three copies of the reissue for her, and he replied with a series of amendments to the title pages, each one as brutally critical as the last. In his covering letter he wrote:

Here are the books with my 'marks' in them. I hardly know what to do in the case of the Peter Pans. I have such a very small opinion of them. But I hope I have added a little to the interest that could be taken in them by expressing my opinion on the title page. Anyhow they are a convenient form in which to read Barrie's charming story. The illustrations have been achieved by clipping down the old (& in some cases almost worn out) blocks regardless of everything except the size of the page of the book. The publishers, though well meaning to an almost unusual degree at least, are blessed with a minus amount of artistic taste.[58]

Rackham goes on to tell Margaret Farjeon that Hodders were also 'putting a preposterously expensive "portfolio" on the market of 12 of the P.P. illustrations – reproduced about the same size as (in some cases larger than) the originals. I cannot believe it will be a

success financially as it certainly is not artistically.' Hodders were prompted to reissue the book, and to assemble the *Peter Pan Portfolio* in 1912, as a response to the popularity of the 1908 London stage production of *Peter and Wendy*, and to follow up their edition of *Peter Pan and Wendy* illustrated by F. D. Bedford for the 1911 Christmas season.[59]

The *Portfolio* was a collection of twelve enlarged reproductions of the *Peter Pan in Kensington Gardens* illustrations, many of which show signs of having been borrowed from owners in a hurry, and re-photographed with the nails and the edges of their frames still visible. The aim of the *Portfolio* was to present a set of reproductions of Rackham's work in mounts ready for framing and hanging at home, an exercise that Rackham condemned on artistic grounds to the extent of consigning his copies to the wastepaper basket.[60] The *Portfolio* did, however, promote his work widely, and ultimately spawned one fine new piece of music. As a little girl, Debussy's daughter, Chouchou (b. 1905), had a reproduction of *The fairies are exquisite dancers ...* hanging above her bed.[61] This will certainly have been taken from the *Portfolio*, and Chouchou, a firm believer in fairies, loved the picture so much that her father composed a Prelude for her, 'Les Fées Sont d'Exquises Danseuses' (Book II, no. 4), which was inspired by the picture.[62]

Rackham's only real rival at this stage was Edmund Dulac (1882–1956).[63] Other artists whose work was being reproduced by three-colour process included Jessie M. King (1875–1949), Charles Robinson (1870–1937), William Heath Robinson (1872–1944) and William Russell Flint (1880–1944). It is significant that Rackham engaged the cuttings agency Romeike and Curtice to send him copies of reviews of

Dulac,[64] the only artist whom he needed to keep the measure of. Both had become masters of the three-colour process, which derived from the half-tone process of black and white printing invented by Meissenbach in 1882, and in general use in Britain by 1904 and 1905.

Though fifteen years Rackham's junior, Dulac had found success at much the same time with a commission from Dent in 1904 to produce sixty watercolour illustrations to the Brontë novels. He subsequently worked, as Rackham had, for the *Pall Mall Magazine*, and in 1907 won the commission from Hodder and Stoughton for *The Arabian Nights*, the book that was to make his name. Comparing the two, in a review of Dulac's *Arabian Nights* exhibition at the Leicester Galleries, *The Observer* decided that Dulac 'owes much to Arthur Rackham.'[65] *The Athenaeum*, however, sounded a warning for Rackham:

Rackham may be said to have invented a beautiful kind of tinted pen drawing ... and we shrewdly suspect that had Mr. Rackham's early efforts been shown alongside these of Mr. Dulac they would have been outshone in public estimation. For Dulac is stronger and more confident in line – the confidence that comes not of research. The essential excellence of

Rackham's work ... is his beautiful feeling for landscape; and this also Dulac does not attempt to rival. But besides these there are secondary qualities with which the older artist pads out his native merit, an industrious neatness and copiousness of finish, a diligent search for amusing material with which to fill out an elaborate drawing; and this sort of thing is done just as well by Dulac, who is technically most accomplished and painstaking.... In the meantime the exhibition is an education for Mr. Rackham, and so well does it do many things that he does, that it may even induce him to purge his art of certain superfluous attractions.[66]

A year later, reviewing Dulac's *Tempest* exhibition, the *Pall Mall Gazette* noted that:

'... if Rackham excells in humour and episode, Dulac takes the palm for scenic beauty and conception in colour from the outset',[67] while *The World* summed the issue up with the observation: 'Mr. Dulac draws with his brush and Mr. Rackham paints with his pen.'[68]

For a few years after *A Midsummer Night's Dream*, Rackham's work began to take an overtly Germanic turn. Reviewers had already noticed the German feeling behind the illustrations in *Rip* and *A Midsummer Night's Dream*, but with *Undine* (1909) and the Wagner books, *The Rhinegold and the Valkyrie* (1910) and *Siegfried and the Twilight of the Gods* (1911), Rackham's

Left: Undine Outside the Window
Pen and ink and watercolour, 1909
280 × 205 mm
Private Collection

Illustration to the line 'Undine, wilt thou for once leave off these childish pranks?' and used as the frontispiece to Undine by Friedrich de la Motte Fouqué. Writing to N. Carroll in 1931, Rackham disclosed that this was one of his favorite drawings. He later (1915) painted a large version of the subject in tempera.

Left: 'Little niece, forget not that I am here with thee as a guide'
Colour process plate, 1909

Illustration to Undine. A variation on the composition of Dürer's Knight, Death and the Devil.

celebration of his German inspiration became specific. In the case of _Undine_, one illustration, '_Little niece, forget not that I am here with thee as a guide_', is a variation on Dürer's _Knight, Death and the Devil_, a print of which hung in the dining room at Chalcot Gardens.

Rackham was aware of the change that this implied for his work, and aware too of the effect it might have on the public's perception of him. In an interview with _The Daily News_ he said: 'The work I have just finished is different from any of my other productions, for the reason that it is of more serious interest.'[69] He spoke of the 'grimness' of much of his _Ring_ series to Z. Merton,[70] and echoed as much to Margaret Farjeon 'I am very glad you like my Ring. I quite expected to make as many enemies with it as friends.'[71] To his child audience he did what he could in damage limitation. Writing to twelve-year-old Rachel Fry he said:

I am very glad you like my illustrations. I am rather afraid that the books of mine that are coming out this year & next, which illustrate Wagner's great Music-stories, the "Ring of the Nibelungs", are not very well suited for those lucky people who haven't yet finished the delightful adventure of growing up, but soon, perhaps, you will know & be fond of Wagner's music and writings, & then you may like these drawings of mine as well as the others.[72]

One particularly sensitive and receptive child, the young C.S. Lewis, had seen one of Rackham's Siegfried illustrations, and longed for more. He proved to be the exception to Rackham's theory that his Wagner illustrations were not well suited to young people.

Above right: Knight, Death and the Devil
by Albrecht Dürer (1471–1528)
Etching

Rackham owned a proof of this etching, which hung in his dining room.

Galloping Valkyrie
Pen and ink and watercolour, 1910
73 × 86 mm
Courtesy of the Board of Trustees of the V&A

A headpiece, later coloured, from The Rinegold and the Valkyrie.

Above: Siegfried Kills Fafner
Pen and ink and watercolour, 1911
375 × 525 mm
Private Collection

Illustration to Siegfried and the
Twilight of the Gods.

**The Wooing of Grimhilde, the
Mother of Hagen**
Pen and ink and watercolour, 1911
335×205 mm
Arthur Rackham Collection, Rare
Book and Manuscript Library,
Columbia University

Illustration from Siegfried and the
Twilight of the Gods.

'Oh Wife Betrayed'
Pen and ink and
watercolour, 1911
239 × 163 mm
Arthur Rackham Collection,
Rare Book and Manuscript
Library, Columbia
University

Brunhilde and Hagen, from
Siegfried and the Twilight
of the Gods.

There, on [my cousin's] drawing room table I found the very book ... which I had never dared to hope I should see, *Siegfried and the Twilight of the Gods* illustrated by Arthur Rackham. His pictures, which seemed to me then to be the very music made visible, plunged me a few fathoms deeper into my delight. I have seldom coveted anything as I coveted that book; and when I heard there was a cheaper edition at 15 shillings ... I knew I could never rest until it was mine.[73]

C.S. Lewis's watery metaphor is particularly apt both for the Wagner books as well as for *Undine*, the story of the water nymph who loved a mortal knight. Both books show Rackham's different approaches to the treatment of water, which he depicts either as stylized metallic waves, like chased decoration on a pewter bowl, or as greeny blue reedy depths with the sun filtering through. Watery subjects, too, gave him the freedom to explore acrobatic movement in the figures, and to achieve this his studio trapeze came into its own as a tool for work rather than play, for his models to pose upon as they mimed a dive into the Rhine.

Rackham was elected to full membership of the Royal Watercolour Society in June 1908, along with

Henry Hopwood and John Singer Sargent. His Diploma work, the obligatory gift of an elected artist, was *A Bargain with the Devil*,[74] in which Rackham once again uses a jovial approach, of the kind that appeared in his earliest illustrations to popular novels, to disguise a demonic subject. He was a member of the RWS Committee from February 1909, becoming Vice President in 1910 and 1911, and was a regular and conscientious attender at meetings. He played a full part in subsequent business, and distinguished himself particularly by leading the defence of his friend Walter Bayes, who had been charged with vilifying the RWS in a published article, and had been threatened with expulsion.[75] Rackham also took it on himself to compose the wording for exhibition advertisements in tube station lifts,[76] and became involved in the hanging of RWS exhibitions. He continued to contribute his services as a lecturer and a hanger until as late as 1932.[77]

He was equally active as a member of the Art Workers' Guild, to which he was admitted in May 1909,[78] coming top of the ballot for that year. Shortly afterwards he was made an Honorary Member of the

Northern Art Workers' Guild in Manchester.[79] The London branch of the Guild held fortnightly meetings at Clifford's Inn Hall, Fleet Street, with lectures on subjects chosen by the members. Rackham's presence as a member soon became felt, as he frequently spoke in the periods of general discussion after lectures such as *The Use of Gold in Painting*,[80] *Methods of Procedure in Figure Composition*[81] and *Persian Miniatures*.[82] He himself gave papers on subjects including *National Character in Art*[83] and *The Value of Literary Motives in Painting and Sculpture*.[84]

The launch of *The Rhinegold and The Valkyrie* gave Rackham the opportunity to air his views not only on Wagner, but on wider issues such as the decline of caricature. The *Daily News* interviewer to whom he spoke about his new book, also caught his views on caricature:

Caricature is almost dead in England. For the last hundred years we have produced little worthy of the name – that of Max Beerbohm being among the few exceptions. E. T. Reed, too, is a genuine caricaturist overflowing with the milk of human kindness.[85] I do not believe there is any lack of original talent for Caricature ... but people have become more sensitive, or at least the guiding spirits of our journals seem to think they have. What English editor would give an artist the chance of developing on the lines of the best works in *Le Rire*, *L'Assiette au Beurre*, *Jugend* or *Simplicissimus*? Would he welcome the immortal Rowlandson, or would he request he tone down the point of his free and delicate fancy?[86]

This view quickly brought correspondence and editorial retort. The *Pall Mall Gazette* politely chided:

[Mr. Rackham] seems to forget that our political and social warfare is not carried out in this country with quite the same rancour and bitterness that infuse the French and German papers named.... The really disturbing point is that ... the *form* of the cartoon seems to have been lost, and its point has evaporated in its method.... Tenniel set a wonderful fashion.... There is no reason ... why English artists should slavishly tie their hands with a method of workmanship popular forty years ago....[87]

A Bargain with the Devil
Pen and ink and watercolour, 1907
350 × 280 mm
By Permission of The Trustees of the Royal Watercolour Society

Illustration to Arthur Morrison's short story 'A Seller of Hate', first published in The Graphic.

The Morning Leader accused German and French caricature as being 'simply a degradation, brutalisation, "uglification" of life',[88] although a few days later it published a letter from a Mr W. Douglas Newton, who complained that 'there is too much plaster cast about English black and white art, whereas that of our

Continental neighbours flows and ripples with the vital fluency of irresistible inspiration....'[89]

In this outspoken statement Rackham says exactly what he thinks. The French and German satirical magazines, in particular the German *Simplicissimus*, had a sharpness that the only British equivalent, *Punch*, rarely matched. *Simplicissimus*, described in *The Studio* in 1901 as 'probably the most pitiless of all the papers now appearing',[90] published drawings by Bruno Paul and Rudolf Wilke which rival in acidity the later satirical drawings of Dix and Grosz.

In his work with the RWS and the Art Workers' Guild and his membership of other arts societies[91] Rackham kept fully abreast of the art life of the capital. He read the magazines, saw the latest books, and visited the current exhibitions. He enjoyed and benefited from regular visits to the National Gallery, a favourite haunt since the days in which he lived in Buckingham Street near Trafalgar Square. He told Clara Mac Chesney that Uccello's *Rout of San Romano* was, with Piero della Francesca's *Baptism* and *Adoration*, one of his three favourite old master paintings, and added that 'Fra Lippo Lippi, yes, all the Italian School, and the Flemish. I often study Michelangelo's Entombment and all the Holbeins and Albert Dürer's wood engravings.'[92] It is rare for Rackham to make direct transcriptions from old masters, such as the one in *Undine*, from Dürer. Instead he makes 'quotations', for example the head of Cesarino in *The Allies Fairy Book* (1916), which Rackham has adapted from the head of the young horseman in Uccello's *Rout of San Romano*. There is a passing reference to Rubens, too, in Rackham's illustration to the Belgian story, 'Last Adventures of Thyl Ulenspiegel' in *The Allies Fairy Book*, but usually Rackham takes the spirit and sense of design from a school or manner of the past, such as the Japanese in *Peter Pan in Kensington Gardens*, or the Dutch in *Rip Van Winkle*, and carefully amends it.

Rackham took his time, and would not release anything he was not fully happy with. He put a disproportionate amount of time even into such small commissions as a book-plate for Z. Merton (see Chapter Seven): '... my failure to send you the bookplate you asked for, so long ago, has not been for want of trying. Still in spite of my efforts I have not been able to do anything that I could pass.'[93] As he wrote to Lewis Melville, 'I'm a very slow and painful worker.'[94]

... Five Books All At Once ...
Pen and ink, ?c1912 or early 1920s
100 × 129 mm
Private Collection

Rackham was at his busiest in the years just before and just after the First World War – as he himself expresses here.

Øm Rackham

CHAPTER FIVE

EVERYONE IN THE WORLD IS SUFFERING 1914–1919

AGAINST THE BACKGROUND OF THE BEGIN-
ning of the First World War, Edyth Rackham
took part in a correspondence that was soon
to put an almost intolerable strain on her emotions, and contributed to the rapid decline in
her health.

Edyth's brother Rex, the officer in the
German Army, had died of tuberculosis in
the 1890s. Edyth had kept in touch with his young
widow, Alle Starkie, and her sister Dr Lili Müzinger,
maintaining a regular and friendly correspondence
with them both, and having Lili to stay when she was
in England before the war. The friendship with Lili,
however, was shattered for the duration of the war by
a misunderstanding caused by the effect on Edyth of
the anti-German propaganda in the British press.

Lili, staying with friends in the Apulian town of
Lecce, had been interned with an Italian family on a
suspicion emanating out of England that she was a spy
and she wrote to Edyth:

Fancy, England has denunciated me to the Italian government
as a spy dressed as a woman and giving all sort of detail about
my person who has been suspicious before during a stay in
England! It is an absurd and ridiculous pretence – yet most
embarrassing in its consequences.... So I am trying all means
to get rid of that monstrous accusation and as most ways are
impracticable I thought perhaps you or Mr. Rackham might
do something in the matter?[1]

Most of Edyth's half of the correspondence does not
survive, but there is enough in what Lili and, later,
Alle wrote to suggest that Edyth had developed a
hatred of Germany,[2] preventing her from being fully
unequivocal in her reply. The violent anti-German

Left: Instantly they lay still, all turned into stone
Pen and ink and watercolour, 1917
299 × 233 mm
Spencer Collection, New York Public Library, Astor, Lenox and
Tilden Foundations

*Illustration to 'The Two Brothers', in Little Brother and Little Sister,
by the Brothers Grimm.*

propaganda which filled the British press masked the fact that only ten or fifteen years before the idea of a war with Germany was, for many, unthinkable. Edyth herself had spent part of her girlhood in Potsdam and Cassel enjoying romantic attachments to young German army officers, to the extent, if her stories to Walter Starkie and her daughter are to be believed, of having duels fought over her. Before the First World War, friendships, marriages, travel and holidays linked Germany with Britain and Ireland, and many of the tragedies of the war stemmed from the shattering of happy bonds made in peace.

The reported destruction of six of Arthur's illustrations and a group of his books when an exhibition of English Illustration at Leipzig Museum was partially destroyed by a fire thought to have been caused deliberately, enforced Edyth's resentment, and Lili expressed a naturally deep dismay that people might take her for a spy:

Just as much as my personal fate oppresses me what you say about Arthur's and your friend's experiences. In Leipzig no doubt his pictures and books were in the part that was destroyed by fire but not burned with intention. The press of each country brings such accidents in a way to arouse scorn and hatred. The sins of journalism will make overflow hell....[3]

Blackberry Gatherers,
Pen and ink and watercolour, 1914
325 × 490 mm
Private Collection

This ominous watercolour, painted at Thurlestone in Devon where the Rackhams were on holiday in the late summer of 1914, was exhibited at the RWS, the following winter. Above a peaceful landscape, a flock of black birds presage war.

Lili was allowed to leave Italy a fortnight later for Switzerland, and wrote again to Edyth from Lugano:

I shall inquire most intensely what happened to the pictures and books of your husband. You can trust me in L.[eipzig] they did not do such a thing as making auto-da-fés of the works of art coming from inimical countries. Your last letter spoke of violated Belgian nuns. Shortly after the Pope declared that he had inquired in the Belgian convents and no such violations occurred. So *were* they nuns the women you saw and were they violated at all?... But what use discussing? Political discussions are presently like religious ones you don't come to an agreement because likewise truth is hidden from you.[4]

Edyth Rackham
Photographed in 1917
Private Collection

Writing from Berlin, via Winterthur, Lili was later able to tell Edyth that 'all the exhibitions of our enemies are *absolutely* safe *nothing* not the slightest thing destroyed or damaged.... So no doubt after the war your husband will have back all his treasures.'[5]

The following month, however, Lili had heard again from Edyth, and replied, again raising the spying accusation via Winterthur: 'I have the feeling that you dare not do anything in my favour because you yourself are not convinced of my *not* being the spy. But that is an awkward and painful revelation.'[6] Shortly after this exchange Edyth suffered a heart attack and was seriously ill for three years. Undoubtedly the tragic misunderstanding with Lili affected her, and caused a deep anguish which helped to weaken her already frail physique.

While helping to nurse Edyth through her serious illness and assuage her understandable anxiety over the spy row, Arthur worked on, both for commercial and war charity publications. In 1914 and 1915 he contributed illustrations to three collections of stories and pictures to be sold to raise money for war charities, *King Albert's Book* (1914), *Princess Mary's Gift Book* (1914) and *The Queen's Gift Book* (1915), and gave six works to the RWS Red Cross Fund collection that Christie's auctioned in 1915.

Rackham's gross income had fallen from the peak of 1910 (£3,979 gross) to £1,178 in 1915. He had published no full-length book in 1914, and, owing no doubt to the uncertainties of publishing as the war began, Heinemann's planned edition of *Comus* was held over from 1915 to 1921.[7] The sales of Rackham's books in the first three months of publication were falling short of the figures that he and his publishers had enjoyed with *Peter Pan* and *Alice*, and, reacting to this, Heinemann became watchful over the print runs of the trade first editions.[8] The slide from the *Alice* peak of 14,322 trade copies sold in Britain in the first three months began with *A Midsummer Night's Dream* at 7,650, and continued at Christmas 1909 with *Undine* (6,325), and at the subsequent Christmases with *Rhinegold* (5,874) and *Siegfried* (4,272).

In an effort to push the sales figures back up, and re-emphasize him as the artist for the popular and 'nursery' market, Heinemann encouraged Rackham away from the Germanic heavyweights by commissioning *Aesop's Fables* in 1912 and *Mother Goose* in 1913. The latter was a collection of traditional nursery rhymes selected and introduced by Rackham, and personalized throughout by means of his self-portrait appearing in decorated initials such as the letter I, in illustrations such as '*As I was going to St. Ives ...*', and in

Above: Scrooge dreams: the father comes home with a porter laden with Christmas toys and presents
Pen and ink and watercolour, 1915
202 × 164 mm
Spencer Collection, New York
Public Library, Astor, Lenox and
Tilden Foundations

Illustration to A Christmas Carol *by Charles Dickens.*

Left: Scrooge dreams: the father comes home . . .
[Abandoned version]
Pencil, pen and ink and
watercolour, 1915
273 × 191 mm
Private Collection

the use of 16 Chalcot Gardens as the model for *The House that Jack Built*. It cannot be a coincidence that in the same year another 'personality' book, *Arthur Rackham's Book of Pictures*, was published, a collection of 54 plates of past work in six sections with titles including 'Of the Little People', 'Some Fairy Tales', 'Some Children' and 'Grotesque and Fantastic'. Whether he liked it or not, Rackham's reputation as a benign and otherworldly gnome-figure, and as the creator of such subjects, was being emphasised again to market him and his personality. This had the effect of putting him firmly back in the Nursery, where his public had first discovered him, and his publishers were able to sell

comfortable quantities of his books. The tactic worked, for in the first three months of publication 6,129 trade copies of *Aesop's Fables* had sold in Britain, and 6,039 of *Mother Goose*.

In place of *Comus*, Heinemann commissioned the more obvious, popular and consumable story, *A Christmas Carol*, to be the Rackham book for Christmas 1915. This was the first Dickens story Rackham had attempted, and despite its ghostliness, and the opportunities for the supernatural that the story presents for its illustrator, Rackham did not exploit these to the full. Although '*The air was filled with phantoms*' or '*Nobody under the bed . . .*' have the doom-laden,

The Sleeping Princess
Pen and ink and watercolour, 1916
251 × 175 mm
The Sutton Place
Foundation/Christie's

Illustration to Perrault's story 'The Sleeping Beauty: A French Tale' in The Allies' Fairy Book. *The illustration demonstrates Rackham's love of combining romance and gorgeous stuffs and settings with a whimsical and throw-away humour, as seen in the supporters to the coat-of-arms at the bed head.*

prescient atmosphere of the best of the *Poe's Tales* images, other illustrations, though charming in a Kate Greenaway manner, do not give him the cutting edge he required to bring his imagination into full play. It is as if, in his choice of subjects, he voluntarily passed by the opportunity to terrify his readers with too many ghosts and images of retribution, and chose instead to calm them with pictures of sliding on the ice in smoky London, dancing with Mrs Fezziwig and children bouncing about on Christmas Eve. Perhaps caught by the mood of national anxiety and tragedy of wartime, Rackham voluntarily softened his interpretation of Dickens's story in a way he might not have done eight

or ten years earlier – or indeed twenty years later with Poe's *Tales*.

His book for 1916, *The Allies' Fairy Book*, published by Heinemann as a contribution to the mood of patri-otism and co-operation between the Allies, is likewise composed of images that thrill and inspire, but do not terrify. Where in *Grimm* Rackham happily includes illustrations of people battering each other to death or hanging by the hair and caught in brambles alive or half dead, this kind of image is not dwelt upon in *The Allies' Fairy Book*. Nor is it, indeed, in his wartime collection of Grimm Stories *Little Brother and Little Sister* (1917), even though some of the stories are as

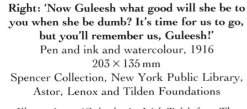

red in tooth and claw as any of their type, and certainly would have allowed a violent interpretation. Reports coming back from the Front, eye-witness accounts of devastation, violation and butchery, were quite enough to suggest to Rackham and his publishers that at this time the Allies could be spared violent images with their family reading at home.

Little Brother and Little Sister is characterized by illustrations of maidens in gorgeous jewelled costume, wide-eyed staring girls in the manner of Frederick Cayley Robinson or vaudeville medieval footsoldiers fretting over a companion whose nose has suddenly grown miles long. Perhaps the most enchanting of all is *'Suddenly the branches twined around her...'*, an illustration to 'The Old Woman in the Wood'. This story, a reversal of the Apollo and Daphne legend, tells of a

Prince, turned into a tree by a witch, who is helped to regain his human form by a beautiful servant girl. The spirit of the book is one of charm and humour, as contrasted with the 1900 edition of *Grimm*, which not only featured violence and imminent terrors, but also set its scenes against some of the German townscapes and landscapes that Rackham had sketched during his pre-war holidays, and which were now inappropriate.

The Romance of King Arthur (1917) was another wartime book, commissioned, like *The Allies' Fairy Book*, to reflect – and cash in upon – the nation's mood of patriotism and martial endeavour. In preparing for the commission, Rackham turned to his own copy of the Beardsley *Morte Darthur* and, following the pattern of the Beardsley version, drew square and rectangular

chapter headings to be set at irregular intervals up and down the pages. As in Beardsley, these have a stark black and white wood-block appearance, though Rackham cannot resist the occasional wryly humorous touch such as a barking dog or a jester's head. The closest Rackham comes to Beardsley, however, is in his illustration of *Sangreal*, a flaming lidded chalice carried by an attenuated golden-haired white-robed maiden. This homage to Aubrey is based closely on Beardsley's own angel in *The Achieving of the Sangreal*, the frontispiece to Volume Two of *Morte Darthur*.

Rackham's work became balm for wounded soldiers, as one mother wrote: 'I am urged to write to you by my son who is wildly fond of your work: and when he was getting better from very bad wounds received near Ypres, your illustrations of Books were his great joy and delight.'[9] A French soldier, Jean Maria Carré, who had published an article on Rackham in 1912, wrote to ask him if he would generously replace his copy of *The Ring of the Nibelung*.

The house has been completely plundered, my books scattered away.... I have been living three years on the front and partaking of all battles, Belgium, Marne, Champagne, Verdun, Somme and Aisne. We have lost everything.... As the Huns have ransacked my library, I would like to secure at least, for my sister, another copy of your Ring of the Nibelung.[10]

At home, Rackham's life moved on, apparently unaffected by the war. Walter Starkie, who stayed with the couple again in 1918, wrote later that his uncle 'had changed little since I had seen him fourteen years before, except that he was more bald and elf-like, with his pale wizened face.... I looked upon him as the only truly happy man I had yet come across because he was absorbed in his work to the exclusion of everything else, and even the grim war news and the air raids left him untroubled. In addition to his detachment he possessed an innate stoicism which made him

Suddenly the branches twined round her and turned into two arms
Pen and ink and watercolour, 1917
366 × 268 mm
Arthur Rackham Memorial Collection, University of Louisville

Illustration to 'The Old Woman in the Wood' from Little Brother and Little Sister, *by the Brothers Grimm.*

Above: The Achieving of the Sangreal
by Aubrey Beardsley.

Frontispiece to Volume II of Morte Darthur *by Thomas Malory, published by J. M. Dent in 1894.*

Left: Sangreal
Pen and ink and watercolour, 1917
Windsor Castle, Royal Library, Her
Majesty Queen Elizabeth II

Illustration to the Macmillan edition of The Romance of King Arthur *by Thomas Malory. The original was bought by HM Queen Mary in 1927.*

endure austerity without complaining.'[11] Edyth, however, her nephew noted, 'showed more clearly the ravages of the years, was completely white-haired and suffered from heart disease. The air raids and the difficulties of catering in London had affected her nerves.... In spite of her ailments and the stress of war she was gay and ironic as I always remembered'.

To ease Edyth's anxieties when the air raids began, Arthur first sent her to lodgings at 134 Victoria Terrace, Littlehampton,[12] where he and Barbara joined her at weekends and school holidays. Subsequently Edyth stayed during term-time at Green Bushes, the house built in nearby Rustington by the Sutherlands as a holiday home for their family[13] – one of whom,

their fourteen-year-old son Graham, later became the highly distinguished painter.

With Edyth safely at Rustington, and Barbara away at school near Petersfield, at Bedales, Arthur was able to give cool descriptions of the air raids he had witnessed in letters to his wife:

We had rough visits from the Germans on Sat. & Sun. Several instalments. But all over before midnight both nights and no damage immediately near. Though I hear that there are 3 or 4 bomb craters on Parliament Hill (last night): and a public house in the Seven Sisters Road Holloway was badly smashed on Saturday.

But last night we appear to have brought one (some say three) down. Great cheering burst out – but the firing was so intense & near that I didn't care to look out until, when in a few minutes the firing died down, there was nothing to be seen.

I went to Wandsworth yesterday. And right through town from here the road is full of groups of kneeling children with all manner of tools gouging & digging out the shrapnel from the wood pavement. Our guns keep going like hell....

It is odd, about dinner time, I have the horrid foreboding uncomfy feeling that makes me want to cut & run out of it. But when it is once bang banging away, I seem to get used to it & indifferent. And mildly curious. And I am quite unaffected after my night's rest.... I will promise you this – I will not be in any exposed place when once the guns have begun to mutter in the distance. The widespread shrapnel is enough to cure one of that desire.[14]

Interspersed in these letters are short paragraphs of information for 'Dearest Edy' about his plans for getting himself, Barbara, Ellen and the French governess Mlle Bellettu down to Littlehampton, and exhortations to his wife not to worry or be anxious if they are delayed as a result of the air raids.

Arthur continued with his social round in London with a detachment developed both through his own inaction and also paradoxically through his actions. In his correspondence as in his private pronouncements he would put himself and his opinions out on a limb, setting himself apart from and sometimes even shocking his friends by his bizarre, anachronistic and often confusing opinions. He wrote to Herbert Farjeon in 1917:

I confess to being very prejudiced about all the modern educational theories I hear about – yes, I think all, but particularly those like Dalcroze &, above all, Montessori, that have got the ear of the newspaper press.

Arthur and Barbara Rackham, c1917
Photograph
Private Collection

They all seem to me to be too taxing of the juvenile intellect, which has been forced far too much in the recent past, & any educational scheme to rouse my enthusiasm would be one that developed the physical & kept back the mental growths. In fact the one thing about Barbara's school that pleased me was to come across its reputation as 'the school where they learnt nothing'.

To learn nothing, to acquire perfect bodily health & physical development, & to have free social intercourse is my ideal education. Indeed except that it usually accompanies insufficient food & supervision, the gutter *must* be the best school. I marvel that any man or woman can achieve any success at all in competition with those of gutter education. But there you are – the world is full of such anomalies.[15]

Rackham's apartness, his neat, bird-like quality did, however, endear itself, as a kind of mascot, to the roistering element of the bohemian London art world. Walter Starkie describes evenings he spent with his uncle in 1918:

[My uncle's] kindliness and broad-mindedness made him very popular among other artists, and I used to look forward to our meetings with Augustus John, who was in those days the most colourful personality in London.... He and my uncle were great friends, but when the former was in his cups it was very funny to see the two of them together. My uncle never lost his timid elf-like expression, even in the most dishevelled Bohemian orgy, and he would cock his head on the side, and peer at the milling revellers of both sexes through his spectacles with such a quaint and puzzled face that Augustus John would give a Homeric roar of laughter, pointing him out to the company, saying: 'Don't shock little Arthur too much, ladies and gentlemen: he is learning about life from you and he must not advance too quickly.' Arthur Rackham never minded his friend's playful bantering, but every now and then he would give a dry chuckle, and then relapse into his puzzled watchfulness. I knew that at the end of the orgy he would play the Good Samaritan and see Augustus John home.[16]

At home at Chalcot Gardens, and in Sussex when air raids threatened, Edyth was gradually recovering from her heart disease, trying new cures of all kinds – patent, herbal, homeopathic, orthodox and quack. She had attempted more than once to make contact with Lili and Alle, by writing to them at the hotel they used to frequent in Locarno. One letter, to Alle, reached home, and prompted Lili to write: 'I want to profit from my stay here to tell you how truly sorry I was to hear from Alle that you have been so badly ill and are still suffering. I do hope you will be able to overcome every shadow of it.'[17] Lili was herself still suffering from the spy misunderstanding, and again pressed Edyth to help her clear the matter up. She ended, however, on a welcome note of understanding and rapprochement:

You know that if you are suffering from a weak heart Locarno is the best place with its Radium containing soil and water. Besides it is lovely in the sunshine which however is scarcer this year than ever before. Just give it a serious thought! Angelica powder is excellent according to Kneipp. You know Kneipp? With fond love, Your Lili.

This hopeful rebuilding of their friendship helped to strengthen Edyth, and at the end of the war she heard from Lili again.[18] Edyth's moving reply, however, at last bearing the explanation for the misunderstanding of four years earlier, failed to reach Lili, and was returned by the Post Office. Even now Edyth was unable to unburden herself and give her side of the story, though the letter's return does enable us to see below the surface of Edyth's suffering and even share it:

I am so sorry to find you are still worried about that false accusation which was made against you, & which re-acted on your friend .... so inconveniently. I cannot get at the person who made it as I do not know who it was, and the person whom you call my 'friend', but who is no friend of mine, would certainly do nothing.... As you know there must have been hundreds of persons wrongfully accused during the war, and the only thing to do is to accept it as one of the hardships of the times, of which there were no end. Innumerable wrongs have had to be borne, for goodness sake let us forget them....[19]

Edyth eventually made contact with Lili and Alle, but not before another letter, this time to Alle, was returned:

I despaired of ever finding Lili or you again.... We are all very well, at least if not very well I am stronger and able to work a little.... It seems to me that everyone in the world is suffering, more or less, & I am anxious on your account, & long that you should not suffer anything.

Your loving sister, Edyth Rackham.[20]

CHAPTER SIX

THE AMERICANS HAVE DONE GREAT THINGS FOR ME 1919–1927

R ACKHAM EMERGED AT THE OTHER END OF the war as a celebrated and respected artist. He was elected Master of the Art Workers' Guild for 1919, a position of authority with the mandate to speak publicly on matters affecting his profession. Early in his term, indeed, he was able to announce an increase in the annual funding for the Gilchrist Trust Scholarship from £100 to £150,[1] and to open discussions on the establishment of an Advisory Committee on War Memorials and a War Memorial Society.[2] He addressed the Guild at intervals during his year of office on *The Art of the '90s*,[3] *Silhouettes*[4] and *Fairy Tale Illustration*,[5] and was also a prominent contributor, as ever, to discussions following the lectures.[6]

His position in the public eye as the master of fairy tale illustration, too, was unassailable. During the course of the war he had been making a collection of Fairy Poems for publication with his illustrations, a book which might have been launched as a personalized collection along the lines of *Arthur Rackham's Book of Pictures*, but in the event was never published. He had been having discussions about it with a publisher, when he was approached by an unidentified writer asking to collaborate with him on a similar venture. Rackham's reply is characteristic of the modest way he bore his talents, but there is also a distinct hint that the friendly gesture with the velvet glove concealed an iron fist:

Curiously, I too have made a collection of Fairy Poems, not yet complete, with the same idea – & I have already talked it over with a publisher & we are only waiting an opportunity to carry it out. I am thus not altogether free in the matter.... For my part, I should be very pleased indeed to have the advantage

Left: Landscape at Houghton
Oil on canvas, c1925
Private Collection

Commissioned for Rackham by his friend and neighbour Sir Henry Royce

Cinderella and the Fairy Godmother
Pencil and watercolour, 1919
321 × 462 mm
Arthur Rackham Collection, Rare book and
Manuscript Library, Columbia University

Preliminary study for Cinderella.

of your kind offer & combine the results of our research....
More than this I can hardly say, for if we are to be rivals we
must henceforth conceal all we can from each other. But, as
you so kindly anticipate, it is a subject quite after my own
heart.[7]

Rackham gave his talk on Silhouettes to the Art
Workers' Guild in November 1919, the month in
which *Cinderella*, the first of his two great silhouette
books, was published. *Cinderella* and *The Sleeping
Beauty* differed from Rackham's preceding books in
relying almost wholly for their effect on silhouette. It
is immediately clear that Rackham is a master of the
medium, being able to evoke character and humour by
profile and gesture alone, and allowing the two-
dimensional effect of his pen work to lead the reader
through the book and keep the story going. Silhouette
books, even with additional colours had lower production costs than their colour plate equivalents, and
so were an attractive option both for publishers and
customers in the uncertain post-war market.

The Prince Presents the Glass Slipper
Pen and ink and body colour, 1919
270 × 418 mm
Spencer Collection, New York Public Library, Astor,
Lennox and Tilden foundations

*Rackham's skill at expressing character through gesture and
profile is evident here.*

By the time the war had ended, Arthur and Edyth had already taken the decision to leave London to live permanently in Sussex. Their last surviving parent, Arthur's mother who was by now in her late 80s, was living out her final years with her youngest daughter, Winifred, in Wandsworth. Arthur wrote to Herbert Farjeon in October 1918.[8] 'We keep pecking at houses in Amberley or near. I wonder whether we shall ever live there....' By early 1920 they had found Houghton House, at Houghton, a village between Arundel and Amberley, with the help of Alfred Mart,[9] who lived in a neighbouring cottage. Houghton House, into which they moved in May 1920[10] on a twenty-year lease from the Norfolk Estates, was 'a beautiful, dignified, warm flint Georgian farmhouse facing on to the village street', as Barbara Edwards later described it. It

**Cinderella and the Fairy
Godmother**
Pencil, pen and ink, 1919
277 × 195 mm
Private Collection

Right: Arthur and Barbara Rackham
c1925 at Houghton House

Below: Sussex Cottages Seen From My Garden
Watercolour, 1926
253 × 364 mm
Arthur Rackham Collection,
Rare Book and Manuscript
Library, Columbia University

The view to the left of Rackham's garden at Houghton House, Eleanor Farjeon lived in the cottage on the right.

had a mature garden, with large elms and beeches, outbuildings, fields sloping down to the river, and a sublime view of the Arun Valley with the Amberley Chalk Pits and Rackham Hill[11] beyond. When P. G. Konody saw the garden in 1926, he described it as 'not an extensive domain, but so cunningly laid out with its different levels, flagged paths, clipped yew hedges, espalier trees, stone steps, flower beds, orchard and lawns and rustic bowers, that it is inexhaustible in variety and creates an impression of quite formidable extent.'[12]

The landscape provided Rackham with subject-matter not only for watercolours but for illustrations too. The 'green sour ringlets', for example, in Act V of *The Tempest* (1926) are being trodden in a meadow below Houghton House,[13] with the Amberley Chalk Pits in the background. Rackham drew his garden trees, too – one such, an apple tree featured in *A Dish of Apples* (1921), stood outside his studio barn, and collapsed very soon after being drawn, having been pushed over by a grazing cow.[14]

The house and its garden was everything that Arthur and Edyth desired: the part of Britain they both particularly loved, the ideal place for the relaxed, expansive, sociable country living that they enjoyed and could now afford, and a quieter atmosphere for Edyth in which she could gradually regain her health.

Their neighbours, as Barbara described them, were 'a congenial mix of farmers, artists and retired colonels', a modest description for a group which included Bernard Weiss, the son of José Weiss, the painter and early pioneer of gliders, the sculptor Francis Derwent Wood and his wife Florence, the motor engineer Sir Henry Royce and his companion Miss Aubin, the zoologist Sir Harry Johnson and his wife, and others. It was, in fact, much the same kind of mix that the Rackhams had attracted around themselves in Hampstead, and included some of the same people, notably Eleanor Farjeon who since 1917 had lived at The End Cottage, Mucky Lane.[15]

Their pleasures were simple, and took full advantage of their surroundings. Although in winter entertainment was limited to good long walks, bridge and ping-pong, it opened out in the summer to embrace fishing, golf, tennis parties on their own and others' 'slow, erratic grass courts', boating parties along the wide reaches of the River Arun and fancy dress dances in gardens bedecked with fairy lights and Chinese lanterns. 'Our house,' Barbara wrote, 'which was primitive in the extreme by modern standards, with a well in the wash-house, candles to see by, and rats scurrying up and down the hollow walls at night, was nevertheless a lovely and gracious environment for entertaining, and on summer weekends, when my mother was well enough, it was often filled with artist friends from the old days in London.'

Top: The River Arun, Sussex
Watercolour, 1926
252 × 358 mm
Arthur Rackham Collection, Rare Book and Manuscript Library,
Columbia University

The view from the bottom of Rackham's garden.

Bottom: The South Downs at Amberley
Watercolour, 1926
Courtesy of the Board of Trustees of the V&A

A view from Houghton House, inscribed verso 'Storm clouds over the Arun Valley.'

Under the Beech Tree, Arundel Park
Watercolour, 1928
240 × 340 mm
Private Collection

The elfin figures seem to have slipped quietly into Rackham's consciousness as he was painting this tree study.

To the right of the house, Rackham kept his studio in a converted medieval thatched barn with an earth floor – from which his handyman had scraped up a gold angel, a coin of *c.*1380.[16] On the wall beside his desk he tested his brushes and nibs, covering a large area with abstract patterns and splashes of paint on the plaster. 'We should sell that one day. It'll be worth a lot of money!' he used to tell Barbara.[17] The barn was Rackham's country studio, where he worked at weekends, having retained a foothold in London by renting, from November 1920,[18] number 6 Primrose Hill Studios, across the courtyard from number 3, the Rackhams' first home after their marriage.

Edyth did not, however, let her weak health defeat her completely, and when she was well threw herself like a whirlwind into domestic activity, to Arthur's despair. He wrote to Eleanor Farjeon:

Barbara is going to a new school & (of course) Edyth must herself make all her clothes, & do all & everything of every kind instead of trusting something to others. But that's her way. I can't change her. And B's Christmas parties & so on – Edyth takes all the work on herself & is half dead. She's resting this minute – for 3 minutes perhaps. I'm sure no more.[19]

For one year at least during their married life, Edyth kept a diary[20] and wrote in it almost every day. The diary begins with a full entry on 1 January 1923, and carries on with only a few blank days until 31 December, implying by its thoroughness that this was not an isolated year, but that there were other diaries, now lost.

Edyth ran Houghton House with the help of the Rackhams' handyman and his wife, Mr and Mrs Sellen (known as Ellen and Sellen), the maid, Alice, and perhaps another maid whose name the diary does not mention. We hear of a New Year's Day ping-pong

game, of getting Barbara's clothes ready – from Edyth's point of view – for her first term at her new school, Queen Anne's, Caversham; of the weather; of bridge parties; of people popping in and out; and of drives around Sussex in the Rackhams' hired car. Nothing of the outside world intrudes apart from a mention of the result of the General Election in December, and of the Japanese earthquake which only draws the comment that their friend Herbert Hughes-Stanton RA survived, when 143,000 people died.

The diary is, however, full of small-scale dramas, describing how they ran over Tojo, the Parishes' dog, in their car, and the subsequent ripples it caused; of Alfred Mart knocking a nail through a water pipe and ruining the kitchen ceiling; of Alice the maid making a fuss about wearing purple; and of Arthur pinching his right hand in a gate. Edyth, too, brings the subtle observation of her painter's eye to bear on some of the characters she meets: 'Friday 9th November: Came home alone [from London] by last train, in smoking carriage. It was full of different class people who argued & nearly fought. Rich lady was one. Three Freemasons, working woman, nice man, nasty man & merchant serviceman & wife. Great fun.' Goodness knows how Edyth could tell that three were Freemasons: perhaps she shook their hands, or just looked them in the eye.

Other entries convey the delight of seeing washing flapping on a 'glorious wild sunny day' in January, of the crocuses in bloom and of drives by the sea. Edyth includes her views on the wireless: 'Went on to Miss Long.... Had a Listening in thing on my ears. Most awful sounds but heard some talking & some music. Shall never want one.' Tensions, of a matrimonial kind, are obliquely noted too: 'Monday 26th February: Arthur went to meet Mrs. Tomlinson at Arundel at 12 O'c. We had a talk which prevented his shaving in time.

Sabrina Rises
Pen and ink and watercolour, 1921
261 × 193 mm
Spencer Collection, New York Public Library, Astor, Lenox and
Tilden Foundations

*Rackham reworked the faces of Sabrina and her leading attendant after
this illustration had been published in* Comus *by John Milton.*

On a roar of merriment until bedtime
Pen and ink and watercolour, 1922
217 × 160 mm
Rare Book Department, Free Library of Philadelphia

Rackham uses shadow here for decorative effect and as a means to convey a theatrical excitement, rather than fear. Illustration to A Wonder Book *by Nathaniel Hawthorne.*

Rather serious I'm afraid. She left by 3.20 train & we tried to have a walk, fearfully windy & wet. Another talk this evening. Feel very strained & tired, but all is well & a momentous day for us, ending very happily.'

Another source of tension was Edyth's intense disappointment and hurt, having spent nearly four weeks overseeing the spring-cleaning of the house, at Arthur's attitude on his return from a working holiday in Italy: 'Sunday 3rd June: Very unhappy house for everyone as Arthur does nothing but undo our work. Lovely weather.'

The diary shows that as late as 1923, when Edyth was still suffering from heart attacks and was frequently sick, she was painting regularly from Joyce, her model, and undertaking new experiments and making discoveries. Tantalizingly, it is not clear what these discoveries are. Like her husband, Edyth was at great pains to have the right sort of glasses for painting, and despaired of the interruptions that pressures of domestic life, of running the house and organizing servants brought: 'Tuesday April 24th: Must try to get some of the sewing off my shoulders or I'll never paint or keep well.'

Edyth's warmth and her courage in the face of her illness are equally revealed by her diary. We can almost hear her flattering and charming tones when

talking to the landlord of Primrose Hill Studios and trying to get her own way in her proposed studio alterations: 'Thursday 8th November: Measured up new sitting room & put screens round. Mr. Healy came at 4 O'c. He is charming & I converted him to my views. He is going to take about a week to consider.'

Edyth's deep affection for Arthur emerges at almost every entry, in a diary which is a gem of understatement, and a unique collection of glances at a special life in Sussex in 1923: 'Sunday 2nd December: Nice day & milder & A & I had long talk on interesting subjects. Went for walk in garden with A & the cats & saw rainbow, all very beautiful.'

It was Arthur's practice to live and work at his Primrose Hill studio in London during the middle of the week, and travel down to Amberley by train on Thursdays or Fridays, returning on Mondays or Tuesdays. In London he involved himself in the daily business of his societies, particularly the RWS and the Art Workers' Guild, though in June 1922 he failed to be elected an Associate of the Royal Academy in the Engraving Section. His application was used by its proposer, Sir Herbert Hughes-Stanton, as a stalking-horse for the ultimate admission of draughtsmen to the RA: 'I am very sorry you did not get elected last

Arthur Rackham signature

Arthur Rackham
by Meredith Frampton RA
(1894–1984)
Oil on canvas, c1920s

*The portrait was destroyed when
Frampton's studio was bombed in 1940.
'I didn't like his portrait of me at all,'
Rackham wrote in 1927 to Kerrison
Preston, 'though I think most highly of
much, of most, of his portraits.'*

evening,' Hughes-Stanton wrote to Rackham. 'You were well supported [11 votes to 26] & ran against Macbeth-Raeburn in the final Ballot. I am very glad I put you down as it has I think settled the eligibility of draughtsmen for the Engraving Section. The matter is to be taken up now.... I hope within the year we may see you in.'[21]

But Rackham was never, in the event, elected to the Royal Academy. Through the great success of his books, however, he had established the same kind of household and way of life as enjoyed by senior Academicians and those who collected his de luxe editions. By 1923 he had a settled fame, and was being referred to by correspondents as 'Sir Arthur' or 'Venerated Master'. 'I am sorry I addressed my letter to you the way I did,' an American correspondent wrote in 1929. 'Everybody here in New York calls you "Sir Arthur".'[22] Edyth saw as her main duty the management of this kind of household for Arthur and their friends, and subordinated her work as a painter to their needs as a family. Her concern extended to the well-being of their friends, too. Edyth

Little Miss Muffet
Pen and ink and watercolour, 1922
38 × 25 mm
Windsor Castle, Royal Library, Her
Majesty Queen Elizabeth II

*One of the collection of miniature works
by eminent artists commissioned in 1922
for Queen Mary's Doll's House at
Windsor Castle.*

Arthur Rackham.
R.W.S.

went to the trouble of having the Houghton House Music Room painted a deep blue so that the near-blind Harry Farjeon, youngest brother of Eleanor, could feel comfortable there when he played the piano.

During the years following the war, Rackham's market in the United States began to take on a life of its own. All his important books, from *Rip Van Winkle* onwards, had enjoyed good sales in America, most of them being published separately by American companies such as Doubleday Page, Dutton or the Century Co. He was less than keen, however, on some of the printing standards, being unable at such a distance to influence them effectively:

I might say that when there are editions in both countries, the English *maybe* better done than the US. At least I fear so. Even our binding is often better – the plates are *usually* the same (printed over here, I think) but on at least one occasion (Irish Fairy Tales) the American edition is printed from electros, & is markedly inferior.[23]

Whereas in 1917 Rackham's US earnings were only 2% of his total gross income for that year, in 1920 they reached 44% of his total of £7,177. This was principally because he had been given a highly successful exhibition of his work at Scott and Fowles Gallery on 5th Avenue in New York in 1919, from which alone he earned sales receipts of £2,865 in 1920. To put them into perspective, Rackham's earnings in 1920 should be multiplied by a factor of 30 or 35 to show their relative values in 1990. Rackham was thus earning the equivalent of around a quarter of a million pounds in 1920, and so was a rich man.

This high proportion of American earning continued throughout the first half of the 1920s, going up to 83% in 1923. Having been a favourite source of charm and escapism for the British during the pre-war and wartime years, Rackham's enchantment had now taken root in America, to the artist's intense relief and pleasure: '…of late years,' he wrote to A. E. Bonser, 'the Americans have done great things for me in buying my pictures – indeed I have mainly lived on them.'[24] It was his major rise in income in 1920 that enabled Rackham to move to Houghton, and the continuation of an American income that enabled the family to stay there.

Although by 1919 he had published three books solely for the American market,[25] Rackham's largest single commission for the US was not for a book but for a series of soap advertisements for the Colgate Co. Colgate commissioned thirty drawings on the theme of the Early English Aristocracy to advertise Cashmere Bouquet Soap, which they billed as 'The Aristocrat of Toilet Soaps'. Spread over the years 1922–25, this commission not only earned him $24,000, but also affected the particular tone of his reputation in America. From being the 'Goblin Master', Rackham was now being seen by the new audience of popular newspaper and magazine readers as the creator of Hollywood style, Jane Austenesque, crinolined fantasies.[26]

During the Colgate advertising campaign, the original drawings were exhibited in art galleries throughout America, including the Metropolitan Museum of Art in New York. The price Rackham paid, however, for spending an extended length of time on the Colgate project – for all its financial and publicity benefits – was that he was diverted from

print. Rackham rose to the occasion, and his nephew's haunting of him was justified. *The Dublin Independent* was particularly warm in welcoming the collection, remarking: 'We read English tales with appreciation because pictures have familiarised us with English imagery. A Fenian tale lacks imagery because we have

book illustration, having to turn down Eleanor Farjeon's request to him to illustrate one of her Sussex stories, possibly *Martin Pippin in the Apple Orchard*: 'The book is quite delightful,' he wrote to her in 1923. 'I had not seen it before, though I saw it well reviewed & hoped that it was doing well. I am very sorry but my engagements will not let me illustrate it. You've got a lot of Sussex into it.'[27]

Rackham's books for the English market in the early post-war years included Flora Annie Steel's *English Fairy Tales Retold* (1918), with its 57 illustrations, for which Macmillan paid an advance – the largest he had yet received – of £1,000, and his friend James Stephens's collection of *Irish Fairy Tales*, also published by Macmillan, for which he produced 37 illustrations in 1920 and received the same advance.

In the latter book, Rackham broke new ground in the illustration of Irish literature. He had been persuaded to tackle Stephens's stories by Walter Starkie, who had vowed to give his uncle 'no peace'[28] until he had agreed to illustrate them. In writing the stories, Stephens had attempted to create an Irish equivalent of *The Arabian Nights*, his own poetic retelling of the stories which existed in the oral tradition and in Gaelic texts, but which had not appeared accessibly in

no art to give it colour and shape to what are presently only names. Some of Mr. Rackham's pictures are pure poems – they set you dreaming.'[29]

The nature of Rackham's exposure and popularity in the British Isles took on a complicated pattern after the war. While his star was rising in America, his position in Britain was shifting in its relation to the

changing artistic and literary worlds. In 1919 he was given the last of his more or less established winter shows at the Leicester Galleries. The public who before the war were avid consumers of the fantasy fairyland with which Rackham's name was associated had had their own fantasies shattered by the realities of war. The Leicester Galleries were now giving exhibitions to modernist artists such as Wyndham Lewis (1921) and Jacob Epstein (1924 and 1926), Vanessa Bell, Roger Fry and Duncan Grant (1926). Theirs was the major London gallery where modern French art could be seen and bought: Van Gogh's paintings were exhibited there in 1923, Gauguin in 1924 and Cézanne in 1925. Roger Fry's Omega Workshop, his Post-Impressionist exhibitions of 1912 and 1913, Vorticism (1913–20) and the impact of Epstein's sculpture had all contributed to fundamental changes in the public's knowledge and appreciation of art. The 'fancy' of Rackham's work, as represented by his gnomes, fairies and imaginative landscapes, was being broken under the heels of the multi-coloured dragon of progressive art of the 1920s. His creatures were suffering the same kind of fate as experienced by Rackham princesses menaced by dragons, and with no sign of rescue.

The book world, too, was changing. A new fashion, for fine books illustrated by black and white wood-engravings and woodcuts, developed particularly in the 1920s through private presses such as Gregynog, Golden Cockerel and the Cresset and Swan Presses.

She went along and she went along and she went along
Pen and ink and watercolour, 1918
260 × 178 mm
Private Collection

Illustration to 'Catskin' from English Fairy Tales *by F. A. Steel*

Girl Beside a Stream
Watercolour, 1920s
368×315 mm
Sheffield City Art Galleries

Drapery Study
Ink wash and
watercolour, c1920s
166 × 237 mm
Arthur Rackham
Collection, Rare Book
and Manuscript Library,
Columbia University

These companies, some of which were managed by artist wood-engravers, were creating a new kind of fine book, complete works of art in themselves, produced to a greater or lesser extent following William Morris's and Eric Gill's tenets of pure craftsmanship.

The Gregynog and Golden Cockerel Presses maintained the highest standards of the movement, but others, as Rackham was only too well aware, were lowering them and having the effect of undercutting the market – his market. He wrote to the American dealer Alwin Scheuer:

In the vogue for limited editions of various classics that Nonesuch & other so called '*presses*' have published, you must bear in mind that no artist or author has to take any considerable share in the profit. The artist may do, & be well paid for, his half-dozen head & tail pieces by a comparatively small proportion of the book's return. All the rest is for the trades. Even the block making is inconsiderable. And the printing is often improperly called the production of that 'press' at all [*sic*] – being merely printed in the ordinary course of business by any good printer for the particular 'press' – which is merely a euphemism for 'publisher'.[30]

This change in the publishing market developed from the new use in mass editions of black and white illustrations, from wood engravings, lino cuts by a younger generation of artists such as Robert Gibbings, Gertrude Hermes, Claire Leighton and Iain MacNab. These new talents brought a new directness

Woman with Spotted Headscarf
Watercolour, c1910–20
252 × 174 mm
Arthur Rackham Collection, Rare Book and Manuscript Library,
Columbia University

Inscribed with Rackham's Chalcot Gardens address, so therefore painted before 1920.

Goats and Mountain, Switzerland
Watercolour, 1930s
340 × 280 mm
Private Collection

Rackham has distilled the jagged edges of the mountain into a decorative Art Deco style.

Right: Enter Several Strange Shapes
Pen and ink and watercolour, 1926
386 × 279 mm
The Art Collection of the Folger Shakespeare Library

Illustration to The Tempest.

of image, a realist and often stark view of the world that contrasted with the primness of some of Rackham's work, and appealed to the more robust end of the inter-war book buying market. Such books also had much lower production costs, because a black and white image needed to go only once through the press as opposed to the three or four times for a colour plate, and so could be sold at a cheaper rate. The change reached its peak in the mid and late 1930s, with such experiments as the *Penguin Illustrated Classics* (1938), a series designed to be sold at 6d a copy, thus putting the best of contemporary book art into everybody's pocket. During the 1920s the trend was already beginning to be felt, to the detriment of the older generation of artists such as Rackham.

Rackham put the position succinctly in his letter to A. E. Bonser, replying to his request for Rackham to illustrate one of Bonser's stories:

I am afraid I can do or *suggest* nothing for your story.... It couldn't anyhow be me, as of late years these matters have so changed that I am not much of interest to the children's book 'market'. Since the war, costs have so changed that the book market has by mutual agreement made a wide cut between children's books, (which must be kept cheap, & therefore nothing to speak of can go towards illustrations), & grown-up books among which it is rather difficult for an illustrated book to find a place at all. It is *just* worth my while going on

illustrating books – but they are of a kind & for a market much smaller & rather different to before the war. There's something artificial & not satisfactory about it. The freely illustrated 'Rackham' book is no longer possible, & I find my way rather precariously & with much less profit into the outskirts of the fashionable 'limited edition' group. What next, I do not know. But as far as I can see looking back into times past, it is not likely that the old 'Rackham book' will ever come back.[31]

With these changes, Rackham was also noting, the change in the nature of illustrators' production, and the destructive effect of Twenties style. About her book of Sussex Stories, he wrote to Eleaner Farjeon:

You have got a lot of Sussex into it. I wonder who will illustrate it for you. I hope you'll get the right kind of person. I am inclined to think some of the women are doing more sympathetic work than the men – not so 'dashing'. There's such an air of experience, & swagger about much magazine illustration nowadays. Extremely able & smart, but unfeeling.[32]

As a cruel counterpoint to the even flow of Rackham's life in the 1920s, two events, the sudden deaths of his elder sister Meg and of his youngest brother Maurice, caused him great anguish. Meg, a single woman living in lodgings in Dorking, stayed with Arthur and Edyth at Houghton for a weekend in June 1925. One morning she walked out of the house and was never seen

Ariel Summoning Fairies
Pen and ink and watercolour, 1926
250 × 175 mm
Private Collection

Frontispiece to The Tempest *by William Shakespeare. Prospero: 'Go bring the rabble, o'er whom I give thee power . . .',* Act IV, sci

alive again, despite searches by police bloodhounds. Her body was found four days later by another walker about eight miles away near Chanctonbury Ring on the Sussex Downs.[33] In January 1927 Maurice Rackham was killed with seven others in an avalanche while skiing in the Tyrol. Both of these tragic reflections in later life of childhood losses of brothers and sisters affected Rackham deeply. He had to give evidence at the coroner's inquest on Meg's death, and kept the many letters of condolence he received after Maurice's fatal accident.

To try to stem his drastic fall in gross income from 1924 to 1926, Rackham prepared during the summer of 1927 to go to America where his most lucrative market now lay. He had been offered his fourth solo exhibition at Scott and Fowles Gallery in New York, and took the opportunity of the opening to visit America for the first time and to follow up contacts.

He sailed to New York from Southampton on the SS *Republic* on 1 November 1927, and to judge from his first letter home, written on board ship, seems to have begun his voyage with a certain wistfulness and an unease that was reflected in his last glimpse of Edyth and Barbara as they waved goodbye:

When the tender moved away at Southampton, you looked such little figures on such a tiny boat – I almost felt that it was you & not me who was setting out into the wide world. This great ship prevents any feeling of being an inconsiderable speck on the nothingness of space – which it must look like from outside.[34]

Although he was caught up in the jovial and energetic deck activities during the voyage, a rather small thin man beside his fat puffing travelling companion Alyn

Williams, he nevertheless slipped into bouts of depression. Mrs Williams commented to her husband on Rackham's seeming very depressed one day: 'Williams asked me if I was built that way – subject to blues on occasion. I thought I might be perhaps.'[35]

Arrival in New York, however, put heart back into him:

This really is a surprising & exciting place. The entrance to the harbour is so full of features, islands, forts, the great statue (which is light greenish – rusted copper I suppose). And the great group of skyscrapers which we saw in a beautiful pinkish glow, partly obscured by drifting smoke.... Such a panting of engines & puffing & clanking & screaming of whistles – to get the ship round to a wharf at right angles with the river, six tugs pushed their noses against her side – abreast. All chug chug chugging away, in the brilliant evening light....[36]

Rackham responded immediately to the sights of New York, the more so because his twelve-day experience of being 'a speck in the nothingness of space' had ceased. His feelings about the city were mixed and, at first, contradictory. The thrill of the landfall at Manhattan gave way to a bewilderment at the noise and the brashness of the city:

And *noise!* I don't think it is ever quiet.... Everything shouts – shop fronts, display windows, architecture. The violence of the competition makes noisy advertisement necessary, I suppose. But everything is overdone. I am wearied with architectural effects & ornament. Great cavernous doorways – all carved & moulded & fluted & adorned like any Rouen Cathedral. *Much* too much – of everything. To live here *must* vulgarise an artist.... Really I feel just like a countryman who comes to London & goes off home by the next train. I could *easily* run off & dump my bags & self on the first ship for Europe.[37]

He stayed at the Yale Club on Vanderbilt Avenue, making forays in his first few days to the Metropolitan Museum 'particularly for the primitives' and Central Park, 'dwarfed & spoiled by the ragged line [of high building] that is seen along the whole length.' His first business call was to the publishers Doubleday Page at Garden City on Long Island. Here he had to battle to get across the importance of printing his work well: '...how the essence of literature did not depend on good printing & book making yet how the very essence of visual art *did*. How it was *futile* to print

Imprisoned Ariel
Pen and ink and watercolour, 1926
187 × 127 mm
The Art Collection of the Folger Shakespeare Library

Originally a vignette page decoration for The Tempest. *The landscape and colour were added later for exhibition and sale.*
'. . . She did confine thee . . .
Into a cloven pine; within which rift
Imprison'd, thou didst painfully remain
A dozen years . . .' ActI, scii.

badly from my work. That it must be given to the public good in quality or not at all. Doubleday Page & Co *need* that realisation. Doran, I am glad to find, did seem to understand it.'[38]

Rackham's main task in his month in New York was to obtain as many good commissions as he could manage to fulfill to keep him in work for the next few years, now that the Colgate series had come to an end. He was looking not only for book subjects, but for contracts for serial magazine illustrations too, of the kind he had been doing for *The Century Magazine* ten years before. In addition he was following up leads which he had heard about in England, one of which at least turned out to be a wild goose chase:

I went up this morning to see the new Cathedral of St. John the Divine, that Miss Massey was going to get for me to decorate. It looks to me as if it would be a very long time before it reached the decorating stage. It will be an enormous place – begun as an arched Byzantine building, & the chancel finished as such, but to be converted into Gothic – whether the old will be pulled down I don't know, but they are at present busy on an enormous Gothic nave which they say will be finished in 1928 – but it hardly looks like it. It looks so remote that I am not sure I shall even bother to call & see Cram the architect.[39]

Before his visit to America was half over, Rackham felt he had done as much as he could in the way of raising commissions. He had arranged a new book with Doubleday, and an illustrated article with the Philadelphia magazine *The Delineator*, and had negotiated for continued publication of Nathanial Hawthorne's *A Wonder Book*, 'but at very poor figures'. He added gloomily: 'I rather fear that there isn't the money in the U.S. market for books that there used to be for us in England. Their books are cheaper, the royalty smaller, the expenses of production bigger.'[40]

The most important result of his visit, however, was probably the least expected. Rackham met E. H. Anderson, the Director of the New York Public Library, who 'propounded a scheme for a book he wants from me, if his committee will agree. Possibly a big job – but probably it will not come off.' A few days later, Rackham had met Anderson again: 'For the New York Library I may do a hand illustrated book, for their collection – to go in the same group as missals & illuminated M.S.S. of old. They have a large bequest which is so limited by restrictions that they will have to exercise their ingenuity almost, to be able to expend it sensibly.... I might have a very interesting thing to do.' This proposal, which was not discussed further until Rackham returned home, became the commission for the manuscript volume of *A Midsummer Night's Dream*, which Rackham designed, illustrated and oversaw in production in 1928 and 1929.

Rackham's depressed mood, and the bewilderment – as expressed to Edyth – of the first two weeks of his US stay gradually began to evaporate as he made new friends and agreed some commissions, at least. He now began to look at New York with a positive eye, at last becoming used to his surroundings:

I am learning a lot about New York.... They are tearing it down & building it up breathlessly. The skyscrapers they are now putting up are only meant to last about 10 years! This is actually the case. There are several reasons – but one is that the requirements of a neighbourhood alter so rapidly. Another is that they are finding out that the structure of these steel cored concrete buildings is acting in a way as yet not fully known on the metal & concrete of the lower stories. Strains & vibrations necessitate renewal of all pipes and sanitary fittings. And the steel cores get 'tired'. So now they are so building them that they can be taken down again. In sight of my bedroom one is going up. I can see men heating rivets to red heat then pitching them over to others who run them into holes prepared for them & crash them into bolts with heads with great whangs of hammers – the holes having been drilled ready with terrific noise.[41]

Rackham had by now had hospitality liberally showered upon him, and had been made a temporary member of four clubs – the Yale, the Century, the Grolier and the Players.

They [the clubs] are far more *picturesque* here – more deliberately determined to collect & gather entertaining possessions & people. More than one man...last night was distinctly gayer than prohibition would wish him to be. Old Jules Guérin (a very well known French decorator & illustrator) was maudlinly affectionate. And there was another member fast asleep in a corner, where the seats made a couch & where I am told there is often a little pile of such nappers.[42]

Above all, he happily experienced the legendary warmth of the Americans: 'Everybody is excessively kind. Everyone was brought up on my work – if young enough – or have brought up their families on it if old enough.'

As the correspondence developed – and Rackham wrote ten long letters home to Edyth – his edginess at being an elderly man in an unfamiliar, foreign and noisy city gradually subsided. When at last he received a letter from Edyth, he released an unusually unrestrained emotion in his reply that is unique in his surviving letters, and seems to hint at past infidelities, now deeply regretted and not unrelated, perhaps, to the difficulties that Edyth's 1923 diary touched upon. The passage also throws a new light on the tone of the previous letters Rackham had written from America, and presents a completely different side of the man from the cool detached professional elf of the popular imagination:

'particularly interested in their experimental branch where students were doing experiments in fresco, tempera &c: & where reputed old masters were x-rayed – revealing great re-painting &c.' He went on to the Gardner Museum, 'filled, in fact built of, all manner of lovely things – bits & scraps of sculpture & so forth put to use – glass – furniture – wall panelling & so on', and the Museum of Fine Arts in Boston, where he was able to see 'the one wonderful Japanese painting of a great Palace on fire of which I knew the existence & have reproductions'.

Rackham's last call, back in New York, was to complete a portrait of the young Jean Ickleheimer, a commission given to him earlier in the trip by her father Henry R. Ickleheimer, a New York businessman:

Have got a likeness at all events. Her pa came in today. He's a nice man, but wants some characteristics I didn't much want to do. I am giving way up to a point. I had intended to put a New York background – as it is now – at this season. He badly wants leaves on the trees. Well, as I am not doing it literally I can manage it. It really only means a mass of dark foliage instead of a mass of black bare trees.... She's a handsome young thing. Dark, in a black velvet dress.... Very amiable & patient fortunately & anxious that her mother for whom it is should have a Christmas present that she will like. *Very* wealthy of course. We talk of treasure hunts & polo....[45]

Despite all the attention he was receiving – being dined at the best clubs in town, taken to major galleries as a special guest, lionized by artists, publishers and booksellers, Rackham was still prey to his emotions three thousand miles from home: 'I'm in much better spirits now I have had your letters, dear dear old Edyth. I'm not sure any New Yorkers have seen tears running down my face but they might have done. I have had some very depressed moments.'[46]

His final evening in New York, however, was as unexpected as it was delightful. He met a boy called Nicholas and his companion Anne Carroll Moore in the Children's Room at the New York Public Library, and, having nothing better to do than 'to kick up my heels until sailing time', spent the evening with the pair riding in a taxi backwards and forwards over the bridges of New York, just for the sheer fun of it, seeing the city lit up against the night sky. The trio dined together in the Brevoort Grill, the most American restaurant they could find, and, as the midnight sailing time approached, Rackham was piped aboard the SS *Olympic* with a present of American chocolates for Barbara and a candle of good luck lit in his cabin by Nicholas.[47]

The letter of yours by me just come is Nov 21. I am very glad to get it. And I can tell you it was not easy to write such impersonal letters as I have been doing. But I understood your instructions were that they were to be so – feelingless records. Oh my dear old Edyth, it is so difficult for me to make you feel, in our troubled grievous time, how close close close, how *one* our lives have been for me. How *outside*, how unrecorded how without influence my wanderings have been to me. Well, I will not go on with that now. Only to say that the reality of *my* life has been that with you, and its happiness has far far exceeded its pain: and *I cannot* damn myself right out & down. I *must* feel, cannot help feeling the pride, growth, joy in my long union with you: & overpowering longing that you too will be able to join me in that realisation.[43]

Arthur's last letters home came from Boston, where he spent three or four days visiting the dealer Lauriat and the publishers Houghton Mifflin, who discussed with him the possibility of 'a small easy child's book ... [and] ... later an important Hans Andersen'.[44] He visited the Fogg Art Museum at Harvard, and was

CHAPTER SEVEN

ALL IS VANITY 1928 – 1939

TOWARDS THE END OF 1929 RACKHAM WENT into hospital for a prostate operation. This came at a time when Arthur and Edyth were preparing to leave Houghton for a new house they were having built at Limpsfield in Surrey. Their idea was to try to have the best of both worlds – a hint of country living and much easier access to London when required. They also hoped to save money by combining their two properties, though in the event Arthur did not relinquish his London studio until 1938 when he was under the constant care of a nurse.[1]

Using her own capital,[1] Edyth commissioned the architect Gerald Unsworth to build a large detached family house for them on land the Rackhams had bought at Pain's Hill overlooking Limpsfield Common, Surrey. The couple were, however, disappointed with the house, which they soon found dull, charmless and too big for them, and whose only abiding grace, they felt, was that it was labour saving and near the golf course on which Arthur could play the nine holes that had been a regular source of exercise for him since his Hampstead days. They called the house Stilegate, in despair of finding a more suitable name, because a footpath ran along the right hand side of the garden, and the front gate had a stile beside it. To soften the crisp modern edges of the house and to add a dying echo of the grotesque, Rackham made a pair of wooden light brackets, decorated with gnomes and dragons, and painted the back of his studio door with a dragon rampant and other ornament.[2] The house that Unsworth had given them was of the type that perfectly suited the business families who were colonizing the South London fringes at the time, but it was by no means the Goblin Master's Ideal Home.

Left: The wall was nearly upon a level with my breast. Unsheathing my rapier, I began to grope with it about the recess
Pen and ink and watercolour, 1935
298 × 204 mm
HRHR Art Collection, Harry Ransom Humanities Research Center, The University of Texas at Austin

Illustration to 'The Cask of Amontillado', from Poe's Tales of Mystery and Imagination.

The Rackhams' social life virtually came to an end in Limpsfield. The informal deep Sussex dwellers were now many miles away, and although they made good friends with new neighbours Edward and Marjorie Pease, the founders of the Fabian movement, and were near, too, to old friends Frank and Rosalie Keen, a different social world went on around them now, and they were both too old and ill to join in properly.

For the first six months of the new decade, Rackham was under medical orders to do nothing but rest. In the late summer, as he was strengthening, and looking forward to working again, Edyth once more became seriously ill, 'an old & threatening trouble of arterial spasms with the heart & all manner of vitalities alarmingly & distressingly involved, and work for me has been out of the question.'[3] Instead, Arthur helped to nurse his wife, and lived and did 'such manner of hackwork as I could'[4] in the room next to Edyth's bedroom.

When Edyth began to recover, Rackham found a new lease of life, and in the 1930s produced a remarkable final series of books. He rarely now went up to Primrose Hill Studios, but instead retreated to the studio he had built among the trees at the bottom of the Stilegate garden, which was 'separate from the house, separate (one felt) from ordinary affairs, very separate from the politely rural suburb in which it was in any case surprising to see him living, and as retired as a wild creature's den'.[5]

In the quietness of his studio, Rackham was able to retreat from his domestic difficulties and the troubles of the outside world and reflect through clouds of pipe smoke on his commissions from his new publisher, Harrap: 'The pipe is here, & it is perfectly splendid,' he wrote to a Mr Wilson, an art teacher whose students he had addressed in London. 'It shall be my regular studio companion & always remind me of you & your students. Actually, I am not *much* of a smoker – unlike most artists – and when I do smoke it is usually (in truth, always) cigarettes, and that not enough to stain my fingers. But I will, again (for I *have* smoked a pipe) fill the bowl, & evoke inspiration with clouds of incense.'[6]

From his studio, from his reading of the newspapers and periodicals, and in his conversations with the Keens and the Peases, he observed the social and

The Thin Person
Pen and ink and watercolour, 1936
Arthur Rackham Collection, Rare Book and Manuscript Library,
Columbia University

A free study for the illustration in Peer Gynt *by Hendrik Ibsen.*

financial changes going on in Britain and America, and the effects these were having. He expressed his views, as ever, through his letters: 'And though outer troubles – unemployment &c cannot be anything like so prominently before us as they are with you,' he wrote again to Wilson:

… all here, even the one time wealthy are not only anxious but experiencing great reductions in business with serious effects. This is a well-to-do "outer dormitory" of London & all round us such things are happening as wealthy people leaving & trying to sell their houses, & moving with their families into their gardeners' cottages. I am sorry most of all for the young people who too often are simply shutting their eyes to the future & becoming almost reckless in their outlook. For myself I am still going on with my work of course, but it is rather in readiness for a recovery than for any great present use. America since the war has been my best "client" – and that has of course absolutely closed down. But an artist is so used to violent fluctuations that I am not particularly anxious on that account.[7]

He tried to pin down his political views, too, in a letter to Alwin Scheuer:

I find in spite of the length of the letter I have just sent off to you that I haven't answered your P.S. about capitalism & socialism.

Really my political knowledge is so rudimentary that I hardly know what is really implied by the terms. But as I certainly believe in full personal responsibility & free opportunities I imagine I should be considered as an opponent by socialists.

But I can't think the world is going to show any great revolutionary changes when once again the cogs & wheels of the great social machine get into gear again.

It is a mysterious thing this worldwide breakdown. But we have been saying these many years that we haven't really *felt* the war yet. And I suppose this is it....

PS If I had been to America (a pretty innocent assumption this) after the war, I think I should have bought up all the purchaseable moveable splendours of all the war-worn countries. That would have restored the equilibrium upset by the war to some extent. It would not have impoverished the European States in the least. It would have made the U.S.A. incomparably rich in the finest fruits of culture, leaving her as well off as ever before in money, with all her industries going like steam and ready to supply whatever the rest of the world needed & could now pay for.[8]

An attachment he discovered to my daughter
Pen and ink and watercolour, 1929
281 × 208 mm
Arthur Rackham Collection, Rare Book and Manuscript Library,
Columbia University

Illustration to The Vicar of Wakefield *by Oliver Goldsmith.*

Rackham's new publishers had tried to keep in step with these social and financial changes, and even if the days of the 'old Rackham book' had gone, a new kind had taken its place. The 1930s Rackham book, as published by Harrap, was now generally slimmer, printed on thinner paper, and had plates printed on coated paper bound in at intervals with the text. The luxury of the tipped-in colour plate was now, largely,

141

a thing of the past. Although these changes reflected advances in printing technology, they equally reflected advances in Harrap's book design. There was still room, however, for Harrap to bring out special, de luxe editions of all their new Rackham books:

There is such a fashion for publishing only limited editions that my books are in a rather curious position. The ordinary editions do not sell so large a number as of old, & the limiteds are vastly over-applied for – whereas, formerly, in one or two cases only happily, the limited editions were not immediately sold out.[9]

Rackham's first two books for Harrap were Washington Irving's *Legend of Sleepy Hollow* (1928) and *The Vicar of Wakefield* by Oliver Goldsmith (1929), though his illness of 1929/30 prevented him from producing anything for 1930. Hodder and Stoughton quickly stepped into this gap in the Rackham market by bringing out yet another version of *Peter Pan in Kensington Gardens*, this time 'retold for little people' by May Byron.

For the next three years Rackham and Harrap had a successful arrangement whereby two Rackham books, a long one and a shorter one, were published together annually. Thus, in 1931, they brought out Walton's *The Compleat Angler* and Clement Moore's poem *The Night Before Christmas*. The limited edition of the latter sold out promptly: 'There was quite a fight over it. America went very strong for it.'[10] The success of this new policy enabled Harrap to publish Hans Andersen's *Fairy Tales* with John Ruskin's fable *King of the Golden River* in 1932, and in 1933 *The Arthur Rackham Fairy Book* with Christina Rossetti's *Goblin Market*. While his publishing was changing for the better, Rackham's sales of originals, too, were holding: 'I could have sold all the Vicar "plates" half a dozen times over,' he wrote to Alwin Scheuer.[11] 'And I did sell them at an *average* of £50 & wish I had asked more. And I already have similar offers for my unfinished & *unbegun* pictures for the Compleat Angler.'

Although Rackham had no shortage of texts to turn his pen and brush to, he and Harrap had to conform to the market pattern. He wrote to Alwin Scheuer, who had been in correspondence with him about titles which Scheuer might publish, and who had suggested *John Gilpin, Hamlet, Macbeth, Tam O'Shanter, The Lady of the Lake* and *Jekyll and Hyde*:[12]

I have to find books that will tempt the public. No very easy thing. My publishers & I are puzzling over it continually, & haven't yet settled on next year's. It is really very difficult indeed. I am so anxious to do only such as give me subjects that I enjoy, while my publishers have to think of vacancies in their lists, & current market conditions, & competitors etc. I *must* have some freedom in the direction of grotesque fantasy, humour & such like. There are not a few books of delicate charm that are outside my natural bent. (Miss Austen, for instance – lovely books but not for me.)

'Aha! a cat, right, plump and fat. You'll make my dinner; count on that'
Pen and ink and watercolour c1934
Private Collection

Illustration from 'Puss in Boots'

The ideal – even the classic – late Rackham commission was Hans Andersen's *Fairy Tales*. Harrap sent him to Denmark for a week in November 1931 to collect Danish atmosphere for the book. Barbara accompanied him, and together they explored Copenhagen, Elsinor, a farm in Zeeland, and visited museums, the cinema ('where I can snooze if I like', he wrote home to Edyth[13]) and the theatre. 'Copenhagen is a very beautiful city. Lots of water, ships, fishing boats, quays – everywhere. Museums, bourse, palaces, &c very handsome renaissance & stately rococo. Slightly provincial grandeur – in fact: all mixed up

Danish Farmhouse Study
Pencil, 1931
Arthur Rackham Collection,
Rare Book and Manuscript
Library, Columbia
University

with narrow old red-roofed houses.... It is rather fatiguing to me. I have to talk so much & behave myself so well all the while taking notes & notes for dear life.'

The Danes, characteristically friendly and accommodating, treated Rackham and Barbara as important foreign guests. One obligatory visit, with their two Danish guides, was to see Andersen's grave. The conversation with the guides was entirely in mime, as Rackham spoke no Danish and the Danes no English. One of the guides, as Barbara described, handed Rackham a wreath, and gestured in a deferential but purposeful way towards the grave. While the deputation stood with their heads bared and bowed, Rackham rather sheepishly laid the wreath on the grave, and as he did so muttered to Barbara out of the corner of his mouth: 'This is the sort of thing an Englishman does very badly, I'm afraid!' The Danes, thinking their guest had offered up a prayer for the soul of their great man, responded with an enthusiastic 'Amen! Amen!' and replaced their hats.

Rackham's Danish sketchbook[14] contains all the 'notes & notes' he took for dear life, studies of cottages, architectural details, courtyards, farm machinery, interiors and so on. The studies appear, as fully dressed drawings, in illustrations such as 'We went hand in hand up the round tower', from *The Elder Tree Mother*, and 'Kay and Gerda in the garden high up on the roof', from *The Snow Queen*.

The studies from the Danish trip were also of great use two years later when Rackham was commissioned to design Basil Dean's production of *Hansel and Gretel* at the Cambridge Theatre, London, for Christmas 1933. Costume notes he made in Denmark found their way into those of the *Hansel and Gretel* characters in his first and only professional theatre production, and the

In the midst of the tree sat a kindly looking old woman
Pen and ink and watercolour, 1932
382 × 285 mm
Courtesy of the Board of Trustees of the V&A

A decorative illustration to 'The Elder Tree Mother' in Hans Andersen's Fairy Tales, *inspired by the wallpaper designs of William Morris.*

145

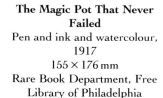

The Magic Pot That Never Failed
Pen and ink and watercolour, 1917
155 × 176 mm
Rare Book Department, Free Library of Philadelphia

Illustrated in black and white in Little Brother and Little Sister, *the colour and exquisite decoration on the fabrics were added later.*

first time he had designed for the stage since his Gilbert and Sullivan days in Highgate. The temperamental atmosphere, long hours, the pressures, the tantrums and the differences of opinion did not suit Rackham's frail physique. 'I assure you,' he wrote to Sydney Carroll, the Manager of the theatre, who was badgering him for progress, 'we are making all possible speed … the revolving stage (which Mr. Dean is at present set on) seems to me to cause trouble *without adding anything* to the effect….'[15]

The show opened on Boxing Day, with Lotte Reiniger's silhouette film *Harlequin and Colombine* as a curtain raiser. 'I think you'll like it. It is too much embroidered with dances &c but very charming. Gretel is delightful.'[16] The press reviews showed enthusiasm for Rackham's venture on to the stage which, to them, was new: 'His drop curtain is a masterpiece with its two impish children so delicately unselfconscious being the centre of an elaborate design … more than once many of [the audience]

'The professor can't stand things of that sort'
Pen and ink and watercolour, 1932
Private Collection/Bridgeman Art Library

Illustration to 'Little Ida's Flowers' in Hans Andersen's Fairy Tales.

'They are only dreams', said the crow
Pen and ink and watercolour, 1932
310 × 255 mm
Private Collection

Illustration in black and white to 'The Snow Queen' in Hans Andersen's Fairy Tales, *and later coloured. ' "I feel as if someone were coming after us," said Gerda, as she fancied something rushed by her. It seemed like a shadow on the wall; horses with flowing manes and thin legs, hunters and gentlemen and ladies on horseback. "They are only dreams," said the crow.'*

showed their appreciation when they should have been silently listening to the music of Humperdinck.'[17] Despite the strains of staging the production, the perfectionist in Rackham would not let the matter rest even when his work was done: 'I noticed a few little points in the costume,' he wrote again to Carroll, 'that I think could easily be bettered in the event of a revival. And I will write to you again about them.'[18]

The pattern of Rackham's career is marked by repeated bouts of late development. He did not marry until he was 36, had to wait until he was 38 for his first public success, Barbara was born when he was 40, and, at 60, an age when nowadays most people would be thinking about retirement, he found himself having to travel half way across the world to America to ginger up support from publishers to keep him in work. His last decade, far from being a time of twilit reflection on his life, became his second great period of creativity in books and, aged 66, also in stage design. Despite his fragility and his incipient illnesses,

Above: Hansel
Watercolour, 1933
Arthur Rackham Collection, Rare book and Manuscript Library, Columbia University, and
Right: Hansel and Gretel: Act Drop
Watercolour, 1933
Private Collection

The Pied Piper
Watercolour, 1934
Chris Beetles Gallery

Illustration to the Harrap edition of The Pied Piper
of Hamelin *by Robert Browning.*

and despite Edyth's invalidity, Arthur managed to find the energy and the spirit not only to move to a new house and environment, but also to create a final sequence of books that are as consistent and inventive as those in his early great period, 1905–16.

It is as if success did not really suit Rackham. Living as an insurance clerk on a meagre income, he struggled to succeed as an artist, and managed it, rising up and up to his pre-war fame. Living as a country gent, however, with a London studio and a rambling Sussex farmhouse, he was cut off from the spectre of discomfort, the fuel that drove him with such urgency to create masterpieces of the calibre of *Grimm* and *Rip van Winkle*. He was kind and loving in his care for Edyth, devoted to her in their final years, and did not like leaving her.[19] 'It is really very cold

today,' he wrote to her from the Arts Club in 1932 on one of his rare visits to London, 'I wonder whether it is so with you. You'll have to have your fire, as well as the pipes. I do hope you have had no more of the slow-heart ... I can't understand your heart getting slower with exercise. Mine responds instantly & gets quicker – even walking along the gardens, say. And soon subsides to normal again.'[20]

Edyth's illnesses, too, fuelled his fire to work and succeed, by isolating and highlighting those periods in his day when he could go to his garden retreat or travel up to London. At Primrose Hill Studios, as in his garden studio, he was his own master, and there slipped into his own more informal style of living. Edyth was very cross when he told her how an important art dealer had arrived unannounced to find

Edyth Rackham, 1930   Arthur Rackham, 1930s

him eating sardines off newspaper at three o'clock in the afternoon. Old friends urged him to come up to London more often. Harry Marillier wrote to say: 'What about coming to lunch with me at the Athenaeum one day and seeing all the pretty bishops? ... I can also show you Ramsay Macdonald, and if you look at him admiringly enough he will give you a knighthood next time.'[21]

Rackham, however, had deeper sadnesses, which no lunch at the Athenaeum, even with a Prime Minister and several pretty bishops in sight, could ever assuage. The passage is not dated, but from the handwriting and the tenor of the accompanying papers in his private notebook we can date what follows to the mid 1930s:

A.R. I began life with two fixed purposes which for many years seemed impossible of achievement. Despairing of success in either, I compromised as middle age drew near and burnt my boats with respect to the more imperatively urgent of the two. Immediately that step was taken, success in the lesser aim followed and has been maintained, and all is vanity. Too late I know the urgency of the injunction 'know thyself'. Neither of my purposes ought to have been lost sight of, or compromised with, on any account whatever.[22]

There is no doubt that this paragraph was set down to be read after his death and understood. In his late sixties, he had not only been pigeon-holed as the master of fantasy, fairy and the grotesque, but had been pressured to continue to serve these delights up to the public. It is perfectly clear that he enjoyed his

The Pied Piper
Watercolour, c1934
203 × 309 mm
Arthur Rackham Collection, Rare Book and
Manuscript Library, Columbia University

Possibly conceived as an illustration for The Pied
Piper, *but not used.*

149

Gold Medals
awarded to Arthur and Edyth
Rackham at the Barcelona
International Exhibition, 1911
59 mm diameter
Private Collection

work, and loved – and felt he justly deserved – the fame and honour he received. Looking back on his life, however, he seems to have reflected that the trappings of fame were as ashes, and all was vanity.

Nevertheless, he carried the responsibilities his fame brought, by replying almost unfailingly to fan mail, giving advice to perfect strangers, signing photographs and even succumbing on occasions to blandishments from people pleading poverty who claimed to be so passionately attached to his work that they wanted to buy a book or a drawing at a specially reduced price. Only occasionally did a mood remotely akin to irritability show through. To a child, asking for a sketch, he wrote:

I get many letters like yours asking for sketches & when they are from grown ups I reply by asking for half-a-guinea in return, for the Artists' General Benevolent Institution. But as I have many people wanting my sketches & pictures, I know you will not be disappointed when I ask you to be content with my autograph alone. Or perhaps a very tiny little sketch:[23]

No diary that Rackham kept has survived, but his correspondence is full of spontaneous expressions about himself and his work. Where these letters have surfaced in public and private collections they have provided a unique view of the man and his work, and of the often contradictory cross-currents in his thinking. 'When I have finished a book,' he wrote to N. Carroll in Massachusetts, 'I wish I could do it all over again, quite different. And invariably the *next* book, the book that as yet consists of blank sheets of paper, is the best that I have ever done. My books are really rather to be regarded as bound up portfolios of pictures – rather than "books". This is a pity but I see no way out of it. They are ungainly books.'[24]

Even in the final year of his life, when he was in and out of hospital and recuperating with a permanent nurse at home, he managed to write to Frank P. Harris at a moment when an injection of morphia was giving him a temporary respite. He described his untidy study with its 'unholy assortment of correspondence,' adding: 'Oh *why* will nice young American ladies write to say such nice things – not that I don't like it.'[25]

To one nice young American lady he wrote a long PS discoursing about the art of ancient man. He hardly needed to, but nevertheless the call of duty to inform and educate was overridingly strong:

Among the other old things at Amberley (my former house) I picked up a flint spearhead. That part of the country is solid chalk on which the top soil is so shallow that every trace of ancient man that is to be found must be in the top few inches. So old flint implements are constantly turning up. They are not very entertaining – in themselves that is. But they tell a tale. How old, nobody knows.

But one thing about them is very interesting to me. And that is that they show that there were artists in those days. That is, people who made things beautifully for no purpose whatever except because they liked doing so. Sometimes they find arrowheads &c of flint made sharp by the neatest prettiest little edging of chips that you could imagine. And all that painstaking skill for prettiness *only*. For the sharpness could much more easily & just as usefully be made with a much more rough chipping. My spearhead is quite coarse workmanship. But this is very dull for you. AR.[26]

For a man whose surviving letters show flashes of insight, wit, opinion and anger, but only very rarely betray any private emotion, Rackham's soliloquy to his Notebook is remarkably frank. It stops short, however, of being a complete revelation, and its meaning remains a tease. If we take it that his 'two fixed purposes' were both concerned with art, and that the 'lesser aim' is book illustration, could the 'more imperatively urgent of the two' be oil painting, and particularly portraiture? In his early career Rackham produced two oil portraits – his *Self Portrait* (1892) and the *Portrait of the Artist's Mother* (1899) – which show an insight and an intensity, and a mature knowledge of the realist portraits of Herkomer. His series of landscape studies at their best are confident and spirited. Even while his fame was breaking he experimented publicly with oil, producing and

Top: Self Portrait – A Transpontine Cockney
Oil on canvas, 1934
390 × 290 mm
Private Collection

Bottom: Portrait of the Artist's Daughter, Barbara
Oil on canvas, 1932
408 × 305 mm
Private Collection

exhibiting a *Rumplestiltskin* in 1903, *Hauling Timber* in 1904, *Undine* in 1916, and others including portraits and self-portraits. He worked with variations of oil, tempera and 'temperoil', and at its best his technique summons up light and atmosphere that always have a chill and telling presence. Rackham struggled with oil painting, never quite relinquishing the discipline, despite the heavy pressures on him to produce more and more startling illustrative images on time for a demanding market expectant of quality. He insisted on high printing standards not simply for his own ends – his publishers and public expected it of him, and expected *him* to whip the printers to their best endeavours.

All this was against the background of Edyth's illnesses and her own struggle to justify and exceed the recognition given to her as a portrait painter. Her inclusions in the Royal Academy in 1907, 1909, 1910 and 1914 show the consistently high level of her professional attainment. When Arthur went to Barcelona in 1911 to collect his First Class Medal for Drawing, Edyth went with him to collect *her own* First Class Medal in the Painting Section for her picture *The Black Veil*, which was later purchased for Barcelona Municipal Museum.

With Arthur, too, her work was chosen for the Luxembourg Gallery in Paris, *The Spotted Dress* being bought for £120 for presentation to the Luxembourg by the collector Edmund Davis in 1913.[27] In her own right, however, Edyth was invited to become a member of the newly formed National Portrait Society in 1910,[28] to show with the Women's International Art Club in 1913,[29] to submit *Reflection* to the Royal Scottish Academy and *Girl's Head* to the Walker Art Gallery, Liverpool in 1914, and to join the International Society of Sculptors, Painters and Gravers in 1915.[30] In 1915, Arthur's account book shows that he spent £25 on model fees for Edyth – sufficient for about 75 sessions: in the same year he spent nearly £22 on 59 sessions with a model for himself. As late as 1923, Edyth wrote in her diary of her despair at having so much sewing to do, fearing that she might 'never paint

The Three Bears
Colour process plate, 1918
Private Collection

Illustration to English Fairy Tales.
Edyth Rackham's The Grebe Hat, *a painting that Arthur hung in his studio, is shown hanging here in Goldilocks' parlour.*

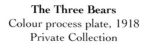

or keep well'.[31] The final trace of Edyth's painting activity comes in Arthur's accounts for 1924: Edyth's model: £5.'

Arthur was always aware of his wife's talent and standing as an artist, and did all he could to encourage her. Writing to Eleanor Farjeon about the text of her forthcoming article, Rackham says:

I *should* like it if you could put in something as prettily as is ever possible about [Edyth] being a companion in craft as well as in the rest of life. The inexorable shutting of the downstairs-studio door during certain hours only conceals a fellowship.... She is at least as distinguished in her own way ... only her work makes such rare appearences that she is very little known.... To give any true picture of our life she should appear, and as a fellow artist.[32]

As Arthur was the first to say, Edyth was no 'artist's wife', but a notable portrait painter in her own right. In *English Fairy Tales Retold* (1918), he paid homage to his wife by including Edyth's painting *The Grebe Hat* in the background of *The Three Bears*.

One is drawn towards the conclusion that in 1903, the year of their marriage, and the year in which Edyth told Arthur not to be so silly and put his fantasy illustrations into the Royal Watercolour Society, there was a private pact between them: illustration for Arthur and portrait painting for Edyth. If this was the 'burning of boats' that Arthur later so bitterly regretted, he did not gainsay the decision, despite the slowing down of Edyth's output, until the late 1920s, when Edyth seems finally to have stopped painting, and Arthur began to show his own portraits at the Royal

Society of Portrait Painters.[33] Rackham's own *Self Portrait* of 1934 reveals a watchful, tense, even tight-lipped man, the Arthur Rackham beneath the veneer of humour and parody that he had brought to his earlier self-caricatures. There are records of Arthur painting at least eight portraits from 1927 onwards, and planning a ninth of the novelist William Locke (1863–1930), a friend of Edward Tinker. This, Rackham suggested in a letter to Tinker, could be either a drawing, watercolour or oil. 'My present habits of thought for portraits lean more & more to the smallish (say half life size), & rather complete work of the early Flemings – or Holbein. With a background that is designed as suggesting interesting associations with the sitter.'[34] Locke, however, died before the commission could be carried out.

Now, once again, the roller-coaster pattern of Rackham's career was moving upwards, making him 'overwhelmingly busy'.[35] In 1935 Harrap published Poe's *Tales of Mystery and Imagination*, the book whose illustrations 'were so horrible I was beginning to frighten myself'.[36] Marita Ross, his one time model, reports that Rackham admitted that he did not enjoy the commission, being afraid that he would be unable to make the illustrations sufficiently gruesome. He need not have worried, however, for not only does he cope masterfully in a Beardsleyesque manner with the *grand guignol* of *The Masque of the Red Death*, but carefully injects a virus of sadistic horror, more appalling than

'Scoundrel! Imposter! Accursed Villain! . . . You shall not dog me unto death!'
Pen and ink and watercolour, 1935
235 × 178 mm
HRHR Art Collection, Harry Ransom Humanities Research Center, The University of Texas at Austin.

Unused illustration to 'William Wilson', from Poe's Tales of Mystery and Imagination.

anything in his 1900 *Grimm*, into two drawings from *Hop-Frog*. In this story, the King and his seven ministers, dressed for a masque as orang-utangs, have been duped by Hop-Frog the Jester and trussed up and set alight in a bundle: 'The eight corpses swung in their chains, a fetid, blackened, hideous and indistinguishable mass.'

This masterly interpretation of Poe's stories is a fine example of the professional illustrator rising and responding to a commission, with a world-weariness

Left: A Descent into the Maelstrom, Centre: In less than half a minute the whole eight were burning fiercely, Right: The eight corpses swung in their chains
HRHR Art Collection, Harry Ransom Humanities Research Center, University of Texas at Austin

Illustrations to Poe's Tales of Mystery and Imagination.

and an almost palpable cynicism at human nature, to resounding decorative and psychological effect. Criticism of it has ignored the fact that its style is just as deeply rooted in Rackham's repertoire as is his fantasy manner – if anything it predates it – but because of the heavy marketing and success of the fantasy subjects, it was a voice that had been silent for decades.

The illustrations to *Poe's Tales* reveal him, once again, to be a master of parody, an aspect of his work which has been barely noticed, still less commented upon. He not only pays homage to Aubrey Beardsley, but he also parodies himself. The silhouette of the great steed of *Metzengerstein* is a decorative version of the horses of the Valkyries which Rackham invented in 1910, while the full-page silhouette in *The Murders in the Rue Morgue* parodies the cut-away house silhouette in *The Sleeping Beauty*. Here the joke is that the drama now moves upwards not to the finding of a spinning wheel in an attic, but to the discovery of a corpse being stuffed up a chimney by an orang-utang.

Rackham's last few years followed a pattern of increasing international veneration and, being diagnosed as having cancer, gradually declining health. Walter Starkie spotted his uncle's influence in Charles Doran's 1921 Dublin production of *A Midsummer Night's Dream*,[37] while Max Reinhardt admitted that he had traced the source of his inspiration for his film version of the *Dream*, then showing at Warner Brothers' Beverley Hills Theater, to 'the eerie paintings of Arthur Rackham'.[38] A retired Lieutenant in the Austrian Navy, Bruno Maria Lancelot Wikingen,

Poe's Tales Title Page Design
Pen and ink, 1935
310 × 210 mm
HRHR Art Collection, Harry Ransom Humanities Research
Center, University of Texas at Austin

154

End Paper Design for Peer Gynt
Pen and ink and watercolour, 1936
Arthur Rackham Collection, Rare
Book and Manuscript Library,
Columbia University

wrote to Rackham as the 'Dear Much Venerated Master' in 1930, asking him where he could find copies of reproductions of his Wagner drawings to insert in a *Ring* manuscrpt that Wikingen was writing out.[39] A Heidelberg Professor of Indology claimed – erroneously as Arthur later maintained[40] – that Rackham had 'so completely mastered the Indian style of painting that when young artists try to imitate [it] what they turn out is merely imitation Rackham.'[41] London, Dublin, Beverley Hills, Vienna, Heidelberg, even, putatively, India: Rackham's art had quietly woven itself into them all. In 1935 he was welcomed back as 'The Goblin Master' by *The Observer*[42] in a review of his first exhibition at the Leicester Galleries

The Distinct Colossal Figure of – a Horse
Pen and ink, 1935
266 × 190 mm
HRHR Art Collection, Harry Ransom Humanities Research Center, University of Texas at Austin

Illustration to 'Metzengerstein', from Poe's Tales of Mystery and Imagination.

Wedding Announcement
for the marriage of Philip Soper and Barbara
Rackham, July 1935
166 × 115 mm
Private Collection

since 1919. The reviewer, Jan Gordon, wrote of how Rackham 'almost miraculously turned into visible image all those subconscious feelings that still are able to haunt us along lonely country lanes, no matter how sophisticated we may be....'

This universal appeal did not put Rackham above wearying himself with relatively trivial commissions for persistent correspondents, and it even increased his insistence on getting printing details right. He continued to demand the highest standards from his printers, to the extent of asking to visit the works where the cover of *Peer Gynt* was to be printed so he could make 'quite small alterations, usually,' to the colour balance on the lithographic stones.[43]

He would willingly make flyleaf illustrations for owners of his books, making it a rule that he was to be entirely free to do whatever suggested itself to him. 'And particularly that it is understood that my little sketches must almost inevitably be of a light hearted or joking nature – & not attempting subtlety. They have to be very spontaneous & free-handed. *The nature of the paper* is such that there can be no preparatory drawing & no alterations.... A jeu d'esprit, a pleasantry, is more in place & attainable, but delicacy & grace need a more deliberate occasion.'[44]

Frank P. Harris was in touch with him in 1938 over some illustrations that he wanted Rackham to put into flyleaves of his books. Five letters from Rackham to Harris,[45] are witness to the care he took over minor commissions, even to the extent of explaining why *Alice* was a particularly tricky book to decorate in this

way because 'the paper is like blotting paper & *a touch* at once soaks in, losing shape a little too & drying quite a different colour.'[46] In October 1938 he was back from hospital and told Harris that the first thing he did 'when I, *ahem*! felt fit (here I slap my chest very gently)' was to look at Harris's books, adding 'I am writing in the garden studio. Have been down since 11 & had lunch with my wife & carved &c like what the Irish call "a well man". But when I have finished this letter I am going quietly back to bed again for the rest of the day.'[47]

Rackham's enforced rest and his periods sitting quietly in his studio gave him the time and peace he needed to read, write and reflect. The notebook into which he stuck newspaper cuttings, postcards from friends and noted down paragraphs he had read or heard on the wireless, reflects his current worries, his particular concern over the political situation in Europe, and his unshakeable belief in the central importance of art and literature in an unheeding world. His own partisan views against modern art slip out too: he notes with glee how Roger Fry confessed to C. J. Holmes 'like a humble art student, how difficult he found it to reconcile his natural straightforward vision with his aesthetic convictions',[48] and he highlights an article in which Kenneth Clark called for 'a new interest in subject matter ... a new myth in which the symbols are inherently pictorial.'[49]

Of the many correspondences that Rackham took part in during his last decade, one, with Robert Partridge over the designs for his book-plate,[50] was

Rip Van Winkle

monumental in its length and trivial in its result, and stretched over two years and at least ten exchanges of letters.[51] Rackham began by offering seven existing drawings which he felt could be well adapted for the purpose, and explained what amendments he was and was not prepared to make to them. He discussed kinds of lettering, their placement and weight, advised Partridge not to get the printing plate made in too much of a hurry, and said no, he had no joke in mind when he sent Partridge a drawing of a Goshawk as a book-plate suggestion. He even went into the matter of paper colour with Partridge, suggesting with razor-sharp precision 'a slightly toned putty colour – not so bright as cream'.[52] 'All this correspondence,' Rackham added to Partridge through gritted teeth, '*perfectly reasonable and necessary*, for such an individual and personal matter as a bookplate, will give you some idea of the reason I have for not jumping at bookplate designing except for a fantastic price. As you see, I am *absolutely* in sympathy with the owner of the bookplate.'[53]

Book-plates had become a minor source of income and a major source of irritation for Rackham. He made designs for at least twelve people during his career, and stretched his patience to the limit in doing so. He wrote to Edward Tinker, the American collector:

I have found some of those who have so kindly asked for a bookplate from me rather under the impression that it is a very small matter, that I could polish them off in an hour or two – & ask a proportionately modest fee. This is unfortunately hardly the case: & I take such commissions as seriously as I do all my work & I do not find them trivial or less exacting ...[54]

He varied his fee and his approach to suit the pocket of the client, naming £100 to Edward Tinker, and 'from – say – £10' at the beginning of his correspondence with Robert Partridge for an existing drawing adapted for the purpose.

> I am not fond of doing them because these isolated imaginative drawings take my mind off my work which usually arranges itself in sequences. So, though I have sometimes done them I have to ask a quite disproportionate fee. £50 or more. Which is absurd (except for the occasional very wealthy persons who ride in Rolls Royces.)[55]

Wet Weather was the Worst
Pen and ink and body colour, 1931
Arthur Rackham Collection, Rare Book and Manuscript Library,
Columbia University

Frontispiece for The Chimes *by Charles Dickens. Rackham wrote to the printer of this edition: 'I wish I had been able to design my decorations for your setting of the text instead of the other way round. I feel my ragged pen-work, very deliberately done for my own lettering, plays Old Harry with your clean neat type.'*

Rackham's letters happily throw back a truer image of the man, without the distortion of his elfin reputation or gnomic self-portraits. He was a compulsive letter-writer, having the ability to form as elegant a written line as a drawn one, and had a turn of phrase that a quickly expressed opinion could neatly hone. His last correspondence, carried on despite the pain of his final illness and operations, and the frustrations of being 'condemned to the companionship of a surgical nurse'[56] for the rest of his days, has a beauty, a courage and a poignancy that gives it a claim to be one of the bravest exchanges of English letters of its period.

Rackham had met George Macy, the Director of the Limited Editions Club of New York, soon after his American visit of 1927. He had illustrated an edition of Dickens's *The Chimes* for Macy in 1931, and in 1935 Macy tried to persuade him to tackle *The Rime of the Ancient Mariner*.[57] 'REGRET IMPOSSIBLE RACKHAM', the artist cabled in reply,[58] adding in a follow-up letter that this was because his time that year was

fully taken up, and also because 'I am not very hopeful of the A.M. as a subject … largely on account of its lack of length.'[59]

Macy called on Rackham at Primrose Hill Studios in the summer of 1936, some months after the artist had begun the Limited Editions Club's *A Midsummer Night's Dream* illustrations, to review progress and to discuss further commissions. The two talked in a desultory way about further ideas, including an edition of James Stephens's *The Crock of Gold*. Nothing really sparked either man, until Macy casually mentioned *The Wind in the Willows*.

Immediately, [Macy wrote] a wave of emotion crossed his face; he gulped, started to say something, turned his back on me and went to the door for a few minutes. When he came back, he said that he had been trying for many years to persuade an English publisher to let him illustrate Grahame's book, having been forced to turn it down due to pressure of other work when Grahame invited him to do it nearly 30 years earlier.[60]

Rackham's subsequent letters to Macy[61] are full of good news of the progress of the *Wind in the Willows* illustrations, alternating with cliffhangers, as it is increasingly clear that this is a race against time, and the question always arises: will Rackham live to finish the book?

Right: She arranged the shawl with a professional fold, and tied the strings of the rusty bonnet under his chin
Pen and ink and watercolour, 1939
Private Collection

Illustration to The Wind in the Willows

Above: Today, however, though they were civil enough, the field mice and harvest mice seemed preoccupied
Pen and ink and watercolour, 1939
Private Collection

Illustration to The Wind in the Willows.

RACKHAM TO MACY, 11.7.37:
Do forgive me for not having written before. And do also please forgive me if I say I would rather not show *any*body, yet, what I am doing for the Wind in the Willows.

I am deep in it – but too experimental to want to show my work. I have not *finished* much yet. And I am not sure that I may not scrap what I have done. This is no unusual thing for me. I get stuck on experimental or off on false lines – and I know by experience that I may be in what seems like a muddle & then get going like a house on fire.

Left: It was a golden afternoon, the smell of dust they kicked up was rich and satisfying
Pen and ink and watercolour, 1939
230 × 185 mm
Private Collection

Illustration to The Wind in the Willows.

I have been down by the River Thames – and out and about in the woods. And discovering canal-barges and all the rest of "stuff" that the book talks of....

RACKHAM TO MACY, 27.8.37:
... I am in the doctor's hands & under orders to do as little as I can – for a short time more only – I am encouraged to know.... I have just been undergoing a course of "deep X-ray therapy" which is to set me up again. It leaves me rather washed out.... I have little completed.... I had already been busy at preliminaries – animal studies, visits to the Upper Thames etc, & when I regain my usual activity I shall be able to go full steam ahead & have no doubt I shall come up to time without question....

RACKHAM TO MACY, 24.1.38:
... two courses of deep X-ray treatment. And also I have made a discovery that I don't like. A threatening to the sight of my right eye. Some months ago, this. And I cannot detect that it is worse, which is hopeful. After these, rheumatism in my hand is a minor matter.

RACKHAM TO MACY, 5.7.38:
... I am very nearly through with the colour work for the Wind in the Willows.... And I think my home conditions are settling down after a long time in which my work has been hopelessly interfered with. It's absurd that one has to be so hampered but I have been crushed by domestic difficulties & what should be insignificant matters have been insupportable. However, I think we are turning the corner now: & I am regaining lost weight.

RACKHAM TO MACY, 13.4.39, *written in a very weak and shaky hand*:
... I should like to see you but my nurse is very strict & limits my time severely. I am still very much in bed.
But I have finished the Wind in the Willows. All the 16 in colour. 12 in pen which I should like used at the beginning of each chapter. And title page.... And I do hope you'll use 3-colour process. It really does facsimile my work best. And done in this country, I hope. The Sun Reproduction Co. I have found the best....
I also wonder whether you are prepared to discuss another book. I have two ideas....
1. A Collection of Fairy Poems.
2. The Water Babies – for which I have often been asked (by USA particularly).
Both of these books would be within my powers now. As I should need very little, if any, work from the living model. And there is no continued character to portray – which, I fear, as yet I could not bear the continuous concentration of. Let me know.

Even on what was fast becoming his deathbed, Rackham worried about reproduction processes, and still insisted on the use of three-colour printing. If barely alive in body, he was unbreakable in spirit. Rackham's last letter to Macy, however, written nineteen days before his death, shows reality beginning to dawn upon him, an acknowledgement of his own mortality, and an old professional's approach to the situation:

... in my last letter to you I fear I talked about possible future books which I am afraid I now doubt the possibility of. I can work a little even when I am in bed. But I think what I shall have to do if I work with a book in view, is to do the work first & then offer it to you or another publisher.... 4 of the Wind in the Willows pictures were done in my Bedroom, & all the line drawings actually in bed. I think some of them are as good as I have ever done.[62]

Left: The gypsy took his pipe out of his mouth and remarked in a careless way 'Want to sell that there horse of yours?'
Pen and ink and watercolour, 1939

Illustration to The Wind in the Willows

'Onion Sauce! Onion Sauce!' he remarked jeeringly
Pen and ink and watercolour, 1939
Arthur Rackham Collection, Rare Book and
Manuscript Library, Columbia University

Illustration to The Wind in the Willows.

The *Wind in the Willows* illustrations, which Rackham did not live to see published have an exuberance of their own, as if in them Rackham is at last skipping free into a commission he always longed for. Owing perhaps to weakening sight, and almost certainly to a new confidence in the ability of the three-colour printing process to reproduce high tone, Rackham consistently uses much brighter and clearer colours than before, creating poignant and indelible images of 'a golden afternoon' in English art and letters.

The current of melancholy which ran through Rackham's surviving letters in his final years was, however, balanced by a faith in the future, and shows a flicker of the youthful Unitarian convictions that he never entirely lost. 'The times are tragic,' he wrote to Sir George Clausen, President of the Royal Academy, in August 1939.

I feel overwhelmingly for our young people, who can see nothing in front of them. We thought, we late Victorians, that we had got past all such criminal folly & expected that those after us would have finer & wiser lives than we had had. And now! ... If by any good fortune we did tide over without a hideous conflagration there is one thing that seems more and more 'in the air' – the realisation that the supremacy of the machine, which is rapidly making robots of humanity, must be faced. And the machine must be put in its place as a servant to do the servile work only, freeing humanity to exercise its birthright of imaginative creative work. One hardly takes up a thoughtful journal without seeing that the danger is at last recognised. That, I think, is the main charge to be laid against the wonderful Victorian days – when the world was so elated at 'conquest of nature &c' that it was not seen what the penalty must inevitably be of this eating of the fruit of the tree of knowledge of good and evil.

Art may indeed be under a cloud. But if it is not the spirit of the Creator working in us I do not know what it is. And it cannot be eternally killed.[63]

Arthur Rackham died at home on 6 September 1939, three days after Britain declared war on Germany. Edyth lived on in Stilegate for 2 years until her death in March 1941. Because of unfounded bombing scares Rackham's undertakers would not drive his coffin into London, and so his final wish, of being cremated at Golders Green, near to the North London haunts of his early manhood and courtship, was denied him, and he was cremated in Croydon. His ashes, however, later to be joined by Edyth's were scattered in the Rose Garden at Golders Green crematorium. A deeper wish, to have a memorial placed on the Artists' Wall in Amberley Churchyard in Sussex, down the hill from Houghton and near the graves of his friends Francis Derwent Wood RA and Edward Stott ARA, remains to be fulfilled.

For an Englishman who contributed so much – and so quietly – to the way children learnt about the world, his official neglect in his own country is disappointing. He was never given any British state honours, and his work is sparsely represented in British public collections. America, however, the country which in Rackham's own words 'kept me alive', is appropriately the greatest public source for his original work, notably in the libraries of New York, Philadelphia, Austin and Louisville, and it was the Americans who gave him the accolade of a 'knighthood'. It was left to the French, Italians and Spanish to give Rackham the gold medals and ribbons for his achievement, and to the Americans to honour him with his Centenary Exhibition at Columbia University, New York, in 1967. If this is a censure on his own countrymen's attitude, it is also indicative of his universal appeal. Late in the day, perhaps, though consistent with the general pattern of Rackham's life, an exhibition of this quiet genius's work was shown in 1979–80 in Sheffield, Bristol and the V & A.

Notwithstanding this tardy recognition in his own country, Rackham's influence on his children's and subsequent generations has been overwhelming. Family tradition has it that he was invited to California by Walt Disney to work with him on *Snow White*, though no record of this invitation has been traced in Disney archives. Filmmakers such as Fritz Lang, Max Reinhardt and Lotte Reiniger – all significantly of German origin – and theatre designers as disparate as Charles Doran in Dublin in 1921 and Robert Israel at Seattle Opera in 1984 have found in Rackham's work an inspiration for their own. Siegfried Wagner, on a visit to London in 1927, expressed a wish to meet Rackham, and 'spoke in great terms'[64] about Rackham's illustrations to his father's operatic

All was a-shake and a-shiver – glints and gleams and sparkles, rustle and swirl, chatter and bubble
Pen and ink and watercolour, 1939
Private Collection

Illustration to The Wind in the Willows, *American edition only.*

cycle. Illustrators working today whose drawings are widely available in mass-produced book and card form carry Rackham's unmistakeable influence. Among these are Michael Foreman, Brian Froud, Kit Williams and Jimmy Cauty.

Rackham was criticized during his lifetime for producing expensive limited editions that were more suited to the drawing room than to the nursery. For every de luxe edition, however, there was a mass-produced trade version, much loved, read, examined and fingered by children and adults. In his poem *Myfanwy*, published in 1940, John Betjeman wrote of 'Finger marked pages of Rackham's Hans Andersen', a book which continues to be enjoyed and collected, and remains a classic of its kind. The rising prices of even the contemporary trade editions of Rackham's books is an indication of how many copies have been read, fingered and simply worn out and thrown away. This, however, is of little consequence, for, as Arthur Rackham himself wrote: 'To end their lives in a nursery ... is the most desired end for my books to reach.'[65]

CHAPTER EIGHT

SO GOOD NIGHT UNTO YOU ALL ARTHUR RACKHAM AND SHAKESPEARE'S *A MIDSUMMER NIGHT'S DREAM*

OWARDS THE END OF HIS LIFE, RACKHAM was invited by the American publisher George Macy to take part in the illustration of the Limited Editions Club's forthcoming complete Shakespeare canon. Macy invited him, in 1936, to list the five Shakespeare plays that he would like now to illustrate,[1] and in his reply Rackham listed: '1. A Midsummer Night's Dream; 2. The Tempest (These two easily first); 3. The Merry Wives of Windsor; 4. Twelfth Night; 5. As You Like It,' adding: 'I have done the *Midsummer Night's Dream* for instance & should like to do it any number of times.'[2] *A Midsummer Night's Dream* returned again and again to Rackham's mind, and it is worth looking closely at the variations of his treatments of it at successive stages of his life.

His first experience of the story as an illustrator came when he provided two images for it in *Lamb's Tales from Shakespeare* in 1899. His first invitation to illustrate the complete text of *A Midsummer Night's Dream*, however, came from Heinemann, who reached an agreement with him on 2 March 1906,[3] seven months before his *Peter Pan* illustrations were due for delivery to Ernest Brown and Phillips, and more than

'. . . . certain stars shot madly from their spheres to hear the sea-maid's music,'
Pen and ink and watercolour, 1908
382 × 265 mm
Courtesy of the Board of Trustees of the V&A/Bridgeman Library

Illustration to ActII sci of A Midsummer Night's Dream. Rackham deliberately used subdued colours which he knew were well within the reproductive capabilities of the 3 and 4-colour printing processes of the day. He has created a modulated beige tone to give the effect of a vellum border to this stylised and literal interpretation of the lines. The medallion of Queen Elizabeth I is based on a portrait at Hatfield House.

two weeks before Hodder and Stoughton made a pre-publication agreement to pay royalties to him on *Peter Pan in Kensington Gardens*. The *Midsummer Night's Dream* contract was also reached more than a year before Rackham's agreement with Heinemann to make his twelve colour drawings for *Alice*, despite a publication date of a year later.[4] It is important to get this perspective clear, as it shows how Rackham's commissions overlapped one another, both in his mind as well as on his drawing-board, and were not produced mechanically in order of publication.

It also shows how thinking about one set of characters, such as the fairies in *Peter Pan*, spawned ideas for another set, such as the largely similar fairies in *A Midsummer Night's Dream* – to the extent that both were in repertoire on his drawing-board in the same period, and part of the cast of one contributed to the cast of the other. It follows that this throws doubt on previous assumptions about the dating of Rackham's drawings. They may well be signed and dated for the year of publication of their book, but this was just the tidy-minded and professional Rackham dating his work forward to its publication date rather than confusingly labelling each with the year in which it happened to have been made.

In his sketchbook for the 1908 *A Midsummer Night's Dream*,[5] Rackham attends to his subject in greater detail than he gives to any other of his books, on the evidence of the sketchbooks that the present writer has seen. Of its 107 pages, 84 are given over to *A Midsummer Night's Dream* studies, some lines of text being given two or more studies to find the right composition, though he is often remarkably quick to reach the idea he wants. He takes the play out of order, suggesting a relaxed approach and a deep

familiarity with the text, and jumps backwards and forwards. Sometimes he leaves twelve pages before going back to a subject, as in the case of studies for *Hermia*,[6] and another 33 before returning to it once again. His technique is direct and immediate, using circular, sweeping pencil lines to brew his figures up like a soup, turning and amending their poses sometimes as he does so. Again, unlike his other sketchbooks, nearly every page is carefully annotated with the line he is illustrating, annotations which give the impression of having been written once the project had been completed.

It is clear that Rackham himself chose the lines he wished to illustrate, to the extent that the illustrations come at awkward points in the text, having to be bound in irregularly, as near as possible to the lines they refer to. As Rackham consistently chose to illustrate groups of lines, and at one point made no fewer than five illustrations to 26 consecutive lines of text at the opening of Act II scene ii, it was impossible for the reader to see both text and picture together. This would normally have been impossible anyway in the de luxe editions, because in the interests of sumptuousness the publishers included tissue interleavings to protect the illustrations, thus effectively masking the text from the illustration and vice versa. Rackham will almost certainly have been referring to this kind of product when, in 1931, he told N. Carroll that his books 'are really rather to be regarded as bound up portfolios of pictures . . . They are ungainly books.'

In his own copy of the book[7] Rackham left a note on the inside front cover listing the sources of some of the illustrations. *The Duke's Oak*, facing the end of Act I, is taken from 'an old sketch' done by Rackham in Wimbledon Park; the churchyard in '*Ghosts wandering here and there ...*' (III, ii) is Ruislip Churchyard in Surrey, and the wool-covered ball hanging from the

'Ere the leviathan can swim a league.'
Pen and ink and watercolour, 1908
272 × 203 mm
Arthur Rackham Collection, Rare Book and Manuscript Library,
Columbia University

Oberon's passing reference to a sea monster in Act II sci of A Midsummer Night's Dream is illustrated by a full blooded and terrifying creature of Rackham's imagination.

baby's cradle in '... *almost fairy time*' (V, i) was Barbara's first toy as a baby. Regarding the illustration '*some war with rere-mice*', Rackham writes: 'The bat was drawn from a stuffed bat belonging to Collier Smithers: I returned it the day of Barbara's birth. I met Miss Chitty while I was carrying it.' Other illustrations include details drawn by Rackham on his and Edyth's autumn holiday to Walberswick in Suffolk in 1907, a few months before Barbara was born.

Gladys Beattie Crozier visited Rackham while he was at work on his 1908 version of the play, and she reported his thoughts on the text and of how Rackham felt that Shakespeare 'dealt with the situation in a spirit of purest fantasy, for it is full of the wildest anachronisms.... Titania seems to have been entirely Shakespeare's own creation, but Oberon is doubtless drawn from the German Elf King, whilst Puck was surely never known in classic times. Then again Demetrius is specially mentioned wearing Athenian dress, Hermia and Helena are described as working on a sampler, popular in the Elizabethan household.'[8]

Heinemann published *A Midsummer Night's Dream* in November 1908, as the exhibition of the original drawings was closing at the Leicester Galleries, and the kind of fulsome reviews that Rackham had now come to expect duly appeared in the papers:

'He has turned out a gallery of sketches which no one else in Europe, probably, could have improved upon for their various distinction and originality, and if the result is not always Shakespeare, it is invariably Rackham.' *Pall Mall Gazette*[9]

'... a delightful land of makebelieve....' *The Daily Telegraph*[10]

'Rackham's name has become a household word and his position firmly established among the greatest illustrators of modern times.... His art appeals with equal strength to the nursery, the drawing room and the studio.... A classic among illustrators ... he speaks a universal language.... He reads the play, and when he comes across a passage or line that stirs his imagination he allows his mind to roam over the whole field of vision suggested by the poet.... He is an artist to his fingertips, equipped with all the gifts that make for lasting fame.' P. G. Konody, *Evening News*.[11]

The Athenaeum, however, once again was critical: '*A Midsummer Night's Dream* affords abundant opportunity for a kind of figure subject for which he has little real aptitude, but which the public insists on demanding from him the moment he takes up a position as interpreter of fairy subjects. Our generation is particularly prone to admiring a good man for the wrong reasons, and putting him to work for which he is constitutionally unfitted; and to condemn Mr. Rackham to live in a sentimental region ... is to stultify him.... We are distressed again and again in viewing the present collection by the sight of landscapes full of fire and vigour spoilt by the introduction of namby-pamby nymphs, whose creation has been, we think, of no pleasure to the artist. We can only suppose that he

'Are you sure that we are awake?'
Pen and ink and watercolour, 1908
292 × 264 mm
The Art Collection of the Folger Shakespeare Library

Demetrius, with Hermia, Helena and Lysander in Act IV, sci of
A Midsummer Night's Dream.

has been led into such paths by the promise of public applause – applause in which his truest well-wishers may refrain from joining.'[12]

In *The Ladies' Field*, Hugh Stokes pointed out: 'Although the scene of the play is "Athens and a wood near it", Mr. Rackham has not handicapped his art with any affectation of the classical, and in this he has followed his author. His interiors are purely Elizabethan, and in his landscapes we catch glimpses of half-timbered dormers, which suggest Warwickshire rather than Attica.... For Puck Rackham has gone to tradition [and] .... follows Reynolds closely.... His drawings will certainly attract as large crowds at the Leicester Galleries as *Peter Pan* or *Rip van Winkle*.'[13]

The Daily Chronicle enlarged on a point made by P. G. Konody: 'He is always at his best when his imagination has a free run: he does not illustrate the play, he prefers to take an idea from the text and turn it into a Rackhamian picture....'[14]

The Outlook made the first considered reference to the special quality of Rackham's trees: '.... a Rackham tree; one of those trees, gnarled and black and twisted .... sprung from seed found in the fancies of Dürer .... but appearing as trees that only one man has ever perceived and drawn....'[15]

Turning to the book, *The Pall Mall Gazette* wrote: 'It is not a luxury that spoils us, so much as the frequency of luxury, and when a fine talent like Mr. Rackham's is turned to the production of a beautiful volume once a year, it is odd that we begin to lose all sense of privilege, and to regard the results as an annual due.... This is the handsomest version of *A Midsummer Night's Dream* we have ever handled.'[16]

The tone of the *Midsummer Night's Dream* reviews, compared with those of *Rip Van Winkle* in which Rackham was essentially welcomed as a newcomer, shows that the critics had by now got Rackham's length, and were able to pigeon-hole him. *The Athenaeum*, warning him about listening too closely to public applause, had looked beyond the fantasy subjects to Rackham's great talent as a landscape painter.

By March 1909, three months after publication, the entire de luxe edition of 1,000 copies had been sold out, and of the 15,000 trade copies, 7,650 had been

Left: 'Oh Monstrous! Oh Strange! We are Haunted.'
Pen and ink and watercolour, 1908
176 × 268 mm
Spencer Collection, New York Public Library, Astor,
Lenox and Tilden Foundations

Quince, Snug, Flute, Snout and Starveling in ActIII, sci.

Right: 'Never so weary, never so in woe.'
Pen and ink and watercolour, 1908
272 × 243 mm
British Museum, London

Hermia re-entering the wood in ActIII, scii. Rackham's pen line has the sharpness of etching, and the contrast of soft flesh and silk with aggressive vegetation is masterly.

Elf Attendant on Bottom
Pen and ink and watercolour, 1908
115 × 155 mm
Courtesy of the Board of Trustees of the V&A

sold.[17] The English edition remained in print and paid him royalties until the end of his life.

Rackham's second venture into *A Midsummer Night's Dream* was commissioned in 1928, a few months after he had returned from New York. Following his meeting with E. H. Anderson, the Director of the New York Public Library, he wrote from home with his proposal:

I should supply 12 full page watercolour pictures illustrating 'Midsummer Night's Dream' and various decorations: which would include design for cover, title page, several 'borders' of pages & headings (at the beginning of Acts & scenes) & other occasional designs. For this my fee would be $7500. I have arranged with *Graily Hewitt* who is the acknowledged head of our 'scribes' & illuminators that he would write the text for £750.[18]

Two months later the Library Committee authorized the commission,[19] which Rackham accepted by letter in May.[20] The following May, the work was reaching completion. Rackham wrote again to Anderson:

Do forgive me for not having written to 'report progress'. Actually I have been so immersed in The Midsummer Night that I quite overlooked that I had promised to. But I am glad to report now that it has gone so well that it is very nearly finished. Graily Hewitt's writing is done: I have less than a week's work to do on minor details: & the design for the cover is done. So it only remains to be put in the hands of the binder which I shall be able to do in a very short time.[21]

Soon after this Rackham's health collapsed and all progress on *A Midsummer Night's Dream* came to a halt. He was forced to go into The Empire Nursing Home in St Vincent's Square, London[22] for a prostate operation,[23] and his doctors ordered him to stop all work for six months. Before the operation, however, he was able to send the completed illustrated pages to New York for a special exhibition in the Public Library in December and January,[24] after which they were returned to him for binding.

As the correspondence shows, Rackham was particularly concerned that this edition of *A Midsummer Night's Dream* should be a complete book, a 'book beautiful' in every respect, to match and pay homage to the beauty and brilliance of the text. To ensure this he oversaw every aspect of its production, down to the last detail, from the choice of paper and calligrapher, through the illustrations and their placing, to the design and execution of the binding, and even to the layout of the spine lettering. As binders he chose Sangorski and Sutcliffe of Poland Street, London, and designed a cover with a heraldic Owl Rampant over a double zig-zag and stylized trees, blocked in gold on olive green leather. Requiring perfection from himself, he expected it, too, from others, and his only disappointment with the volume appeared to be the layout of the lettering on the spine: '... the word Midsummer is too long not to be divided. That's the main difficulty. I do not see any way of making it a thing of beauty. But it *is* necessary for utility.... I want it to have the air of considered finish – but not ornately so.'[25]

The title page of the New York volume, with its wide margins decorated with inhabited vine trails, its full panel on the left, and the illuminated letter A of the title, has a medieval quality that reflects its craftsmanlike manner of production. Rackham was naturally aware of medieval illumination, and although his library is now dispersed and there is no catalogue of it, we can be sure it contained reprints of medieval manuscripts such as those published by the Roxburghe Club and *The Studio*. We do know he had owned, since 1926, a copy of *The Studio*'s reprint of *The Book of Kells*.[26]

Rackham's delight in the gothic contortions of natural forms and in grotesquely fashioned creatures, has a long, sinister pedigree in English and Continental art. An early appearance is in medieval manuscripts, such as bestiaries, psalters and Bibles, where grotesques and frivolities cavort amongst the margins, or writhe painfully in Harrowing of Hell or Last Judgement scenes. Many of these manuscripts were being studied by scholars and published in good quality reproductions, notably by the Roxburghe Club, even as Rackham worked. Northern European fifteenth- and sixteenth-century painters such as Bosch, Dürer, Bruegel, Grünewald and Altdorfer continue the tradition, and their work would undoubtedly have been seen by Rackham on his travels in Europe. Nearer Rackham's lifetime, the work of Richard Dadd, Dicky Doyle, Holman Hunt and Joseph Noel Paton depicted fairies and elves, while the darker side of the subject was developed by Beardsley, William de Morgan, Victor Hugo and Rudolph Bresdin, the French etcher who taught Odilon Redon. Decorative work comparable to Rackham's appears in the buildings of the Gothic Revival architect A. W. N. Pugin, and in the work of the architects of two of Rackham's London residences, Alfred Waterhouse and Charles Voysey.

Cover for the manuscript version of *A Midsummer Night's Dream*, 1930
388 × 286 mm
Designed by Arthur Rackham and made by Sangorski and Sutcliffe, London
Spencer Collection, New York Public Library, Astor, Lenox and Tilden Foundations

The Fairies Sing *ActII sci*
Pen and ink and watercolour, 1928–29
388 × 572 mm
Spencer Collection, New York Public Library, Astor,
Lenox and Tilden Foundations/Bridgeman Art
Library

As Rackham fed upon medieval influences, so medievalists fed upon Rackham. It is no coincidence that one of the great scholars of medieval manuscript painting, Eric G. Millar, owned four Rackham drawings.[27] Rackham did not, however, want his *A Midsummer Night's Dream* to be classed as a 'medieval' production. Writing to Alwin Scheuer, he said in 1931:

So far as I know that is the first book quite of that kind. It hardly groups with illuminated MSS either old or new, and it might well initiate a movement.... I hear the MND is much liked.... The business now done in modern illuminated missals etc though very delightful, is not in the same group. The artists are specialists, & are following a medieval practise. They are not creators. Without being open to the charge of being conceited, I may, to you, claim that my work should be put out in a different way, at a different level, as of a different &, I hope, more original & modern order of creative, imaginative art.[28]

Rackham sent the completed, bound volume off to New York where it was received in December 1930,[29] along with his bill for $8,960, efficiently within his $9,000 estimate of 1928. Sending payment to the binders for their work, Rackham expressed a slight restless dissatisfaction, a creator's licence, born of aiming for, but never quite reaching, perfection. Despite the 'admiration & satisfaction' that he reported had been expressed by the New York Public Library, he told Sangorski and Sutcliffe:

For my part I have nothing but praise for your work – only I wonder if I have such a job to put through again whether you & I together couldn't invent some system of binding which would enable a book to be opened flat – even while it is new.[30]

In technique the illustrations are softer in tone than the 1908 version, and lack the latter's sharply linear quality, the handling that prompted the critic of *The Westminster Gazette* to remark: 'One never sees Mr Rackham's work without an involuntary feeling of regret that he does not etch. He has so keen a feeling for the value of pure line ... that it seems a pity for him to deny himself the conquest of this kingdom.'[31]

The New York illustrations also have less of the feeling of night, less of the visionary spry spookiness that Rackham so brilliantly made his own in 1908. On the other hand there is more stylization in the New York version: Helena and Hermia have short bobbed

hair, and look as if at any moment they might jump up from the cowslip beds and break into a Charleston. If Bottom and his fellow mechanicals seem quite as rustic as their 1908 counterparts, the creatures that invade the borders of their illustration have a Disneyesque quality and sit on Art Deco-out-of-Celtic cloud trails.

Rackham's agreement to undertake what he surely knew would be his final treatment of the play 'in which I should find myself most at home,'[32] delighted George Macy, who wrote in March 1936: 'I don't believe I have written you that I tried to persuade the Trustees of the New York Public Library to let us reproduce the illustrations in their possession, but they were jealous of their monopoly, and would not give us this permission.'[33]

Working very slowly on the illustrations, Rackham was making good progress by Christmas 1936: 'My six drawings will all be in colour. They are well on now & should be done early in the spring at the latest.... I am rather hoping you'll do them in collotype which, at its best, *is* the best. But they will be suitable for 3 or 4 colour also. (I *prefer* 3 colour – but so long as it is good I do not mind either way.)'[34]

Without consulting him, Limited Editions Club chose to ignore Rackham's advice and reproduce his illustrations by lithography, employing the lithographer Fernand Mourlot of Paris, with colouring by Beaufumé.[35] While the plates were being made and the proofs prepared, Rackham had moved on to his series of *Wind in the Willows* illustrations for Macy. He had also fallen very ill again. Writing to Macy in November 1938, he said: 'My doctors tell me I must not be in too much of a hurry – but that's about all they can do for me.'[36] When the proofs for *A Midsummer Night's Dream* came through, Rackham was disappointed and certainly hurt that his friend Macy had

A Fairy Song, Pen and ink and watercolour, 1928–29, Spencer Collection, New York Public Library, Astor, Lenox and Tilden Foundations/Bridgeman Art Library

Act II. Scene II. A Fairy Song.

not listened to him. He had given the advice he did, not to avoid any process that was 'new fangled', and offensive to his rigid conservatism, but because Rackham had developed his technique to his chosen process, and he was certainly too old and ill to change now. If they commissioned him, he expected them to do so on his own terms. He wrote to Macy:

(signature: Arthur Rackham)

Right: 'I go, I go; look how I go, swifter than arrow from Tartar's bow'
Pen and ink and watercolour, 1928–29
388 × 286 mm
Spencer Collection, New York Public Library, Astor, Lenox and Tilden Foundations

Puck, making an exit with a ballet dancer's leap, in ActIII, scii.

Far right: 'So Goodnight Unto You All'
Pen and ink and watercolour, 1937
Arthur Rackham Collection, Rare Book and Manuscript Library, Columbia University

Rackham's final illustration for the 1939 edition, and Puck's last curtain.

I wish I knew what to say about the set of proofs of the 'Dream'. I wish I could say I liked them but I do not. I do not know by what process they are produced, but I think it is one for which my work is not fitted.

I deal in colours that melt into one another, with gradual gradations. This process is granular & spotty, & here & there individual colours start out without any relation to the neighbouring colours.

I do not know what to say to correct them. My work is specially adapted to the 3-col. process, in which each colour is printed in a different strength, over the whole surface.... I am convinced that all efforts to better that process have failed so far – for full colour, modulated paintings, and all my success has been with *3-col.* work, so I believe my best plan is to stick with it, & try no experiments.[37]

For its part, the Limited Editions Club attempted to justify the new medium to its subscribers in a defensive statement in their Club leaflet:

Mr. Rackham ... has usually insisted that his illustrations should be reproduced by the photo-engraving process, by half-tone process blocks. Such a process gives a facsimile reproduction of the drawings; but the fine dots involved in half-tone blocks require that they be printed on coated paper; and we refused to permit the inclusion of coated paper in our Shakespeare. We decided to defy the lightening and to have Mr. Rackham's illustrations reproduced in a different manner this time ... as though the artist himself had made the reproductions with his own brush.... The result is that Mr.

Rackham's reproductions are not facsimiles of the originals.... But we consider they preserve the spirit of Mr. Rackham's drawings, and are infinitely more beautiful in reproduction.

Had Rackham died at this point – as he might well have done – we would inevitably have been left with the nasty taste in the mouth, that he had had his last work abused by his publisher, who had wilfully defied him. Happily, however, only three weeks before he died, Rackham received his copy of the Limited Editions Club *A Midsummer Night's Dream*, whose title page, significantly, carried the line 'Illustrated *from* Watercolours by Arthur Rackham'.[38] He was able to write to Macy: 'Now I have seen the book I do agree with you that the method of reproduction you have chosen is more fitting than the 3-col. process. It is a fine edition. Some of the reproductions are as good as they could be....' Rackham did, however, withhold his *complete* pardon, by adding the parting shot '... – one or two – not so good.'[39]

In all his treatments of *A Midsummer Night's Dream* he returned again and again to the lines that had inspired him in the 1908 version. One scene, however, Rackham left until his last treatment of the play, as if he could not bear to illustrate it before he really meant to hear Puck say these lines for him at his own final curtain:

So, good night unto you all.
Give me your hands, if we be friends,
And Robin shall restore amends.

Building the House for Maimie, Pen and ink and watercolour, 1906, Leeds City Art Galleries

NOTES

ABBREVIATIONS IN NOTES

AR: Arthur Rackham
ER: Edyth Rackham
AWG: Art Workers' Guild
BLCU, NY: Butler Library, Columbia University, New York
GETTINGS: Gettings, Fred: *Arthur Rackham*; Studio Vista, 1975
HRHRC, AUSTIN: Harry Ransom Humanities Research Center, University of Texas at Austin, USA
HUDSON: Hudson, Derek: *Arthur Rackham: His Life and Work*; Heinemann, 1960
LUL: Louisville University Library, Kentucky, USA
NYPL: Rare Book Dept., New York Public Library, USA
PFL: Spencer Collection, Free Library of Philadelphia, USA
RF: Rackham Family Collections
V & A, NAL: Victoria & Albert Museum, National Art Gallery
Abbreviations for dates are given in UK format throughout eg 1.2.03 signifies 1 Feb 1903.

INTRODUCTION

1 Walter Starkie to Derek Hudson, *c.*1959, quoted HUDSON, p. 50.

2 E.V. Lucas writing to AR, 29.3.05. RF.

3 Martin Birnbaum. Introduction to Frederick Coykendall: *Arthur Rackham – A List of Books Illustrated by him*; New York, 1922.

4 Kenneth Clark: *Another Part of the Wood*; 1974, p. 8.

5 C.S. Lewis: *Surprised by Joy*; 1955, p. 74.

6 Roger Berthoud: *Graham Sutherland: A Biography*; 1982, p. 30.

7 AR to N. Carroll, 14.9.31. PFL.

CHAPTER ONE

1 Now renamed Deacon Street.

2 RF.

3 'Dr. Birkbeck' was Dr George Birkbeck (1776–1841), the founder of the mechanics' institutes, one of which, the London Mechanics', developed into Birkbeck College, now part of London University.

4 A Proctor in Doctors' Commons approximated to what we now know as a solicitor.

5 *David Copperfield*, Chapter 23.

6 1871 Census (South Lambeth 673/37) records the household as follows:
Alfred T. Rackham, 41, Civil Service Reg. Clerk Admiralty.
Annie Rackham, 37
Percy Rackham, 6
Margaret Rackham, 4
Harris Rackham, 2
Infant no name, under 1 mo. [i.e. Ethel]
Thomas Rackham, 68
Jane Rackham, 68
Ellen Gooch, 50, Monthly nurse, born London
Lucy L. Darton, 50, Nurse, born New York, British Subject
Mahala Lynds, 21, General Servant, born Kent
Very curiously, Arthur, then aged 4, is not listed in this census. Wherever was the boy?

7 Winifred Adams to Barbara Edwards, 5.7.57.

8 S.J. Kunitz and H. Haycraft: *The Junior Book of Authors*; New York, H.H. Wilson Co., 1934 (2nd edn. 1951), p. 252.

9 Marita Ross: 'The Beloved Enchanter'; *Everybody's Weekly*, 27.9.47, pp. 10–11.

10 Martin Birnbaum: *Jacoleff and Other Artists*; New York, 1946, p. 184.

11 Arthur Rackham: 'In Praise of Water Colour'; *Old Water-Colour Society's Club*, 11th Vol. (1933–34), pp. 51–2.

12 Elizabeth Stevenson to AR, 27.2.77. RF.

13 Gladys Beattie Crozier: 'The Art of Arthur Rackham'; *Girl's Realm*, Nov. 1908, pp. 3–12.

14 Gentleman's Magazine [?], 4.11.81.

15 i, Phil. Trans., vol. xlvi, p. 160. Quoted Blea Allan: *The Tradescants: Their Plants, Garden and Museum 1570–1662*; London, 1964, pp. 227–8.

16 John Loudon: *Arboretum Britannicum*, 1838.

17 Perceval Bequest, Museum Scrapbook, Fitzwilliam Museum. Quoted Blea Allan: *op. cit.*, p. 228.

18 AR to Frederick Mason, 11.1.34. BLCU, NY.

19 2 Samuel, Ch. 18, v. 9–17.

20 Now 5 St Ann's Park Road.

21 Survey of London: Vol. XXVI: *The Parish of St. Mary at Lambeth, Pt 2: Southern Area*; University of London/London County Council, 1956, p. 130. See also the church foundation stone. The building became Our Lady of the Rosary R.C. Church in 1953.

22 *Unitarianism: Some Questions Answered*; Lindsay Press, 1962, para 1.

23 Olive J. Brose: *Frederick Denison Maurice: Rebellious Conformist*; Ohio U.P., 1971.

24 L.E. Elliott-Binns: *Religion in Victorian England*; 1936.

25 31.1.10. See also Chapter 4.

26 Bernard Rackham was to spend his entire career in the South Kensington Museum – later the Victoria and Albert – retiring as the highly distinguished Keeper of Ceramics in 1938.

27 23.8.09. This letter, written to a then aspiring artist, Mr W.E. Dawe, was discovered by Derek Hudson, and published by him in its entirety, HUDSON, pp. 30–6.

28 Rackham family tradition has it that they were descended from the pirate John Rackham, who was hanged for piracy at Port Royal, Jamaica, in 1720.

29 26.12.22. PFL.

CHAPTER TWO

1 A.E. Douglas-Smith: *The City of London School*; Oxford, 1965 (2nd edn.), p. 554.

2 City of London School: *Old Citizens Gazette*; December 1939, p. 4.

3 Winifred Adams to Barbara Edwards, letter *cit*.

4 Letter 28.6.29. Quoted HUDSON, p. 25.

5 City of London School lists.

6 RF.

7 RF.

8 RF.

9 *Old Water-Colour Society's Club, loc. cit.*

10 The 1881 Census (South Lambeth 604/62v), taken when the family were still at 210 South Lambeth Road, lists the household as: Alfred & Annie Rackham; Margaret (14); Arthur (13); Harris (12); Winifred (7); Bernard (4); Stanley (3); Maurice (1); Ann Tucker, servant; Ada C. Barrel, servant.

11 Now the City and Guilds of London Art School.

12 *DNB. Dictionary of National Biography.*

13 AR to Ethel Chadwick, 8.9.09. PFL.

14 AR to Kerrison Preston, 18.2.27. Henry E. Huntington Library, San Marino, California.

15 AR to Mrs Edward Parsons, 10.1.32. PFL.

16 Sturge Moore to AR, 7.6.39. RF.

17 Thomas Herbert Dicksee, the brother of Sir Frank Dicksee PRA, later became an accomplished etcher and Member of the Royal Society of Painter-Etchers and Engravers; Llewellyn became President of the Royal Academy.

18 AR to Mr Wilson, 13.3.32. PFL.

19 AR to Mr Wilson, posted 16.2.33. PFL.

20 Westminster Fire Office, Directors' Minutes, 20.11.84, p. 37. Westminster Borough Libraries, Archives. The Westminster Fire Office (WFO) is now part of the Sun Alliance and London Insurance Group.

21 Reference, from Edwin Abbott, 11.11.84 RF.

22 *loc. cit.*, p. 368.

23 Francis George Ryves, the purchaser of Rackham's *Cottages at Pett*, see below, was another. WFO, 23.12.86, p. 426.

24 WFO 8.8.89, pp. 442–8; and WFO *Rules etc*, May 1897 [WBL 343/112/36].

25 Junior Clerks' starting salaries: Sun Fire Office: £70; Royal Exchange: £90; Law Fire: £50. Figures quoted WFO 8.8.89, pp. 444–5.

26 Old Water Colour Society's Club, *loc. cit.*

27 AR to W.E. Dawe, *cit*. Quoted HUDSON, *loc. cit.*

28 Algernon Graves: *Royal Academy Exhibitors 1769–1904.*

29 AR Sales Book. RF.

30 Antique Collectors Club: *Works Exhibited at the Royal Society of British Artists 1824–93*; 1975.

31 *Scraps*, 4.10.84; *Illustrated Bits*, 15.11.84 and 3.1.85.

32 AR to Frederick Mason, 11.1.34. BLCU, NY.

33 Letter from Amy Tompkins's daughter, Miss May Maitland, 29.9.1969. Miss Maitland dates the romance to 1885–86. BLCU, NY.

34 No name, no date for sale. BLCU, NY files.

35 Information from three letters to Derek Hudson from Walter Freeman's daughter, Mrs Winifred Wheeler, 21.10.57, 6.11.57 and 20.11.57. BLCU, NY.

36 *ibid*, 21.10.57.

37 City and Guilds of London Art School records.

38 WFO 4.2.92, pp. 24–5.

39 Kelly's Post Office London Directory.

40 Kelly's Directory, 1893, p. 239.

41 E.B. Chancellor: *The Annals of the Strand*; London, 1912, p. 105.

42 Kelly's Directory, 1895, p. 233.

43 *Pall Mall Budget* 14.1.92, p. 63.

44 *Pall Mall Budget* 21.1.92, p. 78.

45 *Pall Mall Budget* 4.2.92, p. 170.

46 *Pall Mall Budget* 11.2.92, p. 198.

47 *Pall Mall Budget* 17.3.92, p. 399.

48 *Pall Mall Budget* 2.6.92, p. 794.

49 *Pall Mall Budget* 28.4.92, p. 621.

50 Rackham himself described his eyes as 'grey' in his *Defence of the Realm Permit Book*, 17.7.17. RF.

51 Aubrey Beardsley to G.F. Scotson-Clark, c.15.2.93 [Princeton University]; quoted in Henry Maas: *The Letters of Aubrey Beardsley*; 1970, pp. 43–4.

52 10 of the original drawings for *To the Other Side* are in PFL.

53 AR to N. Carroll, 14.9.31. PFL.

54 AR to M.D. McGoff, 4.5.36. LUL.

55 It seems he travelled with the author, as there is a pen and ink drawing of *Leiston Abbey* inscribed by Arthur: 'Sketched in train from Wells to Overstrand with Mrs. B'. As Leiston Abbey is on the Suffolk Coast and the Wells and Overstrand line ran along the North Norfolk coast, one can only assume that at the time Arthur was drawing the picture from memory or working up an earlier sketch. Perhaps on this trip Rackham also made the small oil on canvas, 228 x 293 mm, s&d 1893, of a village scene with sand dunes. BLCU, NY.

56 H.R. Dent (ed.): *The House of Dent 1888–1938*; London, 1938, p. 70.

57 *Chums*, 23.10.97.

58 *Little Folks* was launched in 1871, in the wake of the Educational Reform Act which stipulated that all children must be taught to read. Its special quality and success lay in the fact that although *Little Folks* had a sound moral tone and the intention to make readers 'good, gentle and industrious', it was 'one degree less didactic, less obtrusively pious, less "goody-goody" than the rival productions of the Sunday School Union and others' [Quotes from Simon Nowell-Smith: *The House of Cassell*; London, 1958, p. 128]. Rackham's illustrations had a suitable robustness and good humour that accorded well with the principles of the magazine and its publishers.

59 Sam Hamer (c.1867–1941). School friend of Rackham's at City of London School. On the editorial staff of Cassell & Co. 1886–1907; Editor of *Little Folks* 1895–1907; Secretary of the National Trust 1911–34. CBE 1935. Writer on travel and Wagner. Amateur musician. [Information from *Who Was Who* and Dr John Andrewes.]

60 Herbert Andrewes (1863–1950): Forestry in India, collector of and writer on beetles; author of the definitive work on *Carabidae* (black beetles). Married to Sam Hamer's sister, Margaret. Percy Andrewes (1866–1940): Schoolmaster. The Hamer and Andrewes families lived near to each other in Highgate, where Rackham was a frequent visitor. [Information from Dr John Andrewes.] Rackham made book-plates for Herbert Andrewes's daughter, Ursula and designs for a book-plate for Percy Andrewes in 1909. BLCU, NY, Sketchbook F7.

61 Percy Andrewes to AR, 21.1.27. RF.

62 Frank Keen to AR, ?.1.08. RF.

63 BLCU, NY, Sketchbook F30. Includes sketches of village scenes, mountain and lake or fjord views, views in England and (?) Germany, and a view of 'Charmouth, Dorsetshire'. Not dated, but certainly in use in 1898.

64 Hans Reusch to AR, 15.11.98. RF.

65 Jean Marie Carré: 'Arthur Rackham'; *L'Art et les Artistes*, Paris, June 1912, pp. 104–12.

66 Quoted in Geoffrey Skelton: *Wagner at Bayreuth*; London, 1967, p. 89.

67 *ibid.*, p. 221.

68 RF.

69 RF.

70 One of the references comes in a letter from Hans Reusch to Rackham, thanking him for sending some published examples of Beardsley's work: 'Beardsley is extremely interesting and Phil May is very good'. 9.12.98. RF.

71 RF.

72 RF.

73 *Westminster Budget*, 20.7.94.

CHAPTER THREE

1 *War Cranks*, March 1900, p. 366.

2 H. R. Dent (ed.): *op. cit.*, p. 101.

3 This and subsequent income and expenditure figures are taken from Rackham's Account Books, RF except where indicated.

4 Dr Hans Reusch to AR, 3.6.98. RF.

5 *Old Water-Colour Society Club*, *loc. cit.*.

6 Kelly's Directory of London.

7 'I often think of the old Highgate days, when I pushed my bicycle up the West Hill'. Letter to A.E. Bonser, 11.1.30. PFL.

8 Algernon Graves: *op. cit.* Alfred Rackham records in his *Personal Recollections* that Edyth exhibited at the Paris Salon in 1884, when she was 17. The present writer has not, however, found trace of her in the Salon catalogues of the 1880s or 1890s.

9 This and subsequent information about Edyth Starkie comes from conversations between the present writer and Barbara Edwards in 1989, and from an unpublished Memoir written *c.*1959 by Mrs Edwards. This was drawn upon by Derek Hudson, pp. 54–5.

10 Walter Starkie claims that Edyth, his Aunt, had been engaged seven times. Walter Starkie: *Scholars and Gypsies*; London, 1963, pp. 18–19, and Hudson, p. 56.

11 'The Worst Time in My Life'; *The Bookman*, Oct. 1925, Vol. 69, p. 7.

12 Barbara Edwards.

13 AR to W.T. Whitley, n.d. [from 54A Parkhill Rd]. BLCU, NY.

14 E.J. Sullivan to AR, 16.7.1900. RF.

15 E.J. Sullivan to AR 14.12.01 and 16.1.02; note in AR's hand recording repayments on reverse of letter 16.7.1900. RF.

16 AR to Mr Barrett, 30.12.02. PFL.

17 Also known as *Sunset, Saas Fee, Switzerland*. It was bought by Harris Rackham.

18 *Outlook*, 24.10.03.

19 *Daily Telegraph*, 30.11.03.

20 1902 Langham Sketching Club Catalogue. V&A, NAL.

21 Three subjects that Rackham tackled with the Club in 1903, 1907 and 1908.

22 Introduction to catalogue of Sketches by Geo. C. Haité, President of the Langham Sketching Club, 1896. V&A, NAL.

23 Ref. Sotheby's 29/30.11.1989, lot 421.

24 RF.

25 I am grateful to Mrs Dorothy Gibbs for bringing this point to my attention.

26 AR to Stanley Rackham, 1.9.03. RF.

27 In a letter to Frank P. Harris, 3.10.38 [PFL], AR writes: '… what laid me low was a haemorrhage, apparently due to an old bladder operation.…'

28 Harris Rackham to AR, 10.7.03. RF.

29 Barbara Edwards.

30 Mina Welland to AR, n.d. [1903]. RF.

31 AR to Stanley Rackham, *cit.*

32 *ibid.*

33 Letter of invitation, 29.9.03. RF. See also letter AR to Z. Merton, 19.1.04, BLCU, NY. The exhibited works included *Andromeda* and *Rumplestiltskin*, exhibited uncoloured. Ref: Royal Commission: *St. Louis International Exhibition, 1904*; compiled by M.H. Spielmann; 1906, pp. 151, 152, 170 and 171.

34 *Birmingham Post*, 9.4.04.

35 Letter from AR to George Routledge & Sons, 5.7.04. PFL.

36 See AR to Robert Bateman, Director of the Whitworth Institute, Manchester, 12.10.05. BLCU, NY.

37 *Birmingham Post*, 9.4.04.

38 *Daily Chronicle*, 11.3.05.

39 Charles Hiatt: 'A New German Designer – Joseph Sattler'; *The Studio*, IV, 1894, pp. 92–97; and *The Studio*, X, 1897, p. 65.

40 *The Times*, 22.9.05.

41 *The Athenaeum*, 25.11.05.

42 AR to Margaret Farjeon, 19.5.06. Private collection.

43 Eleanor Farjeon: 'Arthur Rackham – The Wizard at Home'; *St. Nicholas*, New York, March 1914, pp. 385–9.

44 AR to Eleanor Farjeon, 17.12.13. Private collection.

45 E.V. Lucas to AR, 29.3.05. RF.

46 Clayton Calthrop to AR, 9.10.05. RF.

47 Ernest Brown and Phillips to AR, 11.4.05. RF.

48 Hodder and Stoughton had in 1905 just entered the special art book field. John Attenborough: *A Living Memory: Hodder and Stoughton Publishers 1868–1975*; 1975; pp. 55–6.

49 Rackham's own priced copy of the exhibition catalogue. RF.

50 AR to Routledge, letter *cit.*

51 AR to Robert Bateman, letter *cit.*

52 Alfred Rackham: *Personal Recollections*. RF.

53 Walter Starkie: *op. cit.*, pp. 18–19.

54 J. G. Frazer: *The Golden Bough*; Macmillan, St Martin's Edition, 1957, p. 145.

55 James Barrie to AR, 18.12.06. RF.

56 AR to Eleanor Farjeon, 17 and 18.12.13. Private collection.

57 *Liverpool Post*, 12.12.06.

58 *Manchester Guardian*, 11.12.06.

59 *The Times*, 14.12.06.

60 *Daily Express*, 18.12.06.

61 *The Star*, 11.12.06.

CHAPTER FOUR

1 Rackham gives this information on a loose sheet inside his Account Book. **RF**.

2 AR to Routledge, *cit.*

3 Invitation, n.d. [1905], with added note in Rackham's hand. **RF**.

4 AR to Bateman, *cit.*

5 Duncan Simpson: *C.F.A. Voysey: An Architect of Individuality*; 1979, p. 149.

6 The address is omitted from the 1906 *Kelly's Directory*, suggesting that for part if not all of that year it was between occupants and being altered.

7 'Celebrities at Home'; *The World*, 17.12.07.

8 Gladys Beattie Crozier: *op. cit.*

9 Clara T. Mac Chesney: 'The Value of Fairies – What Arthur Rackham Has Done to Save them for the Children of the Whole World'; *The Craftsman*, New York, Vol. XXVII, Dec. 1914.

10 AR to Alfred Mart, 2.10.09. **BLCU, NY**.

11 Conversations with Barbara Edwards, 1989, remembering her father as he was when she was aged about ten, i.e. *c.*1918.

12 G.B. Crozier: *op. cit.*

13 Clara T. Mac Chesney: *op. cit.*

14 A.L. Baldry: *The Practice of Watercolour Painting*; 1911, p. 112.

15 AR entered into a contract on 2.3.06, later cancelled, with Heinemann to produce 12 colour and 4 black and white drawings for a proposed edition of *The Sleeping Beauty*. **RF**.

16 AR to E.A. Osborne, 21.7.35. **HRHRC, AUSTIN**.

17 *The Bookman*, New York, Vol. XXX, Sep. 1909.

18 G.B. Shaw to AR, 15.3.11. **RF**.

19 Charles Holroyd to AR, 20.3.11. **RF**.

20 Walter Starkie: *op. cit.*, p. 18.

21 A.E. Douglas-Smith: *op. cit.*, p. 271.

22 Eleanor Farjeon: *op. cit.*

23 *ibid.*

24 AR to Eleanor Farjeon, 18.12.13. Private collection.

25 His experience of a press cuttings agency was not as brief as Rackham suggests. Romeike and Curtice supplied him with cuttings for at least seven years, from 1903 to 1910. **RF**.

26 'The Value of Criticism'; *The Bookman*, London, Vol. 71, Oct. 1926, p. 11.

27 *The Sphere*. (Reference not traced)

28 *Evening Standard*, 14.12.39.

29 Reproductions of some of these illustrations are collected in Graham Ovenden and John Davis: *Illustrators of Alice*; 1972.

30 *Punch*, 4.12.07, p. 411.

31 *ibid.*, p. 414.

32 *The Times*, 5.12.07.

33 As it happened, Macmillan's had already invited Rackham to illustrate *Through the Looking Glass*, of which they still held the copyright, for an edition to be produced uniform with the coming Heinemann *Alice*. Letter to Rackham, 22.10.07. **RF**. Rackham did not take the offer up.

34 *Daily Telegraph*, 27.11.07.

35 Rackham's Sales Book. **RF**.

36 7,364 copies of the trade edition of *Peter Pan* sold in the first 9 months from publication. *Loc. cit.*

37 H.R. Robertson to AR, 11.12.07. **RF**.

38 Claude Shepperson to AR, n.d. [Jan. 1908]. **RF**.

39 Ernest Brown and Phillips to AR, 18.1.08. **RF**.

40 Hugh Rivière to AR, 20.1.08. **RF**.

41 It was reported in the *Daily Mail*, *The Times* and the *Morning Post*.

42 *St. Nicholas*, New York, Vol. XLI, Dec. 1913, p. 163.

43 *Daily Mirror*, 23.11.08. Photograph 24.11.08.

44 31.1.10. Quotations taken from the report in the *Morning Post* 1.2.10.

45 AR's Account Books. **RF**.

46 Bernard Rackham to AR, 17.1.08. **RF**.

47 Letter, n.d. [1907]. **RF**.

48 Clara T. Mac Chesney: *op. cit.*

49 AR to Mr Clare, 15.3.09. **BLCU, NY**.

50 AR to Z. Merton, 5.3.12 and 23.10.12. **BLCU, NY**.

51 AR to Alfred Mart, 26.5.09. **BLCU, NY**.

52 *Morning Post*, 7.11.07.

53 AR Account Books. **RF**.

54 *Loc. cit.*

55 AR to Alfred Mart, 9.6.09. **BLCU, NY**.

56 Certificate of Associateship. **RF**.

57 18.5.12, as translated by AR and sent to W.T. Whitley, 30.5.12. **BLCU, NY**.

58 AR to Margaret Farjeon, 17.11.10. **HRHRC, AUSTIN**.

59 John Attenborough: *op. cit.*, pp. 69–70.

60 AR to E.A. Osborne, 27.10.36. **BLCU, NY**.

61 Try as I might, I have not been able to retrace the source for this information, which I picked up from the back of a record cover during an idle moment in the 1970s. JH.

62 Writing to Debussy in 1914 about Chouchou, Paul-Jean Toulet says: 'She firmly believed in fairies the last time I saw her, perhaps when I see her next she will be a Bergsonian.' Edward Lockspeiser: *Debussy: His Life and Mind*; 1965, Vol. II, p. 198.

63 Colin White: *Edmund Dulac*; 1976. James Hamilton and Colin White: *Edmund Dulac 1882–1953: A Centenary Exhibition*; Sheffield City Art Galleries, 1982.

64 **RF**.

65 *The Observer*, 24.11.07.

66 *The Athenaeum*, 23.11.07.

67 *Pall Mall Gazette*, 27.11.08.

68 *The World*, 17.12.08.

69 *Daily News*, 6.10.10.

70 AR to Z. Merton, 23.10.12. **BLCU, NY**.

71 AR to Margaret Farjeon, 17.11.10. **HRHRC, AUSTIN**.

72 AR to Rachel Fry, 21.9.10. Quoted **HUDSON** pp. 90 and 92.

73 C.S. Lewis: *op. cit.*, p. 77.

74 Illustration to Arthur Morrison's short story *A Seller of Hate*, published in *The Graphic*, 23.2.07.

75 Ref. letters to AR from Cayley Robinson, Herbert Hughes-Stanton, T.M. Rooke, Henry S. Tuke and William T. Wood, 31 [*sic*].6.20–4.7.20. **RF**.

76 RWS Minutes, 15.11.11.

77 AR to ER, 13.10.32. **RF**.

78 AWG Minutes, 7.5.09. Votes cast: **AR**: 42; S.J. Cartlidge: 38; A.J. Mavrogordato: 24. Rackham's sponsors were C.F.A. Voysey and Robert Anning Bell.

79 Will Mellor to AR, 7.6.09. **RF**.

80 Given by J.D. Batten, 5.5.09.

81 Given by T.M. Rooke, 5.11.09.

82 Given by Laurence Binyon, 18.3.10.

83 Given with W.K. Shirley, 4.11.10.

84 Given with S. Finberg, Anning Bell and Spence, 17.3.11.

85 Rackham seems to be lacing his words with irony here. It was Reed who had lampooned Rackham's *Alice* in *Punch*, *loc. cit.*

86 *Daily News*, *loc. cit.*

87 *Pall Mall Gazette*, 10.10.10.

88 *Morning Leader*, 15.10.10.

89 *Morning Leader*, 18.10.10.

90 Hans W. Singer: 'German Pen Drawings'; *Modern Pen Drawings: European & American – Studio Special Number*, 1900–1, p. 160.

91 In 1915, the first year from which detailed accounts of his expenses survive [RF], Rackham was a paid-up member of eight arts societies: National Portrait Society, International Society, Art Workers' Guild, International Arts League, Arts Club, Langham Sketch Club, Society of Artists and the Royal Watercolour Society.

92 Clara Mac Chesney: *op. cit.*

93 AR to Z. Merton, 6.3.05. BLCU, NY.

94 AR to Lewis Melville, 1.4.11. PFL.

CHAPTER FIVE

1 Lili Müzinger to ER, 6.6.15. RF.

2 Alle Starkie to ER, 3.12.16. RF.

3 Lili Müzinger to ER, 12.7.15. RF.

4 Lili Müzinger to ER, ?.7.15. RF.

5 Lili Müzinger to ER, 24.8.15. RF.

6 Lili Müzinger to ER, 20.9.15; postmarked 7.1.16. RF.

7 AR's Account Book. RF.

8 Print runs of English first edition (trade): *Alice* (1907): 21,000; *Midsummer Night's Dream* (1908): 15,000; *Undine* (1909): 10,000; *Rhinegold and Valkyrie* (1910): 10,100; *Siegfried and the Twilight of the Gods* (1911): 10,000; *Aesop's Fables* (1912): 15,000; *Mother Goose* (1913): 10,000; *Book of Pictures* (1913): 6,000. [Information from AR's Account Books. RF.]

9 Millicent Jacob to AR, 24.2.191?. RF.

10 J.M. Carré: *op. cit.* Letter J.M. Carré to AR, 15.10.17. RF.

11 Walter Starkie: *op. cit.*, p. 166.

12 AR's Defence of the Realm Permit Book, 10.8.17. RF.

13 Roger Berthoud: *op. cit.*

14 AR to ER, Monday, n.d. [1917]. RF.

15 AR to Herbert Farjeon, 16.5.17. BLCU, NY.

16 Walter Starkie: *op. cit.*, p. 167.

17 Lili Müzinger to ER, 30.1.17. RF.

18 *ibid.*, 25.7.19. RF.

19 ER to Lili Müzinger, 11.8.19. RF.

20 ER to Alle Starkie, 9.11.19. RF.

CHAPTER SIX

1 AWG Minutes, 21.2.19.

2 *ibid*, and 2.5.19.

3 4.4.19.

4 7.11.19.

5 19.12.19.

6 AR spoke after F.D. Bedford's lecture on *Art for Children*, 11.7.19, and after Prof. E. Gardiner's paper on *Silhouette in Greek Art*, 7.11.19.

7 Ref. letter AR to an unidentified recipient, 6.1.19. PFL.

8 AR to Herbert Farjeon, 28.10.18. PFL.

9 Letters AR to Alfred Mart, 18.3.18–[?]1920. Sotheby's 1–2.12.1988, lot 332.

10 AR paid rates for Houghton House from May 1920. AR's Account Books. RF.

11 AR to Catharine Jones, 20.4.35. PFL. '... The Down beyond ... is called Rackham Hill. There is a hamlet of the name below it, but I cannot trace my family back to it though it is more than likely that we did originally live there & took the name when we migrated to Suffolk where there are lots of us....'

12 P.G. Konody: 'The Home of the Wee Folk: Where Arthur Rackham Lives and Works in the Heart of the Sussex Downs'; *House Beautiful*, Sep. 1926. Reprinted in *The Horn Book*, May–June 1940, pp. 159–62.

13 AR to Catharine Jones, letter *cit.*

14 *ibid.*

15 Annabel Farjeon: *Morning Has Broken: A Biography of Eleanor Farjeon*; 1986, pp. 130–2.

16 AR to Adèle Von Blon, 20[?].7.36. PFL.

17 This was extant in 1980, when it was seen by Mr Jeremy Maas. It now, to my certain knowledge, no longer exists. JH.

18 AR's Account Books. RF.

19 AR to Eleanor Farjeon, 1.1.23. Private collection.

20 RF.

21 Sir Herbert Hughes-Stanton to AR, n.d. [June 1922]. RF.

22 Two letters Ruth Rackham to AR, 14.11.29 and n.d. [late 1929]. RF.

23 AR to Walter Delaney, 15.3.34. BLCU, NY.

24 AR to A.E. Bonser, 11.1.30. PFL.

25 *Puck of Pook's Hill*, (1906); *Good Night* (1907) and *Snickerty Nick* (1919).

26 William P. Gibbons: 'Sir [*sic*] Arthur Rackham's Adventure in Advertising Art'; *The Artist and Advertiser*, Jan. 1931, pp. 6–8. The article reports that only 'about ten' of the originals survived a fire in the Colgate offices in the late 1920s.

27 AR to Eleanor Farjeon, 1.1.23. Private collection.

28 Walter Starkie: *op. cit.*, p. 90.

29 *The Dublin Independent*, 12.12.20.

30 AR to Alwin Schleuer, 21.10.31. BLCU, NY.

31 AR to A.E. Bonser, letter *cit.*

32 AR to Eleanor Farjeon, 1.1.23, *cit.* Private collection.

33 *The Times*, 24.6.25.

34 AR to ER, 2–9.1.27. RF.

35 AR to ER, 12.11.27. RF.

36 AR to ER, 12.11.27. RF.

37 AR to ER, 14.11.27. RF.

38 AR to ER, *c.*16.11.27. RF.

39 AR to ER, 18.11.27. RF.

40 AR to ER, 20.11.27. RF.

41 AR to ER, 18.11.27. RF.

42 AR to ER, 29.11.27. RF.

43 AR to ER, 1.12.27. RF.

44 AR to ER, 3.12.27. RF.

45 AR to ER, 3.12.27. RF.

46 AR to ER, 1.12.27. RF.

47 Anne Carroll Moore: 'A Christmas Ride with Arthur Rackham'; *The Horn Book*, Christmas 1939, pp. 369–72.

CHAPTER SEVEN

1 Ref. Alfred Rackham *Personal Recollections*. A note in Harris Rackham's hand reads: '... moved to a house which he [crossed out] his wife had built.'

2 The present [1989] owners of Stilegate, Mr & Mrs Adrian Baulf, have carefully preserved *in situ* the painted dragon which they discovered on the back of Rackham's studio door. I am grateful to them for showing it to me. JH.

3 AR to Edward Tinker, 27.11.30. HRHRC, AUSTIN.

4 *ibid.*

5 R.H. Ward. Letter to Derek Hudson, c.1959. Quoted HUDSON, pp. 136–7.

6 Letter *cit.*, AR to Wilson, 13.3.32. PFL.

7 AR to Wilson, posted 16.2.33. PFL.

8 AR to Alwin Scheuer, 8.4.31. BLCU, NY.

9 AR to Alwin Scheuer, 14.3.31. BLCU, NY.

10 AR to E.A. Osborne, 17.9.35. HRHRC, AUSTIN.

11 AR to Alwin Scheuer, 11.2.31. BLCU, NY.

12 AR to Alwin Scheuer, 8.9.31 and 21.10.31. BLCU, NY.

13 AR to ER, 12.11.31. RF.

14 Sketchbook F29. BLCU, NY.

15 AR to Sydney Carroll, 2.11.33. BLCU, NY.

16 AR to J.C.C. Taylor, 28.12.33. BLCU, NY.

17 H.E. Wortham, *Daily Telegraph*, 27.12.33.

18 AR to Sydney Carroll, 8.2.34. BLCU, NY.

19 AR to Frederick Mason, 11.1.34. BLCU, NY.

20 AR to ER, 13.10.32. RF.

21 Harry C. Marillier to AR, 1.1.31. RF.

22 RF.

23 AR to Miss Lomar, 21.1.07. PFL.

24 AR to N. Carroll, 26.7.31. PFL.

25 AR to Frank P. Harris, 3.10.38. PFL.

26 AR to Adèle von Blon, 20.7.36. PFL.

27 Edmund Davis to ER. 5[?].1.13. RF.

28 Letter of invitation, NPS to ER, 17.6.10. RF.

29 G.M. Curtis, Sec. of WIAC, to ER, 10.2.13. RF.

30 ISSPS to ER, 10.2.15. RF.

31 24.4.23.

32 AR to Eleanor Farjeon, postmarked 18.12.13. Private collection.

33 1929: *Alfred Mart* (76) and *Lieut. Cdr. T. Wontner Smith, J.P.* (78); 1931: *A Lady in a Black Shawl* (19); 1932: *The Artist's daughter, Barbara*; 1934: *Self Portrait: A Transpontine Cockney* (53).

34 AR to Edward Tinker, 26.6.29. HRHRC, AUSTIN.

35 AR to E.A. Osborne, 21.10.35. BLCU, NY.

36 Marita Ross: 'The Beloved Enchanter'; *Everybody's Weekly*, 27.9.47, pp. 10–11.

37 Walter Starkie to AR, 21.2.21. RF.

38 'Drawing Director's Inspiration'; Los Angeles, paper unknown, Nov. 1935. RF.

39 B.M.L. Wikingen to AR, 28.11.30. RF.

40 AR to Bernard Rackham, 22.9.36. Quoted HUDSON, p. 46.

41 Bernard Rackham to AR, 20.9.35. RF.

42 *The Observer*, ?.12.35.

43 Undated note [1936], PFL.

44 AR to J.C.C. Taylor, 6.8.31. BLCU, NY.

45 Dated July and October 1938. PFL.

46 AR to Frank P. Harris, 30.7.38. PFL.

47 AR to Frank P. Harris, 27.10.38. PFL.

48 RF.

49 Kenneth Clark: 'The Future of Painting'; *The Listener*, 2.10.35.

50 Original drawing at University of Louisville Library, Rare Books Room.

51 AR to Robert Partridge 11.8.35 – 10.9.38. BLCU, NY, and LUL.

52 Note on preliminary book-plate proof. LUL.

53 AR to Robert Partridge 2.9.36. BLCU, NY.

54 AR to Edward Tinker, 26.6.29. HRHRC, AUSTIN.

55 AR to Robert Partridge, 11.8.35. LUL. Since HUDSON, more Rackham book-plates have come to light. Rackham made book-plates for the following individuals: P. L. Andrewes; Ursula Andrewes; Emma Williams Burlington; Francis P. Garman; Mabel Brady Garman; George Lazarus; Robert Partridge; Barbara May Rackham; Mrs Edward Tinker; Edith Clifford Williams; Barbara Jean Woolf; and Arthur Rackham himself. The book-plate of Eugene Grosman at PFL, an uninspired re-drawing of a figure of Ariel from *The Tempest*, was not, in the present writer's view, drawn by Rackham himself.

56 AR to George Macy, 8.11.38. HRHRC, AUSTIN.

57 AR to George Macy, 18.4.35. HRHRC, AUSTIN.

58 AR to George Macy, 30.4.35. HRHRC, AUSTIN.

59 AR to George Macy, 30.4.35. HRHRC, AUSTIN.

60 George Macy: 'Arthur Rackham and the Wind in the Willows': *The Horn Book*, May–June, 1940, pp. 153–8.

61 The collection is kept at HRHRC, AUSTIN.

62 AR to George Macy, 19.8.39. HRHRC, AUSTIN.

63 AR to Sir George Clausen, 18.8.39. Royal Academy Library, CL/1/169.

64 Percy Pitt to AR, 6.4.27. RF.

65 AR to M.D. McGoff, 4.5.36. LUL.

CHAPTER EIGHT

1 George Macy to AR, 13.1.36. HRHRC, AUSTIN.

2 AR to George Macy, 23.1.36. HRHRC, AUSTIN.

3 AR's Account Books. RF.

4 The *Alice* agreement was reached on 26.4.07. AR's Account Books. RF.

5 Sketchbook F2. BLCU, NY.

6 Pages 26r, 38r and 71r.

7 RF.

8 Gladys Beattie Crozier: *op. cit.*

9 *Pall Mall Gazette*, 3.10.08.

10 *Daily Telegraph*, 3.10.08.

11 *Evening News*, 5.10.08.

12 *The Athenaeum*, 10.10.08.

13 *The Ladies' Field*, 17.10.08.

14 *Daily Chronicle*, 20.10.08.

15 *The Outlook*, 21.11.08.

16 *Pall Mall Gazette*, 27.11.08.

17 AR's Account Books. RF.

18 AR to E.H. Anderson, n.d., recd 23.2.28. NYPL.

19 NYPL Minutes, 11.4.28, p. 42.

20 AR to E.H. Anderson, 15.5.28. Ref. NYPL Minutes, 11.6.28, p. 66.

21 AR to E.H. Anderson, 27.5.28. NYPL.

22 Ref. postcard to J.C.C. Taylor, 18.11.29. LUL.

23 Ref. letter to Edward Tinker, 27.11.30. HRHRC, AUSTIN.

24 NYPL Minutes 9.12.28, p. 213.

25 AR to Sangorski and Sutcliffe, 28.5.30. NYPL.

26 Ref. letter to *The Studio*, 26.10.26, PFL, fearing that the copy of their Book of Kells reprint that he had ordered might have been sent to Houghton, Essex, rather than Houghton, Sussex.

27 Three of these are in the British Museum.

28 AR to Alwin Scheuer, 8.4.31. BLCU, NY.

29 'The most important announcement ... is the arrival of Mr Arthur Rackham's illustrated *A Midsummer Night's Dream*.' NYPL Minutes 12.1.31, p. 325.

30 AR to Sangorski and Sutcliffe, 1.1.31. NYPL.

31 *Westminster Gazette*, 9.10.08. Two etchings by Rackham, dateable to the 1890's, a landscape and a portrait, have, in fact survived.

32 AR to George Macy, 13.1.36. HRHRC, AUSTIN.

33 Copy letter, George Macy to AR, 6.3.36. HRHRC, AUSTIN.

34 AR to George Macy, 16.12.36. HRHRC, AUSTIN.

35 Notes for Subscribers to the Limited Editions Club's Shakespeare *A Midsummer Night's Dream*, 1939.

36 AR to George Macy, 8.11.38. HRHRC, AUSTIN.

37 AR to George Macy, 7.3.39. HRHRC, AUSTIN.

38 My italics.

39 AR to George Macy, 19.8.39. HRHRC, AUSTIN.

CHRONOLOGY OF ARTHUR RACKHAM'S LIFE

1867	Born, 19 September, at 210 South Lambeth Road, London, third surviving child of Alfred Rackham, then Clerk at the Admiralty Registry, Doctors' Commons, and his wife, Annie.
1868	Harris, his brother, born.
1871	Ethel, his sister, born and died.
1872	Leonard, his brother, born and died.
1873	Winifred, his sister, born.
1875	Alfred Rackham promoted to Chief Clerk at the Admiralty Registry. Mabel, Arthur's sister, born. She died in 1876.
1876	Bernard, his brother, born.
1877	Stanley, his brother, born.
1878	Percy, his elder brother, died.
1879	Maurice, his youngest brother, born. Arthur entered City of London School, at same time as his younger brother, Harris.
1881	Early surviving watercolour, *Castle Rising, Norfolk.*
1882	Family moved to 27 Albert Square, Clapham Road, Lambeth. Family summer holiday in Lancing, Sussex.
1883	Won school prize for best Memory Drawing and class prize for Algebra and Trigonometry, summer term. Family summer holiday in Lancing. Won school prize for Drawing, Christmas term. Left City of London School.
1884	Voyage to Australia to improve his health, January–March. Stayed in Sydney, March–May. Voyage home to England, May–July. Family summer holiday in Lancing. Enrolled at Lambeth School of Art, autumn. Passed exam to enter Westminster Fire Office, as a clerk, but not appointed to post. First illustrations published in *Scraps*, October and November.
1885	Family moved to 3 St Ann's Park Road, Wandsworth, in March. Appointed Junior Clerk, 4th Class, at Westminster Fire Office, autumn. Salary £40, p.a.
1888	First work in public exhibition at Royal Academy.
1889	Summer holiday in Cornwall with Walter Freeman.
1890	Harris graduated from Christ's College, Cambridge, with 1st in Classical tripos. Arthur left Lambeth School of Art.
1891	Regular contributor of illustrations to *Pall Mall Budget.*
1892	Resigned from Westminster Fire Office. Moved to 12 New Court, Carey Street, Lincoln's Inn Fields. Painted *Self Portrait.*
1893	Left *Pall Mall Budget* at beginning of year to work on *Westminster Budget* and *Westminster Gazette.*
1894	Already working for the publishers J.M. Dent. Took part in exhibition of Dent's black and white artists to mark the publication of *Morte Darthur* illustrated by Aubrey Beardsley at Institute of Watercolour Painters, Piccadilly, September–October.
1895	Moved to Buckingham Chambers, 11 Buckingham Street, The Strand.
1896	Alfred Rackham appointed Admiralty Marshal. *The Zankiwank and the Bletherwitch* published by J.M. Dent.
1897	Illustrating for Cassell's magazines *Chums* and *Little Folks*, and other Cassell publications. Visited Bayreuth to see Wagner's *Ring* cycle. Went on walking trips in Northern Europe and Scandinavia with the *Fünfverein* during the summers of 1896–99.
1898	*Ingoldsby Legends* published by J.M. Dent. Art Editor of *The Ladies' Field* for three months. Bernard Rackham, with 1st class Classics degree, appointed to staff of South Kensington Museum. Arthur moved to 8 Brecknock Studios, 114A Brecknock Road, Tufnell Park. Met Edyth Starkie around this time.
1899	Alfred Rackham retired as Admiralty Marshall. Second visit to Bayreuth to see *The Ring* and other Wagner operas. Painted *Portrait of the Artist's Mother.* *Feats on the Fjord* by Harriet Martineau and *Lamb's Tales from Shakespeare* illustrated by Rackham published by J.M. Dent.
1900	*Gulliver's Travels* published by J.M. Dent and Grimm's *Fairy Tales* by Freemantle & Co.
1901	Became engaged to Edyth Starkie. Included in loan exhibition of Modern Illustration at Victoria and Albert Museum and Edinburgh.
1902	Elected Associate of the Royal Watercolour Society. Began to exhibit at the RWS summer and winter exhibitions. By 1902 he was a member of the Langham Sketching Club.
1903	In hospital for surgery, possibly on his bladder. Married to Edyth Starkie on 16 July. Honeymoon in North Wales. Moved with Edyth to 3 Primrose Hill Studios.

1904 First child stillborn, March.
Received commission for 51 illustrations to *Rip Van Winkle* from Ernest Brown and Phillips.
Exhibited at St Louis International and Düsseldorf International exhibitions.
Spent summer holiday in Italy with his father.

1905 Elected Chairman of Langham Sketching Club (until 1907).
Rip Van Winkle exhibition held at Leicester Galleries, and contract for *Peter Pan in Kensington Gardens* agreed, April.
Article about him by A. L. Baldry published in *The Studio*, April.
Rip Van Winkle published by Heinemann, September.

1906 Contract for *The Sleeping Beauty* and *A Midsummer Night's Dream* agreed with Heinemann, March.
Won Gold Medal at Milan International Exhibition.
Bought 16 Chalcot Gardens, Hampstead, and moved in after extensive alteration of house.
Peter Pan in Kensington Gardens published, December, with accompanying exhibition at Leicester Galleries.

1907 Contract for *Alice in Wonderland* agreed, April.
Contract for *The Sleeping Beauty* cancelled, after some preliminary drawings had been done.
Holiday with Edyth in Walberswick, Suffolk, autumn.
Alice published, November, with accompanying exhibition at Leicester Galleries.
Profiled in *The World* in their feature 'Celebrities at Home', December.

1908 Barbara born, January.
Views on dolls published in *The Daily Mirror*, November.
A Midsummer Night's Dream published, November, with accompanying exhibition at Leicester Galleries.

1909 Elected to Art Workers' Guild, May.
Gulliver, *Grimm* and *Lamb's Tales* reissued.
Undine published, November, with accompanying exhibition at Leicester Galleries.

1910 Addressed Authors' Club on the role of Illustration, January.
Contract for two volumes of *The Ring* agreed with Heinemann, January.
Elected Vice President of RWS (held the office for two years).
Views on the decline of caricature published by *The Daily News*, October.
Rhinegold published, November, with accompanying exhibition at Leicester Galleries.

1911 Won 1st Class Medal at Barcelona International exhibition.
Siegfried published, November, with accompanying exhibition at Leicester Galleries.

1912 His father, Alfred Rackham, died, April.
Elected Associate of the Société Nationale des Beaux Arts, Paris.
Aesop's Fables published, October, with accompanying exhibition at Leicester Galleries.

1913 Work bought by Edmund Davis for presentation to the Luxembourg Gallery, Paris.
Mother Goose published, with accompanying exhibition at Leicester Galleries.

1914 Included in exhibitions at the Louvre, Paris, and in Leipzig, both exhibitions closed on the outbreak of war.
Contributed to *King Albert's Book* and *Princess Mary's Gift Book*.

1915 *A Christmas Carol* published.
Contributed to *The Queen's Gift Book*.

1916 Edyth suffered serious heart attack.
Allies' Fairy Book published.

1917 Barbara at Bedales School, Petersfield.
Edyth moved temporarily to Rustington, Sussex, to escape air raids.
Grimm's *Little Brother and Little Sister* and Malory's *Romance of King Arthur* published.
Rackham's use of models now at its height.

1918 *English Fairy Tales Retold* and *The Springtide of Life* published.

1919 Elected Master of the Art Workers' Guild.
Cinderella published.
First exhibition at Scott and Fowles, New York.

1920 Moved to Houghton House, near Amberley, Sussex, May.
Rented 6 Primrose Hill Studios as his London base, November.
Irish Fairy Tales published. *Sleeping Beauty* published.
Correspondence with Eden Phillpotts, 1920–21, concerning *A Dish of Apples*.
Second exhibition at Scott and Fowles.
His mother, Annie Rackham, died, December.

1921 *A Dish of Apples* and Milton's *Comus* published.

1922 Failed to be elected to RA, June.
Nathaniel Hawthorne's *A Wonder Book* published.
Commissioned by Colgate Soap to draw 30 illustrations for advertisements.
Third exhibition at Scott and Fowles, New York.

1923 Barbara started at Queen Anne's School, Caversham, January.
Spent May in Italy alone.

1924 Took part in British Empire Exhibition, Wembley.

1925 Death of elder sister, Meg Rackham, June.
Two books, primarily for the US market, published, *Where the Blue Begins* and *Poor Cecco*.

1926 Exhibited oil painting, *The Step Daughter*, at Royal Academy.
The Tempest published.
Took Barbara on her first visit to Paris.

1927 Death of youngest brother, Maurice, in skiing accident, January.
Visit to New York, Boston and Philadelphia, fourth exhibition at Scott and Fowles, New York, November.

1928 Commissioned by New York Public Library to oversee and illustrate MS version of *A Midsummer Night's Dream*.
Begins to exhibit portraits at Royal Society of Portrait Painters.
Commissions for books from Harrap begin.

1929 A new detached house in course of construction for the Rackhams at Pain's Hill, above Limpsfield in Surrey.
The Vicar of Wakefield published.
Undergoes prostate operation and convalescence, November and December.
Completed but unbound illustrations for *A Midsummer Night's Dream* shown at New York Public Library.

1930 Moved with Edyth to Stilegate, Pain's Hill, Limpsfield.
Edyth seriously ill for three months.
Completed *A Midsummer Night's Dream* delivered to New York, December.

1931	*The Compleat Angler, The Night Before Christmas* and *The Chimes* published. Visited Denmark with Barbara to gather material for *Hans Andersen's Fairy Tales.*
1932	*Hans Andersen's Fairy Tales* published.
1933	*Arthur Rackham Fairy Book* and *Goblin Market* published. Worked on stage and costume designs for *Hansel and Gretel*, autumn and winter.
1934	*Pied Piper of Hamelin* published.
1935	Barbara married Philip Soper. The couple moved to Johannesburg. *Poe's Tales of Mystery and Imagination* published. Exhibition of illustrations to *Hans Andersen* and other books, Leicester Galleries, December.
1936	*A Midsummer Night's Dream* and *The Wind in the Willows* commissioned by Limited Editions Club of New York, March. *Peer Gynt* published.
1937	Completed *A Midsummer Night's Dream.*

Visited the Thames in Berkshire with Elspeth Grahame to gather material for *Wind in the Willows.*
Underwent deep X-Ray therapy, August.
Barbara and Philip Soper moved back to London, November.

1938	The Rackhams' first grandchild, Martin, born. Continued to work on *The Wind in the Willows*, between extended periods in hospital. Permanently under the care of a surgical nurse. Relinquished his Primrose Hill studio.
1939	*The Wind in the Willows* illustrations completed, April. *A Midsummer Night's Dream* published, July. Edyth in hospital with broken arm, and Arthur with internal bleeding, summer. Arthur Rackham died of cancer at home, 6 September. Cremated at Croydon. Memorial exhibition, Leicester Galleries, December.
1940	*The Wind in the Willows* published in the US.
1941	Edyth Rackham died, March.
1950	*The Wind in the Willows* published in UK.

ARTHUR RACKHAM'S
FAMILY TREE

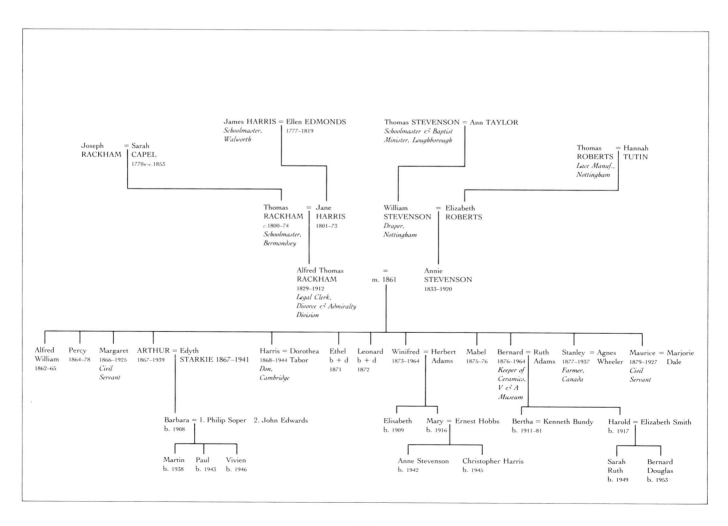

BOOKS ILLUSTRATED
BY ARTHUR RACKHAM

In compiling this bibliography, which aspires to completeness but may not reach it, the author acknowledges his debt to the excellent bibliographies compiled by Bertram Rota and revised by Anthony Rota (HUDSON, 1960 & 1974), and Fred Gettings (GETTINGS, 1975). The numbers after each title indicate colour/black and white illustrations in each book.

1893 Thomas Rhodes, *To the Other Side*, George Philip and Sons **20/0**

1894 Annie Berlyn, *Sunrise-Land Rambles in Eastern England*, Jarrold and Sons **73/0**

Fydell Edmund Garrett, *Isis Very Much Unveiled, Being the Story of the Great Mahatma Hoax*, Westminster Gazette **1/0**

Anthony Hope *The Dolly Dialogues*, Westminster Gazette **4/0**

Washington Irving, *The Sketch-Book of Geoffrey Crayon, Gent.*, G. P. Putnam's Sons (Holly Edition, New York and London) **3/0**

Lemmon Lingwood *Jarrold's Guide to Wells-next-the-sea*, Jarrold and Sons **51/0**

1895 Walter Calvert, *Souvenir of Sir Henry Irving*, Henry J. Drane, Chant & Co. **2/0**

William Ernest Henley, *A London Garland. Selected from Five Centuries of English Verse*, Macmillan & Co. **1/0**

Washington Irving, *Tales of a Traveller*, G. P. Putnam's Sons, London and New York **5/0**

Washington Irving, *The Sketch-Book of Geoffrey Crayon, Gent.*, G. P. Putnam's Sons (Van Tassel Edition, New York and London) **4/0**

'The Philistine' (pseud.), *The New Fiction and other Papers*, Westminster Gazette **1/0**

Henry Charles Shelley, *The Homes and Haunts of Thomas Carlyle*, Westminster Gazette **1/0**

1896 Shafto Justin Adair Fitzgerald, *The Zankiwank and the Bletherwitch*, J. M. Dent & Co., London; E. P. Dutton & Co., New York **41/0**

Hulda Friederichs, *In the Evening of his Days. A Study of Mr Gladstone in Retirement*, Westminster Gazette **10/0**

Washington Irving, *Bracebridge Hall*, G. P. Putnam's Sons, London and New York **5/0**

Henry Seton Merriman, (pseud. Hugh Stowell Scott), and S. G. Tallentyre, *The Money-Spinner and other Character Notes*, Smith, Elder & Co. **12/0**

1897 Maggie Browne, (pseud. Margaret Hamer), *Two Old Ladies, Two Foolish Fairies and a Tom Cat*, Cassell & Co. **19/4**

William Carlton Dawe, *Captain Castle. A Tale of the China Seas*, Smith, Elder & Co. **1/0**

Thomas Tylston Greg, *Through a Glass Lightly*, J. M. Dent & Co. **2/0**

Charles James Lever, *Charles O'Malley, The Irish Dragoon*, Service & Paton, London; G. P. Putnam's Sons, New York **16/0**

Henry Seton Merriman, (pseud. Hugh Stowell Scott), *The Grey Lady*, Smith, Elder & Co. **12/0**

1898 Frances Burney, *Evelina, or the History of a Young Lady's Entrance into the World*, George Newnes **16/0**

Thomas Ingoldsby, (pseud. Richard Harris Barham), *The Ingoldsby Legends: or Mirth and Marvels, by Thomas Ingoldsby, Esquire*, J. M. Dent & Co. **80/12**

Stanley John Weyman, *The Castle Inn*, Smith, Elder & Co. **1/0**

1899 George Albemarle Bertle Dewar, *Wild Life in the Hampshire Highlands*, Haddon Hall Library, J. M. Dent & Co. **19/0**

Sir Edward Grey, *Fly Fishing*, Haddon Hall Library, J. M. Dent & Co. **19/0**

Samuel Reynolds Hole, *Our Gardens*, Haddon Hall Library, J. M. Dent & Co. **26/0**

Charles and Mary Lamb, *Tales from Shakespeare*, J. M. Dent & Co. **11/1**

Harriet Martineau, *Feats on the Fjord*, J. M. Dent & Co. **11/1**

Lady Rosalie Neish, *A World in a Garden*, J. M. Dent & Co. **15/0**

William James Tate, *East Coast Scenery*, Jarrold & Sons **7/0**

1900 Country Life Library, *Gardens Old and New (Vol. 1)* **9/0**

Jacob Ludwig Carl Grimm and Wilhelm Carl Grimm, *Fairy Tales of the Brothers Grimm*, (trans. Mrs Edgar Lewis), Freemantle & Co. **95/2**

John Nisbet, *Forests and Woodlands*, Haddon Hall Library, J. M. Dent & Co. **11/0**

John Otho Paget, *Hunting*, Haddon Hall Library, J. M. Dent & Co. **19/0**

Jonathan Swift, *Gulliver's Travels into Several Remote Nations of the World*, J. M. Dent & Co. **11/1**

1901 May Bowley (*et al.*), *Queen Mab's Fairy Realm*, George Newnes **5/0**

Arthur George Frederick Griffiths, *Mysteries of Police and Crime*, Cassell & Co., 3 vols. **13/0**

Edwin Hodder, *The Life of a Century. 1800 to 1900*, George Newnes **6/0**

Charles Richard Kenyon, *The Argonauts of the Amazon*, W & R Chambers, E. P. Dutton, New York **6/0**

Robert Henry Lyttelton, *Out-Door Games. Cricket and Golf*, Haddon Hall Library, J. M. Dent & Co. **12/0**

Edmund Selous, *Bird Watching*, Haddon Hall Library, J. M. Dent & Co. **14/0**

Animal Antics, Partridge, London **1/0**

1902 Horace Bleackley, *More Tales of the Stumps*, Ward, Lock & Co. **9/0**

John Leyland (ed.), *Gardens Old and New (Vol. 2)*, Country Life Library **9/0**

Alexander Innes Shand, *Shooting*, Haddon Hall Library, J. M. Dent & Co. **13/0**

1903 Louisa Lilias Greene, *The Grey House on the Hill*, Thomas Nelson & Sons **8/0**

George Alfred Henty (*et al.*), *Brains and Bravery*, W & R Chambers **8/0**

Miranda Hill, *Cinderella*, Little Folks plays series. Cassell & Co. **2/2**

Barthold Georg Niebuhr, *The Greek Heroes*, Cassell & Co. **8/4**

Marion Hill Spielmann, *Littledom Castle and other Tales*, George Routledge & Sons **9/0**

William Montgomery Tod, *Farming*, Haddon Hall Library, J. M. Dent & Co. **8/0**

1904 Maggie Browne, (pseud. Margaret Hamer), *The Surprising Adventures of Tuppy and Sue*, Cassell & Co. **19/4**

Mary Cholmondeley, *Red Pottage*, George Newnes **8/0**

Richard Henry Dana, *Two Years Before the Mast*, Collins' Clear-Type Press, London; The John C. Winston Co., New York (Illustrations not coloured by Rackham) **0/8**

William Price Drury, *The Peradventures of Private Pagett*, Chapman & Hall **8/0**

Sam Hield Hamer, *The Little Folks Picture Album in Colour*, Cassell & Co. **0/1**

Henry Harbour, *Where Flies the Flag*, Collins Clear-Type Press **0/6**

1905 Washington Irving, *Rip Van Winkle*, William Heinemann, London; Doubleday, Page & Co., New York **3/51**

Sam Hield Hamer, *The Little Folks Fairy Book*, Cassell & Co. **9/0**

Myra Hamilton, *Kingdoms Curious*, William Heinemann **6/0**

Arthur Lincoln Haydon, *Stories of King Arthur*, Cassell & Co. **2/4**

Arthur Lincoln Haydon (*et al.*), *Fairy Tales Old and New*, Cassell & Co. **2/4**

Laurence Houseman and W. Somerset Maugham (ed.), *The Venture. An Annual of Art and Literature*, John Baillie, London **1/0**

1906 James Matthew Barrie, *Peter Pan in Kensington Gardens*, Hodder & Stoughton, London; Charles Scribner's Sons, New York **3/50**

Ralph Hall Caine (ed.), *The Children's Hour: An Anthology*, George Newnes **1/0**

Rudyard Kipling, *Puck of Pook's Hill*, Doubleday, Page & Co., New York **0/4**

1907 Alfred E. Bonser, Emma Sophia Buchheim and Bella Sidney Woolf, *The Land of Enchantment*, Cassell & Co. **37/0**

Lewis Carroll (pseud. Charles Lutwidge Dodgson), *Alice's Adventures in Wonderland*, William Heinemann, London; Doubleday, Page & Co., New York **15/13**

Eleanor Gates, *Good Night*, Thomas Y. Crowell Co., New York **0/5**

Thomas Ingoldsby(pseud. Richard Harris Barham), *The Ingoldsby Legend of Mirth and Marvels*, J. M. Dent & Co., London; Doubleday, Page & Co., New York **77/23**

J. Harry Savory, *Auld Acquaintance*, J. M. Dent & Co. **2/0**

J. Harry Savory, *Sporting Days*, J. M. Dent & Co. **2/0**

Pamela Tennant, *The Children and the Pictures*, William Heinemann **1/0**

1908 Robert Burns, *The Cotter's Saturday Night*, J. Hewetson & Son, London **1/0**

Bertram Waldron Matz (ed.), *The Odd Volume, Literary and Artistic*, Simpkin, Marshall, Hamilton, Ken & Co. **1/0**

William Shakespeare, *Henry IV, Part II* (Intr. A. Birrell) Vol. xxiv of *The University Press Shakespeare*, George G. Harrap & Co. **1/0**

William Shakespeare, *Macbeth*, (Intr. Henry C. Beeching) Vol. xxxiii of *The University Press Shakespeare*, George G. Harrap & Co. **1/0**

William Shakespeare, *A Midsummer Night's Dream*, William Heinemann, London; Doubleday, Page & Co., New York **34/40**

1909 Friedrich De la Motte Fouqué, *Undine*, (adapted by W. L. Courtney) William Heinemann, London; Doubleday, Page & Co., New York **41/15**

Jacob Ludwig Carl Grimm and Wilhelm Carl Grimm *Fairy Tales of the Brothers Grimm*, (trans. Mrs Edgar Lucas) Constable & Co., London; Doubleday, Page & Co., New York **62/40**

Charles and Mary Lamb, *Tales from Shakespeare*, J. M. Dent & Co., London; E. P. Dutton & Co., New York **37/12**

Mabel Hill Spielmann, *The Rainbow Book*, Chatto and Windus **15/1**

Jonathan Swift, *Gulliver's Travels into Several Remote Nations of the World*, J. M. Dent & Co., London; E. P. Dutton & Co., New York **34/12**

1910 Maggie Browne (pseud. Margaret Hamer), *The Book of Betty Barber*, Duckworth & Co. **12/6** (coloured by Harry Rountree)

Arthur Lincoln Haydon, *Stories of King Arthur*, Cassell & Co. **2/4**

Agnes Crozier Herbertson, *The Bee-Blowaways*, Cassell & Co. **17/0**

Richard Wagner (tr. Margaret Armour), *The Rhinegold and the Valkyrie*, William Heinemann, London; Doubleday, Page & Co., New York **8/30**

1911 Richard Wagner (tr. Margaret Armour) *Siegfried and the Twilight of the Gods*, William Heinemann, London; Doubleday, Page & Co., New York **8/30**

1912 Aesop (intr. G. K. Chesterton), *Aesop's Fables*, William Heinemann, London; Doubleday, Page & Co., New York **82/13**

James Matthew Barrie, *Peter Pan in Kensington Gardens*, Hodder & Stoughton, London; Charles Scribner's Sons, New York **12/50**

Arthur Rackham, *The Peter Pan Portfolio*, Hodder & Stoughton; Brentano's, New York **0/12**

1913 Clifton Bingham (*et al.*), *Faithful Friends. Pictures and Stories for Little Folk*, Blackie & Son **1/0**

Arthur Rackham, (intr. Sir Arthur Quiller-Couch), *Arthur Rackham's Book of Pictures*, William Heinemann, London; The Century Co., New York **11/44**

Arthur Rackham, *Mother Goose. The Old Nursery Rhymes*, William Heinemann, London and New York **78/13**

1914 Hall Caine (intr.) *King Albert's Book*, The Daily Telegraph **0/1**

Julia Ellsworth Ford, *Imagina*, Duffield & Co., New York **0/2**

1915 Charles Dickens, *A Christmas Carol*, William Heinemann, London; J. B. Lippincott Co., Philadelphia **17/12**

John Galsworthy (Foreword) B. Harradey (text), *The Queen's Gift Book*, Hodder & Stoughton **2/1**

Lady Sybil Grant (*et al.*), *Princess Mary's Gift Book*, Hodder & Stoughton **5/1**

1916 Edmund Gosse (intr.), *The Allies' Fairy Book*, William Heinemann, London. J. B. Lippincott Co., Philadelphia **23/12**

1917 Jacob Ludwig Carl Grimm and Wilhelm Carl Grimm, *Little Brother and Little Sister*, Constable & Co., London; Dodd, Mead & Co., New York **45/13**

Sir Thomas Malory, *The Romance of King Arthur and his Knights of the Round Table*, (abridged by Alfred Pollard) Macmillan & Co., London and New York **70/16**

1918 Flora Annie Steel, *English Fairy Tales*, Macmillan & Co., London and New York **43/16**

Algernon Charles Swinburne, *The Springtide of Life. Poems of Childhood*, William Heinemann, London; J. B. Lippincott Co., Philadelphia **58/8**

Francis James Child (*et al.*), *Some British Ballads*, Constable & Co. **23/16**

1919 Julia Ellsworth Ford, *Snickety Nick and the Giant. Rhymes by Witter Brynner*, Moffat, Yard & Co., New York **10/3**

Charles S. Evans, *Cinderella*, William Heinemann, London; J. B. Lippincott Co., Philadelphia **53/8**

1920 Charles S. Evans, *The Sleeping Beauty*, William Heinemann, London; J. B. Lippincott Co., Philadelphia **57/9**

Jacob Ludwig Carl Grimm and Wilhelm Carl Grimm, *Snowdrop and Other Tales*, Constable & Co., London; E. P. Dutton & Co., New York **29/20**

Jacob Ludwig Carl Grimm and Wilhelm Carl Grimm *Hansel and Gretel and other Tales* Constable & Co., London; E. P. Dutton & Co., New York **28/20**

James Stephens, *Irish Fairy Tales*, Macmillan & Co., London and New York **20/16**

1921 John Milton, *Comus*, William Heinemann, London; Doubleday, Page & Co., New York **35/22**

Eden Phillpotts, *A Dish of Apples*, Hodder & Stoughton **26/3**

1922 Nathaniel Hawthorne, *A Wonder Book*, Hodder & Stoughton, London; George H. Doran Co., New York **21/24**

1923 L. Callender (ed.), *The Windmill: Stories, Essays, Poems and Pictures*, William Heinemann, London **0/1**

1924 A. C. Benson and Sir Lawrence Weaver (ed.), *The Book of the Queen's Dolls' House*, Methuen & Co. **0/1**

1925 Christopher Morley, *Where the Blue Begins*, William Heinemann, London; Doubleday, Page & Co., New York **16/4**

Ernest Rhys (*et al.*), *The Book of the Titmarsh Club*, (printed by J. Davy & Sons) **2/0**

Margery Williams, *Poor Cecco*, Chatto & Windus, London; George H. Doran Co., New York **12/7**

1926 Erica Fay (pseud. Marie Stopes), *A Road to Fairyland*, G. P. Putnam's Sons **0/1**

William Shakespeare, *The Tempest*, William Heinemann, Ltd; Doubleday, Page & Co., New York **20/20**

1927 Sir Robert Baden-Powell (*et al.*), *Now Then! A Volume of Fact, Fiction and Pictures*, C. Arthur Pearson **1/0**

1928 Abbie Farwell Brown *The Lonesomest Doll*, Houghton Mifflin Co., Boston and New York **26/4**

Washington Irving, *The Legend of Sleepy Hollow*, George G. Harrap & Co., London; David McKay Co., Philadelphia **32/8**

Lewis Melville (pseud. Lewis S. Benjamin), *Not All the Truth*, Jarrolds **1/0**

J. C. Eno, *A Birthday and Some Memories*, Spottiswoode, Ballantyne, London **1/0**

1929 May Clarissa Byron, *J. M. Barrie's Peter Pan in Kensington Gardens, Retold for Little People*, Hodder & Stoughton, London; Charles Scribner's Sons, New York **16/6**

Oliver Goldsmith, *The Vicar of Wakefield*, George G. Harrap & Co., 23 12 London; David MacKay Co., Philadelphia **23/12**

1930 William Shakespeare, *A Midsummer Night's Dream*, Unique copy, text written out by Graily Hewitt. Spencer Collection, New York Public Library **0/12**

1931 Charles Dickens, *The Chimes*, Limited Editions Club, New York **19/0**

Clement Clarke Moore, *The Night Before Christmas*, George G. Harrap & Co., London; J. B. Lippincott Co., Philadelphia **19/4**

Izaak Walton, *The Compleat Angler*, (ed. Richard le Gallienne) George G. Harrap & Co., London; David McKay Co., Philadelphia **22/12**

1932 Lewis G. Fry (ed.), *Oxted, Limpsfield and Neighbourhood*, (printed: W & G Godwin) **5/0**

Hans Christian Andersen, *Fairy Tales*, George G. Harrap & Co., London; David McKay Co., Philadelphia **52/12**

John Ruskin, *The King of the Golden River*, George G. Harrap & Co., London; J. B. Lippincott Co., Philadelphia **13/4**

1933 Arthur Rackham, *The Arthur Rackham Fairy Book*, George G. Harrap & Co., London; J. B. Lippincott Co., Philadelphia **64/8**

Christina Rossetti, *Goblin Market*, George G. Harrap & Co., London; J. B. Lippincott Co., Philadelphia **19/4**

Walter Starkie, *Raggle-Taggle. Adventures with a Fiddle in*

Hungary and Roumania, John Murray, *The Best Books of the Season 1933–34* Simpkin, Marshall Ltd. **2/0**

1934 Robert Browning, *The Pied Piper of Hamelin*, George G. Harrap & Co., London; J. B. Lippincott Co., Philadelphia **16/4**

Walter Carroll, *River and Rainbow. Ten Miniatures for Pianoforte*, Forsyth Brothers Ltd **1/0**

Walter Starkie
Spanish Raggle-Taggle. Adventures with a Fiddle in North Spain, John Murray **2/0**

1935 Julia Ellsworth Ford, *Snickerty Nick. Rhymes by Whitter Brynner*, Suttonhouse, Los Angeles & San Francisco **11/0**

Edgar Allen Poe, *Tales of Mystery and Imagination*, George G. Harrap & Co., 28 12 London; J. B. Lippincott Co., Philadelphia **28/12**

1936 Henrik Ibsen, *Peer Gynt*, George G. Harrap & Co., London; J. B. Lippincott Co., Philadelphia **38/12**

Walter Starkie, *Don Gypsy*, John Murray **2/0**

1938 Percy Mackaye, *The Far Familiar*, Richards Press **1/0**

Maggs Bros, *Costume through the Ages* **6/0**

1938 Percy Mackaye, *The Far Familiar*, Richards Press **1/0**

1939 William Shakespeare, *A Midsummer Night's Dream*, The Limited Editions Club, New York **0/6**

1940 Kenneth Grahame, *The Wind in the Willows*, The Limited Editions Club, New York; The Heritage Press, New York (not published in England until 1950, by Methuen) **1/16**

RACKHAM
IN PUBLIC
COLLECTIONS

Original drawings and paintings by Arthur Rackham can be seen in
the following public and semi-public collections, usually by
appointment only.

AUSTRALIA
National Gallery of Victoria, Melbourne.

FRANCE
Musée Nationale d'Art Moderne (Edmund Davis Collection)

GREAT BRITAIN
Cecil Higgins Museum, Bedford.
Beverley Art Gallery, North Humberside.
Cartwright Hall, Bradford.
Brighton Art Gallery and Museum.
Townley Hall, Burnley.
Cambridgeshire Collection, Cambridge City Libraries.*
Fitzwilliam Museum, Cambridge.
Derby Art Gallery.
Harrogate Art Gallery.
Leeds City Art Gallery.
University of Liverpool Art Collections.
Art Workers' Guild, London.
British Museum, London.
Royal Watercolour Society, London.

Tate Gallery, London.
Victoria and Albert Museum, London.
Castle Museum, Nottingham.
Harris Museum and Art Gallery, Preston.
Sheffield City Art Galleries.

SPAIN
Barcelona Municipal Museum

UNITED STATES OF AMERICA
Harry Ransom Humanities Research Center Art Collections,
University of Texas at Austin.
Harvard University Library, Cambridge, Mass.
Mary Harbage Room, Wright State University Library,
Dayton, Ohio.
Rare Book Room, University of Louisville Library, Kentucky.
Berg and Spencer Collections, New York Public Library.
Butler Library, University of Columbia, New York.
Pierpont Morgan Library, New York.
Rare Book Department, Free Library of Philadelphia.
Folger Shakespeare Library, Washington D.C.

*This collection comprises Rackham's books, and is probably the most
important single collection in public hands in Great Britain. It
belonged to the artist's brother Harris Rackham and was then
bequeathed to Cambridge City Library by C. D. Rackham in 1944.

THE BUSINESS OF ILLUSTRATION AND HOW RACKHAM MADE IT PAY

THROUGHOUT HIS CAREER, RACKHAM KEPT detailed records of his income from royalties, publishers' advances and sales of pictures, professional expenses, and of where his work was exhibited, to whom sold, for how much, and the names and addresses of purchasers. That he regularly kept his list of purchasers up to date, to keep track of the whereabouts of sold work, is evidenced by his recording changes of address and writing DEAD against some of the names as time went on.

Four quarto notebooks, half bound in leather, survive,[1] and together these give a unique insight into Rackham's organization of his business as an artist, for part of his career at least, and his successes and disappointments.

One of the books holds his Income and Professional Expenditure accounts from 1915 until his death in 1939. This gives a working, month-by-month picture, and at the end of each year he calculates his net earnings for his accountant. The entries are often speedily written, and can be untidy, but it follows from this that we can be assured that they were written more or less near the time of receipt of income or expenditure, when he had more pressing things on his mind. The entries go into such close detail that their accuracy can certainly be guaranteed.

Among the expenditure headings are hire of models, travel, materials, postage and stationery, telephone, rent and rates, messengers, coal, professional fees and so on, while the income figures reveal the major fluctuations in his receipts, and thus, despite his fame, the precarious nature of his profession. Although always living modestly, and prudently investing in stocks and shares when he was doing well financially, he worried throughout his life about his commissions drying up (which they did), about his becoming ill and unable to work, and about Edyth's illnesses.

A side issue which the Account Book illuminates is the state of Rackham's eyesight and of his confidence – or lack of it – in the future. Not only does he enter as legitimate business expenses his oculist's fees, new spectacles and repairs to spectacles, but there are also entries from 1930 onwards recording him selling off his own collection of rare books. These begin with payments from Lauriat, the Boston bookdealer, and Alwin Scheuer, the New York dealer, of £50 and £10 respectively in 1930, and include payments of £25 from the London dealer E. A. Osborne in 1935 for Rackham's own copy of his first illustrated book *To the Other Side* by Thomas Rhodes (George Philip & Sons, 1893), and £400 from Bertram Rota for 'old books from my own collection of rare books' in 1937. Rackham counts these entries, shrewd businessman to the last, as unearned income and thus not liable for tax.

His eyesight had been poor for many years. It had been particularly bad in 1920 and 1921 when he was bombarded by letters from an importunate Eden Phillpotts, eager to obtain his services to illustrate his new collection of poems about apples (eventually published by Hodder and Stoughton at Christmas 1921 as *A Dish of Apples*, with Rackham's illustrations). Phillpotts apologized for his tone in previous letters when he became aware that Rackham's silence and apparent lack of regard for his talents as a poet had a reason: 'I am much concerned to know that Mrs. Rackham is ill, but very thankful to hear that your eye tremble has been got under. I am venturing to send her a pound of Devonshire cream....'[2]

Rackham's accounts show regular entries for treatment and spectacles, because for a man whose eyes were his means to a livelihood his frequent and comparatively substantial payments (average about £2 per year. Highest payments £15 in 1936) indicate an extreme prudence over the welfare of his eyesight, if not a real anxiety about it.

Rackham's payments to his models are also pointers to the activity of his studio and the way he went about his business. The information he gives is fuller in some years than in others, but it is clear that his use of models reached a peak of 107 sessions in 1917, when he was working on Malory's *Romance of King Arthur and his Knights of the Round Table* for Macmillan (rights purchased 31 May 1917) and the Brothers Grimm's *Little Brother and Little Sister* for Constable (advance paid 17 Oct. 1917).

YEAR	NO. OF SESSIONS	MODEL FEES £ s. d.	FOOD FOR MODELS £ s. d.
1915	59	21.17. 3	4. 1. 0
1916	99	41. 8. 2	3. 0. 0
1917	107	40. 9. 6	4. 0. 0
1918	90 [*est*]	32.18. 6	6. 0. 0
1919	80/90 [*est*]	34. 6. 0	2. 0. 0
1920	30 [*est*]	19.19. 6	2. 0. 0
1921	33 [*est*]	22. 7. 0	2. 0. 0
1922	26	22.11. 6	2. 0. 0
1923	25 [*est*]	23.13. 6	Food cost not separately listed by A. R. from here on.
1924	25 [*est*]	25.12. 6	
1925	20/25 [*est*]	23. 9. 6	
1926	........*no breakdown given*........		
1927	20 [*est*]	22. 6. 0	
1928	40 [*est*]	34. 0. 0	
1929	........*no breakdown given*........		
1930	20 [*est*]	21. 0. 0	
1931	15 [*est*]	18.10. 0	
1932	........*no breakdown given*........		
1933	........*no breakdown given*........		
1934	20 [*est*]	25. 0. 0	

YEAR	NO. OF SESSIONS	MODEL FEES £ s. d.	FOOD FOR MODELS £ s. d.
1935	........*no breakdown given*........		
1936	20 [*est*]	23. 0. 0	
1937	........*no breakdown given*........		
1938	10 [*est*]	11. 0. 0	
1939	None.		

(*est*: figure estimated by the author on basis of total annual payment.)

Models were essential for Rackham, for both his nude and costume subjects. When she was old enough and not at school, Rackham used Barbara regularly, to pose for anything from a little girl to a witch.[3] For daily purposes, however, he required his own 'stock' of people. A small black notebook,[4] which he kept for more than forty years, records over 300 names and addresses of men, women and children of all types and all ages whom he would pay to come and sit, stand, dance and make faces for him.

Rackham was forced to give up working from the model at the end of 1938 or 1939 because of his ill health, and confided to Sir George Clausen:

... In general health & spirits I continue to get stronger, but the basic trouble keeps on up and down, & I doubt whether I may hope for anything better. However, I can still work – if not very much. I can no longer use models which will limit me, but I shall get along somehow.[5]

The 1915–39 Account Book gives close detail of Rackham's finances at this period. Inside it are a few loose sheets from another notebook which contain details of his capital holdings up to *c*.1935 and of his professional income over earlier years. He records that before 1901 he earned under £300, but from then on his total gross income dropped to £271 in 1902 and rose to a peak of £3,979 in 1910, dropping down again to £2,064 in 1914. As the Account Book shows, it dropped further to £1,178 gross in 1915, before picking up again and reaching its 1920 peak. (*See Graph.*)

Meanwhile, however, he was investing carefully on the Stock Market, against the lean years. According to the loose sheets, his capital invested grew from £1,500 in 1903 to a total of £14,550 in 1914, having dropped back to £1,500 in 1906 when he bought the lease on 16 Chalcot Gardens. By *c*.1935 he had added a further £22,800 to his capital invested, bringing it to around £37,000. It was the income from these investments, and not current professional earnings, that enabled the Rackhams to live in the manner to which they had become accustomed, with a London studio, servants, and, from 1920 onwards, a good-sized country house.

From 1915 to his death, Rackham's professional expenses remained more or less constant within the three distinct periods:

YEARS		MAX £	MIN £	AVERAGE
1915–19	16 Chalcot Gardens	363	330	349
1920–29	Houghton House, Amberley	524	408	463

[*Exceptional expenses omitted:*
1920: £298 for building work at Houghton
1927: £200 for trip to USA]

1930–38	Stilegate, Limpsfield	572	418	501

In his expenses he included not only his models, materials, art society subscriptions, his servant, reference books, travelling costs – both up and down to London from Houghton and Stilegate, and abroad – occasional expenses for Edyth for her painting, spectacles and so on, but also one-third of the rent and rates at Houghton and, later, at Stilegate, two-thirds of rent and rates at Primrose Hill Studios, and an allowed proportion of telephone, electricity, coal and so on, and half the cost of their car.

It is clear that Rackham took sensible advantage of the tax laws by being sure to claim for everything allowable, down to spectacles, messengers, models' food, brushes and, in January, February and March 1915 for six, ten and four eggs respectively, at one penny each. These, one dares to hazard, were the crucial ingredients in the tempera and oil painting of *Undine* (30″ x 20″), exhibited at the Liverpool Autumn exhibition of 1915, and sold at the Scott and Fowles exhibition in New York in 1919. The appearance in January and disappearance by April 1915 of eggs in Rackham's precise and literal accounts, suggests that we can date the large *Undine* almost to the week.

Rackham's earned income, less expenses, during this period fluctuated wildly, however, reaching a lifetime peak of £6,409 net in 1920. In this rosy year, in which his net income was over five times that of the previous year (£1,260), he received £2,865 as the proceeds from the sale of 65 out of the 102 works exhibited at his Winter Exhibition at Scott and Fowles. Added to this were two new advances, of £1,000 from Macmillan for *Irish Fairy Tales* and £200 from Heinemann for *The Sleeping Beauty*. Royalties from past books did well, too: Heinemann paid £1,055.16.2 and Constable £748.3.5.

1920 was also the year in which Rackham first rented Houghton House, near Amberley, as a country house for the family, and sold 16 Chalcot Gardens. The rent of Houghton House was the – even then – ridiculously low figure of £26.10.0 p.a., one third of which Rackham set off against tax. By 1927 the rent had risen to only £60 p.a., less by £10 than the annual rent on Rackham's small Primrose Hill studio.

Income for 1921, compared to 1920, was disappointing, falling to £1,847.4.8 net. A second exhibition at Scott and Fowles in the winter of 1920 had brought only £515 by February 1921, and the one advance he received that year was £150 from Hodder and Stoughton for Phillpotts' *A Dish of Apples*. Annual income, however, climbed over the next three years to £4,615.14.10 net in 1924, fuelled especially by a third winter exhibition at Scott and Fowles in 1922 (£2,292), and by the first four payments totalling $18,000 (£4,119.19.3) from Colgate for Rackham to make a series of drawings to advertise soap. A fifth and final Colgate payment ($6,000 : £1,248.14.0) came in 1925.

This was to be the final peak in Rackham's earnings. He had no agent, and all the contacts he made he had to cultivate himself. Age and illness, however, were slowing him down, and the tide of fashion was running resolutely against him. Despite the immediate appeal of his *Hans Andersen Fairy Tales* (Harrap, 1932), it paid him only £788.6.6 in royalties, spread out over the last seven years of his life, a figure that includes £25 paid for a Spanish edition. In 1938 his income, after deduction of professional expenses, was £20 – mere pin-money for a hobbyist. If he had lived to do his accounts at the end of 1939 he would have seen he had made a loss for the first time in his life, earning nothing that year from new work except £22.19.5 from a picture sold in June at the RWS. He had been paid a $600 (£121.9.1) advance on *The Wind in the Willows* by the Limited Editions Club of New York in May 1937, but that, more than two years before he died, was his final advance.

In his last two years, when both he and Edyth were in and out of hospital, his main income came from royalties on past books, and that dwindling (1938: £181.15.5; 1939: £46.3.7), as well as from a few picture sales and fees for drawing flyleaf pictures for purchasers of his books (1938: £256.16.6; 1939: £66.5.8). Significant among these latter fees was Frank P. Harris's payments totalling £159.19.0 in 1938 for books 'from my own collection of rare books' and for flyleaf sketches in them.

At the end of a career dedicated to creating illustrations which, in his own lifetime and beyond, enchanted and enriched adults and children all around the world, he makes a sad final entry in his account book: 'Imp. Art League Policy: Saunders & Gibson: 2 pictures presumed stolen (Not earned income) £80'. As if in compensation for this robbery, however, every year from 1906 until his death, Rackham received sums from Hodder and Stoughton for sales of the book that never grew out of paying him royalties: *Peter Pan in Kensington Gardens*.

1   RF.

2   Eden Phillpotts to AR, 23.3.21. RF.

3   Barbara Edwards: 'Try to Look Like a Witch!'; *Columbia Library Columns*, May 1968, Vol. XVII, no. 3, pp. 3–7.

4   RF.

5   AR to Sir George Clausen, letter *cit*.

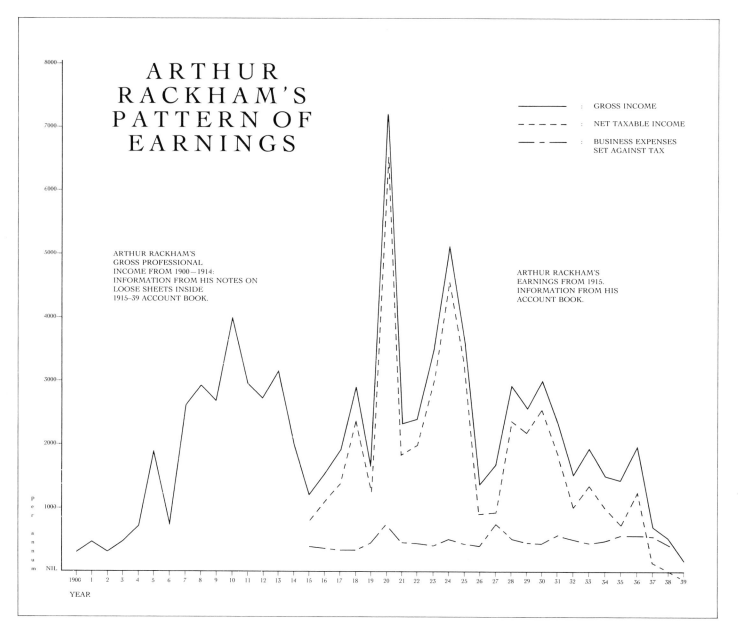

ARTHUR RACKHAM'S PATTERN OF EARNINGS

——————— : GROSS INCOME

– – – – – : NET TAXABLE INCOME

– — – — : BUSINESS EXPENSES SET AGAINST TAX

ARTHUR RACKHAM'S GROSS PROFESSIONAL INCOME FROM 1900–1914: INFORMATION FROM HIS NOTES ON LOOSE SHEETS INSIDE 1915–39 ACCOUNT BOOK.

ARTHUR RACKHAM'S EARNINGS FROM 1915. INFORMATION FROM HIS ACCOUNT BOOK.

YEAR.

SELECT
BIBLIOGRAPHY

Philip Loring Allen, 'The Sketch-Books of Wonderland', *The Bookman*, New York, Feb. 1908, pp. 648–51.

Anon, 'Celebrities at Home: Arthur Rackham', *The World*, 17.12.07.

John Attenborough, *A Living Memory: Hodder & Stoughton Publishers, 1868–1975*, London: Hodder & Stoughton, 1975.

A. L. Baldry, 'Arthur Rackham: A Painter of Fantasies', *The Studio*, Vol. 25, May 1905 (pp. 189–201).

A. L. Baldry, *The Practice of Water-Colour Painting*, London: Macmillan, 1911 (pp. 109–13).

Roland Baughman, *The Centenary of Arthur Rackham's Birth*, New York: Columbia University Libraries, 1967.

Gladys Beattie Crozier, 'The Art of Arthur Rackham', *The Girl's Realm*, Nov. 1908 (pp. 3–12).

Roger Berthoud, *Graham Sutherland: A Biography*, London: Faber, 1982.

Martin Birnbaum, *Jacoleff and Other Artists*, New York: Paul A. Struck, 1946 (pp. 183–92).

David Bland, *A History of Book Illustration*, London: Faber, 1958.

Jean Marie Carré, 'Arthur Rackham', *L'Art et les Artistes*, June 1912 (pp. 104–12).

Ethel M. Chadwick, 'Arthur Rackham', *Dekorative Kunst*, Dec. 1909 (pp. 105–13).

John Christian (ed.), *The Last Romantics*, London: Lund Humphries, Barbican Art Gallery, 1989.

Kenneth Clark, *Another Part of the Wood*, London: John Murray, 1974.

Frederick Coykendall, *Arthur Rackham – A List of Books Illustrated by Him*, New York: Privately Printed, 1922. With an introduction by Martin Birnbaum.

Gillian Darley, *Octavia Hill*: Constable, 1990.

Margery Darrell (ed.), *Once Upon a Time: The Fairy-Tale World of Arthur Rackham*, London: Heinemann, 1972.

J. M. Dent, *The House of Dent 1888–1938*, London: Dent, 1938.

A. E. Douglas-Smith, *City of London School*, Oxford: Basil Blackwell, 1965.

Barbara Edwards, 'Try to Look Like a Witch!', *Columbia Library Columns*, May 1968 (pp. 3–7).

Eleanor Farjeon, 'Arthur Rackham – The Wizard at Home', *St. Nicholas*, New York, March 1914, pp. 385–9.

J. Garner, 'The Wizardry of Arthur Rackham', *International Studio*, July 1923.

Fred Gettings, *Arthur Rackham*, London: Studio Vista, 1975.

William P. Gibbons, 'Sir [*sic*] Arthur Rackham's Adventure in Advertising Art', *The Artist and Advertiser* (US), Jan. 1931 (pp. 6–8).

Eleanor Grahame, *The Story of the Wind in the Willows*, London: Methuen, n.d. [1950].

James Hamilton, *Arthur Rackham 1867–1939*, Sheffield City Art Galleries, 1979. [Exhibition catalogue.] Introductory essay reprinted in *Antique Dealer and Collectors Guide*, March 1980 (pp. 72–6).

James Hamilton and Colin White: *Edmund Dulac 1882–1953 A Centenary Exhibition*; Sheffield City Art Galleries, 1882 [Exhibition catalogue]

A. S. Hartrick, 'Arthur Rackham 1939–1940 [*sic*] – An Appreciation', *Old Watercolour Society's Club*, 1940.

Derek Hudson, *Arthur Rackham: His Life and Work*, London: Heinemann, 1960 [2nd edn. 1974].

Diana L. Johnson, *Fantastic Illustration and Design in Britain, 1850–1930*, Rhode Island Museum of Art, 1979.

P. G. Konody, 'The Home of the Wee Folk – Where Arthur Rackham Lived and Worked in the Heart of the Sussex Downs', *House Beautiful*, Sept 1926. Reprinted in *The Horn Book*, May–June 1940 (pp. 159–62).

S. J. Kunitz and H. Haycraft, *The Junior Book of Authors*, New York: H. H. Wilson & Co., 1934 (pp. 252–3).

S. B. Latimore and G. C. Haskell, *Arthur Rackham: A Bibliography*, 1936.

Robert Lawson, 'The Genius of Arthur Rackham', *The Horn Book*, May–June 1940 (pp. 147–51).

C. S. Lewis, *Surprised by Joy*, London: Geoffrey Bles, 1955.

Clara T. Mac Chesney, 'The Value of Fairies: What Arthur Rackham Has Done to Save Them for the Children of the World', *The Craftsman*, New York, Dec. 1914 (pp. 248–59).

Haldane Macfall, 'English Illustrators of Juvenile Books', *The Girls' Realm*, Nov. 1908.

George McWhorter, 'Arthur Rackham: The Search Goes On', *The Horn Book*, Feb. 1972.

George McWhorter, *The Arthur Rackham Memorial Collection*, University of Louisville, Kentucky, 1988.

George Macy, 'Arthur Rackham and The Wind in the Willows', *The Horn Book*, May–June 1940 (pp. 153–8).

H. J. L. J. Massé, *The Art Workers' Guild: 1884–1934*, London: AWG, 1935.

Susan E. Meyer, *A Treasury of the Great Children's Book Illustrators*, New York: Abrams 1983.

Anne Carroll Moore, 'A Christmas Ride with Arthur Rackham', *The Horn Book*, Nov–Dec 1939 (pp. 368–72).

Simon Nowell-Smith, *The House of Cassell 1848–1958*, London: Cassell, 1958.

E. A. Osborne, 'Some Early Illustrated Books of Arthur Rackham', *The Bookman*, London, Dec. 1933.

Jennifer Phillips, 'The Arthur Rackham Collection', *The Library Chronicle*, University of Texas at Austin, May 1971 (pp. 19–28).

Vittorio Pica, 'Un Nuovo Illustratore Inglese: Arthur Rackham', *Emporium*, Nov. 1907 (pp. 325–40).

Arthur Rackham, 'How I Spend Christmas', *The Bookman*, London, Dec. 1909 (p. 135).

Arthur Rackham, 'The Ideal Christmas', *The Bookman*, London, Dec. 1910 (pp. 141–2).

Arthur Rackham, 'The Worst Time of My Life', *The Bookman*, London, Oct. 1925 (p. 7).

Arthur Rackham, 'The Value of Criticism', *The Bookman*, London, Oct. 1926 (p. 11).

Arthur Rackham, 'In Praise of Water Colour', *Old Water Colour Society's Club*, 1933–34 (pp. 51–2).

G. M. Ray, *Illustrators of the Book in England, 1790–1914*, New York: Pierpont Morgan Library and Oxford University Press, 1976.

Marita Ross, 'The Beloved Enchanter', *Everybody's Weekly*, 27.9.47.

Walter Starkie, *Scholars and Gypsies*, London: John Murray, 1963.

Nancy Vanderglass, *The Arthur Rackham Collection*, Wright State University, Dayton, Ohio, 1987.

Colin White: *Edmund Dulac*; Studio Vista, 1976.

INDEX